Praise for

Beware the Roadbuilders
Literature as Resistance

"Paul Thomas is the conscience of American education. He is our North Star. He writes about a 'pedagogy of kindness,' an idea unknown to policymakers these days. In these essays, he demands that we see the world through the eyes of others, that we open our minds and our hearts to the children and families left behind by our culture, that we place the demands of social justice above the demands of accountability and testing. You need to read his work, think about it, incorporate it into your sense of what is right and just. 'Where there is no vision, the people perish.' Paul Thomas has the vision we need now."

Diane Ravitch, *Research Professor of Education at New York University, Historian of Education*

"Literature, Professor Thomas shows us, can and should be a source of ideas that challenge us to think critically about the world around us—especially the ways that we educate our children. Thomas uses this wonderfully written book to engage readers with these ideas and to further the much-needed conversation concerning education policy."

Kevin Welner, *Director, National Education Policy Center*

"Paul Thomas is the master of the pithy, pointed essay, and this collection should provoke readers to think hard about educational issues that matter. His 2013 recognition as NCTE's George Orwell

Award winner for public commentary that gets to the heart of the matter was well-earned and suggests the quality of the pieces collected in this volume. If you're not acquainted with his work, now's a great time to meet him in this book; and if you are familiar with his writing, then you know what a treat you're in for."

Peter Smagorinsky, *Distinguished Research Professor of English Education Department of Language and Literacy Education, The University of Georgia*

"In *Beware the Roadbuilders: Literature as Resistance*, P.L. Thomas reveals the intersections among oppression, education, and literature. Drawing on canonical and contemporary texts, he lifts them into the light, exposing surface cracks and deep crevices, both of which have the potential to leverage transformation. Thomas challenges teachers, parents, policymakers, and readers everywhere to rethink what literature can show us about society, and how such learning can lead to a more just future."

Julie Gorlewski, *Assistant Professor, State University of New York at New Paltz, Co-editor English Journal (NCTE)*

"Boldly imagined, brilliantly powerful, Thomas' collection of 'reimagined' blog posts originating at his blog, the becoming radical, illuminates the power of critical literacy to reread and rewrite our worlds. The scholarship on what texts matter and what texts reveal support the status quo of power is impressive and well handled. This is the kind of writing that truly calls for the examination of self, of personal beliefs, biases."

Jeanne Marcum Gerlach, *Associate VP for K-16 Initiatives, Dean, Professor, University of Texas-Arlington*

"This book demonstrates the wide ranging critical perspectives of Paul Thomas. His insightful critical discussions of areas as diverse as art, literature, race, education, class and others provide readers with insights that allow for engaging our critical consciousnesses. The material is provocative and timely. A must read."

William M. Reynolds, *Associate Professor, Curriculum, Foundations & Reading, Georgia Southern University*

"Dr. Thomas taught me that when I am successful as a teacher, an equal part of the success belongs to my student. I believe that the same is true in the other direction: when I am successful as a teacher, I attribute a large part of that success to the influence his mentorship has had on the way I conceive of education, students, and my role as an educator. His passion for social justice advocacy and art -- and the occasional bad joke -- creates a space in which freedom of expression fosters a sense of responsibility to be critical of the power of a single voice. Dr. Thomas' is a powerful voice for change, but ultimately, his greatest influence is in the way he empowers others to speak."

Alison H. Williams, *Furman University 2014, First-year ELA teacher*

BEWARE THE ROADBUILDERS
LITERATURE AS RESISTANCE

P.L. THOMAS

BEWARE
THE ROADBUILDERS
LITERATURE
AS RESISTANCE

P. L. THOMAS

GARN PRESS
NEW YORK, NY

Published by Garn Press, LLC
New York, NY
www.garnpress.com

Book and cover design by Benjamin J. Taylor

Cover photo by Benjamin J. Taylor

Library of Congress Control Number: 2014959054

Publisher's Cataloging-in-Publication Data

Thomas, P. L. (Paul Lee), 1961-
    Beware the roadbuilders : literature as resistance / P. L. Thomas.
        pages cm
Includes bibliographical references.
ISBN: 978-1-942146-07-0 (pbk.)
ISBN: 978-1-942146-08-7 (e-book)
        1. Education and state. 2. Social justice. 3. Critical pedagogy. 3. Literature—
Study and teaching. 4. Racism in education.   I. Title.
LB2806.36 . T487 2015
379`.73—dc23
                                2014959054

child (Skylar) of my child (Jessica)

child of my child
not yet here among us

we have not made this world
as we should have as we could have

you will be among us though
in a world a beautiful possibility still

a world a beautiful possibility still
just as you are and will always be

when you arrive we will all hold hands
reach for you and cry and smile and cry and smile

and then together we will all look skyward
because all above us is the limit the sky

the sky
the sky

nearly as wide and forever infinite
as the exponential love for you child of my child

P.L. Thomas
13 November 2013

Table of Contents

Foreword

Beware the Dam Builders, Too

I could write in short space about how much I admire and look up to Paul Thomas for the public scholarship he creates. Many thousands of people read and share his public writing each day, from blog posts to op-eds to journal articles to tweets. He's constantly engaged in the discourse on public education for the sake of the students and teachers involved in it. I could share that he's also a genuine and good-natured human, someone I'm proud to call a friend. He's never been too busy to respond to an email or answer a phone call. I save bits and pieces of advice he's provided and return to it, timely reminders of how to respond in difficult situations.

Instead, let me start by saying just how important I think this book is. Based on the coalescence of his writings on education and deep literary knowledge, Thomas blends the two in ways equal parts beautiful for their craft and terrifying for their truths in revealing the current situation. Every educator and parent needs a copy of this book. The consequences of people not reading and understanding the attacks on learning, children, and teachers outlined here are grave, embodied in the powerful and diverse literary imagery he uses to describe them.

Reading this book reminded me of a story that hits close to my home of Fayetteville, Arkansas, one that played out a century ago. William Hope 'Coin' Harvey, convinced that a greed-based society (later known as unbridled capitalism) would ultimately perish, made plans to build an obelisk in his resort at Monte Ne, Arkansas, to hold a time capsule, preserving for future societies the story of how America fell. Coin's pyramid was to preserve copies of his financial book, *The Remedy*, as well as other cultural artifacts of a once great society.

Ill health eventually thwarted Mr. Harvey's building plans, but the model he provides is one that I urge public educators and parents to follow after reading *Beware the Road Builders*. Whether we build an obelisk or the modern day version of making sure something lasts forever, the story of America and our education system is one presently imperiled by faux education reformers. If the current trends are not subverted and reversed, trends that we should all, following Giroux, bear witness to, books like this one will tell the story well, making it simple to tie the end of the American experiment to the loss of its system of public education.

Recognized by the National Council of Teachers of English in 2013 with the George Orwell Award for the defense of public language, Thomas is unflinching and unflappable, unequivocally taking corporate and government figures and ideas to task. Standing above other accounts as one of the most literary of the education reform whistleblower texts, metaphors and images borrowed from our literary kin are expertly wielded by Thomas, axes driving into our collective psyche a strong counter-narrative to prevailing and well-financed forces.

Beware the Roadbuilders? Despite egregious wealth inequity in America today, Coin's fatalistic predictions are not yet realized. His resort town was sunk beneath the waters of manmade Beaver Lake in 1966, and only rarely are the ruins seen when the water recedes in drought. One erect structure, part of two hotels built on the site, is surrounded with barbed wire and covered with decades of graffiti, a building with no capstone of books and artifacts for the future, only its crumbling self. The water I drink and bathe in daily originates from the lake, a public good that was certainly part of the campaign to dam the river and build the lake. But it is the same water covering Coin's resort town and dreams that is now primarily the embodiment of consumerism, expensive boats racing back and forth in front of million-dollar houses, a well-off personal playground to the rich enabled by the government vis-à-vis the US Army Corps of Engineers. So, beware the dam builders, too.

Christian Z. Goering
University of Arkansas
www.edusanity.com

Prologue

Education in Black and White
Beware the Roadbuilders

Despite efforts to ignore, despite efforts to deny, the U.S. has been forced to look closely, look hard at the stark and disturbing realities of race and racism in 2014. One city has become nearly mythic, in part due to the power of social media, simply evoked as *Ferguson*.

The list grows and remains equally incomplete, but the social consciousness now includes not just the name of a city in protest, but the names of young black men shot and killed, often by the exact police force charged to serve and protect: Trayvon Martin, Jordan Davis, Tamir Rice, Eric Garner…

And just as the mainstream media has been exposed for 24/7 coverage of missing young white females while ignoring missing young black females, this growing list of sacrificed young black men remains haunting as well because the numbers of young black men discarded, ignored, or abandoned dwarfs the short list above, the names serving both the media feeding frenzy and as rallying cries for those seeking justice *deferred*.

As I have been preparing this volume, Ferguson has answered Langston Hughes's searing question about "a dream deferred"— "*Or does it explode?*" And since the following chapters of this book tend to reach for the carefully crafted and published *word*, I have watched as James Baldwin's essays and public talks have returned in the social media of many who are outraged by the callous relationship between the U.S. police and legal system and young black males; who are outraged about the swift and deadly consequences of justice at the end of a gun; who are outraged about the now tarnished shields on police officers' chests that seem not to represent their service but to protect them from the consequences of their too often dark and swift deadly force, while they remain above the law they represent.

Like Hughes, Baldwin in "They Can't Turn Back" (*Mademoiselle*, August 1960) was prescient about Ferguson: "a gesture can blow up a town," although he was discussing specifically the South ("A gesture," 2011). A year later in an interview by Studs Terkel, Baldwin (2014a) explained: "The question that really obsesses me today is not whether or not I like violence, or whether or not you like it—unless the situation is ameliorated, and very, very, quickly, there *will* be violence" (p. 17). Further, Baldwin could have easily been speaking about Ferguson as he confronted the racial tension in Birmingham:

> There will be violence...one day in Birmingham. And it won't be the fault of the Negroes in Birmingham. It is the fault of the administration of Birmingham, and the apathy of Washington. An intolerable situation. It has been intolerable for one hundred years. (pp. 17-18)

Now we add fifty-plus years, and we must consider that protesters in Ferguson have been slurred as "rioters" and "looters." And then, the 1984 Julius Lester interview with Baldwin (2014a) revealed Baldwin as a maverick:

> **Lester:** What do you see as the task facing black writers today, regardless of age or generation?
>
> **Baldwin:** This may sound strange, but I would say to make the question of color obsolete.
>
> **Lester:** And how would a black writer do that?

Baldwin: Well, you ask me a reckless question, I'll give you a reckless answer—by realizing first of all that the world is not white. And by realizing that the real terror that engulfs the white world now is visceral terror. I can't prove this, but I know it. It's the terror of being described by those they've been describing for so long. And that will make the concept of color obsolete. Do you see what I mean? (pp. 52-53)

In his discussion with Lester, Baldwin clarified his identifying himself as a witness, not a spokesperson. In that role as witness, Baldwin confronted the white gaze as blame, but with Terkel, Baldwin (2014a) also challenged the calls for patience: "When people talk about *time*, therefore, I can't help but be absolutely not only impatient but bewildered. *Why* should I wait any longer? In any case, even if I were willing to—which I am not—how?" (p. 13).

This prompted Terkel to quote Baldwin's essay on Faulkner: "'There is never time in the future in which we will work out our salvation. The challenge is in the moment, the time is always now'" (Baldwin, 2014a, p. 13).

Ferguson could easily carry that refrain, "the time is always now."

This volume is, in that context, a collection and reimagining of posts originating at my blog, *the becoming radical.* They represent both the *act* of critical literacy as well as a *case* for critical literacy. The following chapters use texts of many genres, forms, and media to initiate confrontations of social and educational norms. Since the thread holding this volume together is *text*, I often quote at length, despite scholarly conventions against such a practice—both to honor the voices from whom I draw inspiration, *to stand on the shoulder of giants*, and to invite you to continue to those original works beyond the passages I share here.

While each chapter can stand alone as a separate reading, my intent was to produce a cohesive theme or motif about the power of critical literacy to read and re-read the world, to write and re-rewrite the world (Freire, 1993, 1998). Supporting that larger message are several key ideas and questions:

- What are the confrontational texts we should be inviting students to read, that anyone should read?

- Instead of reducing texts to the narrow expectations of New Criticism or "close reading," how do we expand those texts into how they inform living in a free society and engaging in activism?

- How do traditional assumptions about what texts matter and what texts reveal support the status quo of power?

- And how can texts of all types assist in the ongoing pursuit of equity among free people?

I have also sought ways to include some of the power of blogging as I reframed the work for a more traditional book. In this re-imagining, I have tried to add another layer of meaning to the pieces collected. And one blog post serves as the guiding image for the entire book, the image of the roadbuilders culled from Alice Walker—now an image, I think, that is not unlike the specter of the police from Ferguson to New York City.

In *The Color Purple* (Walker, 1982), Nettie sees the world in stark black and white once she faces and confronts the *missionary zeal being done to* the people who are native to Africa. The letters exchanged between Nettie and Celie are literally the lived stories of oppression and the oppressed right there in black and white for readers: "The first thing I should tell you about is the road," explains Nettie, continuing:

> The road finally reached the cassava fields about nine months ago and the Olinka, who love nothing better than a celebration, outdid themselves preparing a feast for the roadbuilders who talked and laughed and cut their eyes at the Olinka women the whole day. In the evening many were invited into the village itself and there was merrymaking far into the night. I think Africans are very much like

white people back home, in that they think they are the center of the universe and that everything that is done is done for them. The Olinka definitely hold this view. *And so they naturally thought the road being built was for them* [emphasis added].

In the wake of Ferguson, can we not imagine this same exchange about the contrast between how whites and blacks view the police and the legal system in the U.S.? And then Nettie's letter grows more and more ominous:

Well, the morning after the road was "finished" as far as the Olinka were concerned (after all, it had reached their village), what should we discover but that the roadbuilders were back at work. They have instructions to continue the road for another thirty miles! And to continue it on its present course right through the village of Olinka. By the time we were out of bed, the road was already being dug through Catherine's newly planted yam field. Of course the Olinka were up in arms. But the roadbuilders were literally up in arms. They had guns, Celie, with orders to shoot!

The image of the roadbuilders with guns resonates as I revisit my posts, as I shape this volume, and as I re-read both my own words and the letter from Nettie:

It was pitiful, Celie. The people felt so betrayed! They stood by helplessly—they really don't know how to fight, and rarely think of it since the old days of tribal wars—as their crops and then their very homes were destroyed. Yes. The roadbuilders didn't deviate an inch from the plan the headman was following. Every hut that lay in the proposed roadpath was leveled. And, Celie, our church, our school, my hut, all went down in a matter of hours. Fortunately, we were able to save all of our things, but with a tarmac road running straight through the middle of it, the village itself seems gutted.

Immediately after understanding the roadbuilders' intentions, the chief set off toward the coast, seeking explanations and reparations. Two weeks later he returned with even more disturbing news. The whole territory, including the Olinkas' village, now belongs to a rubber manufacturer in England. ...The ancient, giant mahogany trees, all the trees, the game, everything of the forest was being destroyed, and the land was forced to lie flat, he said, and bare as the palm of his hand. (pp. 174-176)

And then there is a scene in the problematic film (Smyth, 2014) *Gandhi* (itself both an unmasking of imperialism and the embodiment of paternalism and privilege) when Gandhi expresses his idealism about the potential for non-violent resistance to overcome oppression:

Brigadier: You don't think we're just going to walk out of India!

Gandhi: Yes. In the end, you will walk out. Because 100,000 Englishmen simply cannot control 350 million Indians, if those Indians refuse to cooperate. (Attenborough, 1982)

As a work of art (*The Color People*) and a film recreation (and appropriation) of history (*Gandhi*), these scenes speak to the current state of education and education reform, especially when those contexts are viewed through the lens of the 60th anniversary of *Brown v. Board* (Thomas, 2014, May 16). Unlike Gandhi, I am not optimistic that oppressive privilege will simply walk away. Like Nettie, I watch as the roadbuilders court the people they plan to bulldoze. In New Orleans, the roadbuilders are charter school advocates and Teach For America recruits are the missionaries filled with zeal.

And 60 years after *Brown v. Board*, New Orleans has replaced its public schools with charter schools in the wake of firing all of the public school teachers—a 21st century separate but equal:

White students disproportionately attend the best charter schools, while the worst are almost exclusively populated by African American students. Activists in New Orleans joined with others in Detroit and Newark last month to file a federal civil rights complaint, alleging that the city's best-performing schools have admissions policies that exclude African American children. (Layton, 2014, n.p.)

Privilege remains white and inequity remains black. I invite you, then, to read, to listen—a call that black and brown people have offered in the aftermath of young black men being shot and killed, in the aftermath of justice denied as police remain above the law, pressed like a boot on the throats of blacks.

First, listen to Andre Perry (2014, June 2) in "The education-reform movement is too white to do any good":

But let's also stipulate that overwhelmingly white movements pursuing change for black and brown communities are inherently paternalistic. ...Reform is being done to communities of color. That's why saying you're a black education reformer effectually elicits charges of "acting white" from black communities....

So when black and brown people are largely absent from positions of power, the entire reform movement loses credibility and accrues suspicion. Black education reformers struggle to connect with the very communities we're members of. The overarching sentiment among attendees at the aforementioned meeting was that black leadership is missing from education reform. Consequently, "reform" has become a dirty word in some communities....

We need less "reform" and more social justice. (n.p.)

And then, listen to Tressie McMillan Cottom (2014) in "No, college isn't the answer. Reparations are":

For some, reparations to African Americans for enslavement and state-sanctioned apartheid (more benignly known as "Jim Crow") is a shocking case to make....For Darity, Hamilton, and many other serious scholars of race, history, and inequality, the matter of reparations is anything but novel or shocking. Neither is it hyperbolic....*If you have never heard of them, that is likely by design* [emphasis added]. Few powerful persons or institutions have ever been willing to seriously put a reparations program before the American people.

But I wager that you *have* heard a lot about how education and opportunity can be, through hard work and moral fortitude, the path to greater equality for African Americans. In many ways, when the formerly enslaved asked first for a national program to redress the forced, free labor that made the United States the nation we know it to be, they were given schooling instead of redress; opportunity instead of compensation. It is an attitude that persists in our policy and our cultural lexicon. When the demand is for justice, we are most likely to respond with an appeal, instead, to fairness. And in no institution is that more clearly evident than education. (n.p.)

Also, listen to Mia McKenzie (2014) in "The White Teachers I Wish I Never Had":

Black children need teachers who can reflect the history of our people to them in an honest and empowering way. They also need teachers who *see* them, who don't think of them as deficient, as problems to solve, or as thugs-in-training, when they are really just children, innocent and eager and as capable of learning as anyone else. They need teachers who can love them. In a world that tells them they are less, having authority figures, from an early age, who believe in their humanity, in their goodness, in their extraordinariness, is everything.

Ms. Reisman was the first terrible white teacher I had, but after her there were others. Mr. Fleischman, my seventh-grade homeroom and math teacher, was one. He disliked me and he showed it. He punished me for things more popular kids got away with daily. He seemed to like only the Black kids who were hip and cool but not smart, and then only if they were also boys. My awkward girl presence bugged him, particularly because I wasn't silent or invisible. (n.p.)

And then finally, listen to Margaret Kimberley (2014) in "Police Target Black Children":

Americans should take a long look in the mirror before criticizing other nations for human rights abuses. The law enforcement system in the United States ranks among the worst in the world in the cruel treatment meted out to its citizens. Even children in this country are not safe if they are black and unlucky enough to interact with the police. Of all the various ethnic and national groups in the United States, only black people have to worry that their child may be pushed through a glass window by officers of the law. (n.p.)

A study published in the *Journal of Personality and Social Psychology* (Goff, et al., 2014) demonstrated what black people have always known and lived. Black children are dehumanized to such an extent that they aren't perceived as children at all. They are assumed to be older, less innocent, and inherently guilty of some wrong, some breach of law. Study co-author Matthew Jackson said, "With the average age overestimation for black boys exceeding four-and-a-half years, in some cases, black children may be viewed as adults when they are just 13 years old" (McDonough, 2014).

Recurring high-profile shootings of unarmed young black males in the U.S. remind us of what this research confirms and what the following chapters seek to examine, to investigate—and as Baldwin would say, to witness: Beware the roadbuilders. They are not here to serve you, they are on their way to bulldoze right over you.

Author's Note: As mentioned above, this volume is drawn from my blog posts, work that serves as a drafting process for a wide variety of my work. Some posts have been integrated in a number of different publications—some more formal public work and some much more formal scholarly work. The result is that my work is recursive, consciously so, in that pieces are blended into a variety of publications as I continue to wrestle with the ideas and texts that both inform me and my view of the world.

1

New Criticism, Close Reading, and Failing Critical Literacy Again

When the Common Core debates drift toward advocacy or critiques of the standards themselves, I have refused, mostly, to engage with that conversation because I believe debating the quality of Common Core concedes too much. I remain opposed to Common Core regardless of the quality of the standards because of the following reasons:

1. Common Core cannot and will not be decoupled from the caustic influence of high-stakes testing;

2. all bureaucratic and mandated standards de-professionalize teaching;

3. accountability/standards/testing as a reform paradigm has failed, and nothing about the Common Core iteration offers a different approach, except that this is called "national";

4. there is absolutely nothing in the Common Core agenda that addresses social or educational inequities such as disproportionate discipline policies, course access, and teacher assignment (Mathis, 2012).

So with due trepidation, I want to wade into the few but needed challenges being offered about how Common Core encourages "close reading" of texts. First, let me highlight that my primary field of teaching writing offers a powerful and disturbing parallel model of how the accountability/standards/testing movement has supplanted and destroyed evidence-based pedagogy.

I have detailed that the rise of best practice in the teaching of writing in the 1970s and 1980s was squelched by the accountability era begun in the 1980s (Thomas, 2013, December 3). As well, Applebee and Langer (2013) offer a chilling refrain of best practice in writing wilting under the weight of standards and testing in their *Writing Instruction That Works: Proven Methods for Middle and High School Classrooms*. We must acknowledge that reading instruction and reading experiences for children will suffer the same negative consequences under Common Core and the related high-stakes tests, because there are no provisions for adopting Common Core that change how standards and tests are implemented. Often, each round of standards and tests is simply infused into the current practices, and in reality, Common Core approaches to reading are nothing more than new names for traditional (and flawed) reading practices.

Next, I strongly recommend the following perspectives that essentially confront the central problem with Common Core's focus on close reading. Also, as I'll expand on below, close reading continues the traditional view of text-based analysis that is grounded in New Criticism—and thus excludes critical literacy and the powerful contributions of marginalized writers and critics, as highlighted in the work of Louise Rosenblatt (1995).

In "Reading Without Understanding — Common Core Versus Abraham Lincoln," Alan Singer (2013) concludes this about the flaws of close reading: "When Common Core ignores the context behind the Gettysburg Address, it does students, Americans, and Abraham Lincoln a great disservice" (n.p.).

And Daniel E. Ferguson (2013/2014) rejects the claim that implementing Common Core is a civil rights issue; instead, Ferguson argues:

To force a discussion of King's letter to remain "text dependent" may make it easier to test, but it also forces out its entire social and historical context....

Critical literacy argues that students' sense of their own realities should never be treated as outside the meaning of a text. To do so is to infringe on their rights to literacy. In other words, literacy is a civil and human right; having your own experiences, knowledge, and opinions valued is a right as well. Despite praise for King's rhetoric, Coleman promotes a system that creates outsiders of students in their own classrooms. (n.p.)

I want to add just a few more thoughts on why committing to Common Core and close reading fails against the gains we have made in understanding the complexity of responding to texts in the context of the words on the page, the intent and biography of the writer, the biography of the reader, and the multiple historical contexts that intersect when *anyone* reads *any* text.

Let me start with an example. I always began my poetry unit with "The Red Wheelbarrow" that William Carlos Williams details "so much depends/upon." My instructional goals with starting here were many, but in part, this poem was ideal to make a key point about how we respond to text. I would read the poem aloud and then ask students to close their eyes and envision a wheelbarrow. Then I would ask several students to describe what they saw.

The exercise highlighted that many students pictured wheelbarrows in various positions. I always shared with students that I always see any wheelbarrow turned up on its front edge, leaning against a tree because my father was adamant that a wheelbarrow must not sit with the body of the wheelbarrow turned so that it can gather water, which leads to rust forming. This activity allowed us to discuss what readers can say about the text of a piece, distinguish that from their personal responses (the text says nothing of how the wheelbarrow is sitting, but states that it is red, for example), and tease out how writer intent, text, and reader affect create the possibility of dozens of credible, although different, interpretations.

From there we began to confront what counts as "right," as well as who decides what is "right" as an interpretation. I made certain my students understood how to conduct a New Criticism analysis and stressed that school, teachers, and many testing situations (notably Advanced Placement) honor *only* such approaches to text. Next, however, we challenged that dynamic and began exploring how each student's empowerment and autonomy rested on having a broad set of lens through which to engage with text, and through which to unmask the power dynamics embedded in authoritative interpretations of text (see Chapter 16).

This, of course, is the province of critical literacy.

Ironically, if we use a critical reading of Common Core and its calls for close reading (Ferguson, 2013/2014), we discover that close reading is simply a repackaging of text-only approaches to text embraced by New Criticism (Thomas, 2012).

Like the mechanistic and reductive ways in which New Criticism has been implemented in formal schooling in order to control and measure objectively how students respond to text, Common Core and the focus on close reading are poised to serve efficiency models of high-stakes testing, while also failing students who need and deserve the complex and challenging tools afforded with critical literacy. Common Core and close reading—if we wade into debates about the quality of the standards—are nothing new. In fact, advocates of Common Core are ironically proving why instead of close reading, we actually need critical reading.

Context matters.

2

On Jeffrey Eugenides's *Middlesex*

With *Middlesex*, Jeffrey Eugenides (2003) garnered popular and critical attention for, in part, the controversial focus on the biological sex of the central character. But the novel also offers a powerful exploration of Detroit—the setting nearly a character itself—as well as an unmasking of the sociopolitical, racial, and sexual history of the U.S. throughout the mid-twentieth century.

Below, I briefly consider how the novel speaks to the status of workers in the U.S. (notably teachers) and then to issues of class, race, and cultural heritage.

21st Century Teachers: Easy to Hire, Easy to Fire

Detroit rises to the status of a major character in Jeffrey Eugenides's *Middlesex*. About a fifth of the way into the novel, the narrator, Calliope/Cal Stephanides makes this observation about the arrival of the automotive industry in the Motor City:

Historical fact: people stopped being human in 1913. That was the year Henry Ford put his cars on rollers and made his workers adopt the speed of the assembly line. At first, workers rebelled. They quit in droves, unable to accustom their bodies to the new pace of the age. Since then, however, the adaptation has been passed down: we've all inherited it to some degree, so that we plug right into joysticks and remotes, to repetitive motions of a hundred kinds.

But in 1922 it was still a new thing to be a machine.

...Part of the new production method's genius was its division of labor into unskilled tasks. That way you could hire anyone. And fire anyone. (Eugenides, 2003, p. 95)

This is a chilling passage about the dawning of the assembly line era of American manufacturing, but equally as chilling is that this passage offers a clue to where we now are heading in U.S. public education and the fate of the American teacher.

A Teacher Is a Teacher Is a Teacher...

Like Henry Ford, Bill Gates has ushered in a new era in U.S. public education, shifting the already robust accountability era—that began in the early 1980s and accelerated in 2001 with the passing of No Child Left Behind (NCLB)—from focusing on school and student accountability for standards and test scores to demanding that teachers be held accountable for student test scores addressing those standards. Gates has been assisted by Michelle Rhee and Secretary of Education Arne Duncan as the "No Excuses" Reformers (Thomas, Porfilio, Gorlewski, & Carr, 2014) who have perpetuated narratives conjuring the myth of the "bad" teacher, which Adam Bessie (2010) has confronted by suggesting we hire hologram teachers in order to remove the greatest problem facing education: Humans.

Just as the assembly line rendered all workers interchangeable, and thus easy to hire and easy to fire, the current education reforms focusing on teacher accountability, value-added methods (VAM) of evaluating teachers, and the growing fascination with Teach For America (TFA) are seeking the same outcome for teachers: a de-professionalized workforce and teaching as a service industry (Thomas, 2010, November 14), easy to hire and easy to fire.

All of the following are key elements of the "No Excuses"

Reformers' plans to eradicate teaching as a profession in the U.S.:

- Secretary Duncan leads the chorus of "teachers are the most important factor in student achievement" despite ample evidence that teacher influence on measurable student outcomes, i.e. tests, is only about 10-15% (Di Carlo, 2012). This refrain serves two purposes for the "No Excuses" Reformers: (1) it deflects attention from the 60-80% influence that out-of-school factors play in student achievement, and (2) ensures that teachers are de-professionalized, thus creating a cheap labor force for a privatized education system.

- The propaganda continues to increase, calling for TFA recruits to serve high-poverty schools. The evidence on the effectiveness of TFA recruits is sparse, but once reviewed (Heilig & Jez, 2010), the research doesn't support using uncertified and inexperienced teachers to address the main problem faced by many high-poverty schools: a lack of certified, experienced teachers. Thus, TFA recruits can only be attractive because they represent the Ford ideal of workers easy to hire and easy to fire (exceptionally easy to fire, in fact, because they leave of their own accord in a short time).

- From *The New York Times* (Lowry, 2012) to President Obama in his 2012 State of the Union Address, VAM propaganda remains powerful, calling for holding teachers accountable for their students' test scores. Yet, after careful examinations of the Chetty et al. study praised by Lowry (Baker, 2012, January 7), any claims that VAM is effective remain unfounded (see Thomas, 2013, January 3; Thomas, 2014, April 13). Again, we must conclude that seeking ways to quickly hire and fire teachers is more important than whether or not any method achieves the claimed goals of seeking higher student achievement. VAM is a terrible tool for identifying and rewarding excellent teaching, but, like the assembly line, it is an effective (as in efficient) tool for reducing any worker to a cog in the machine.

- While 50 states have implemented accountability, standards, and testing without satisfactory results, "No Excuses" Reformers are committed to national standards, Common Core, and the expected national tests to follow. While there is no national or international evidence that standards and testing improve education (Mathis, 2012), this call for federalizing standards and testing proves to be an important lever for completely removing teacher autonomy and creating the platform upon which teachers are easily fired.

- And now a long-time mantra coming from self-proclaimed reformers wedded to school choice ideology— "All parents deserve the same choices as the wealthy," a mask for their real intentions, privatizing schools, and a perverse idealizing of "choice" (Thomas, 2012)—is being bolstered by the rise of parent-trigger laws and legislation aimed at giving parents direct oversight of what is being taught. "The trouble with the consumer movement as embodied in the New Hampshire law is that it makes public schools vulnerable to the whims of fringe groups," explains Gardner (2012). The medical profession has already seen what happens when professionals abdicate their expertise to the consumer when the overuse of antibiotics created MRSA and other "superbugs" (DeBellis & Zdanawicz, 2000; Ong, et al. 2007). But parental oversight, again, is not about doing what is best for students; it's about using free market rhetoric to create teaching as a service industry.

The ultimate evidence that "No Excuses" Reformers want to de-professionalize teaching, however, is the issue of professional autonomy. Accountability must be preceded by autonomy; otherwise, accountability is tyranny. Instead of creating professional autonomy for teachers, every aspect of the "No Excuses" Reform movement is bent on removing autonomy from teachers, while reducing further all student achievement to tests so that teacher quality can be easily and quickly quantified as well.

In the wake of Obama's continued support of the current reform movement and the prospect of where "No Excuses" Reform will continue to go, I think it isn't much of a stretch to consider the possibility of this sentence coming to pass: *Historical fact: teachers stopped being professionals in the twenty-first century.*

It is the path we are on, and it is a path that must be avoided.

Class, Race, and Cultural Heritage

Fiction offers avenues to Truths, often *hard* Truths, that otherwise remain closed or less often traveled. While many people associate *Middlesex* (Eugenides, 2003) with themes addressing sexuality and gender, this novel also offers readers a vivid and insightful consideration of class, race, and cultural heritage. Toward the middle of the novel, the life of the main character, Calliope/Cal Stephanides, intersects with the 1967 race riots in Detroit, a moment in history reframed by the narrator: "[I]n Detroit, in July of 1967, what happened was nothing less than a guerrilla uprising.... It turned out that when it finally happened, the revolution wasn't televised. On TV they called it only a riot" (pp. 248, 251).

Here, the narrative contextualizes events of history within the tensions of race, class, and culture, emphasizing the role of power in how we perceive Truth—the media, as an extension of white middle-class power, were in control of how the events were characterized.

In the reality of a riot/"guerrilla uprising," Calliope/Cal, as a child, slips from her home and rides her bicycle behind a tank to find and rescue her father, who has jumped up in the middle of the night to barricade himself in his diner and protect his business. As the confrontations between African Americans and the police bolstered by the National Guard and the military intensify, Calliope/Cal confronts the power dynamics that lay beneath mid-twentieth century America (and remain today, as I will discuss below):

> Up until that night, our neighborhood's basic feeling about
> our fellow Negro citizens could be summed up in something
> Tessie said after watching Sidney Poitier's performance in
> *To Sir with Love*, which opened a month before the riots.
> She said, "You see, they can speak perfectly normal if they
> want." That was how we felt. (Even me back then, I won't
> deny it, because we're all the children of our parents.) We
> were ready to accept the Negroes. We weren't prejudiced
> against them. We wanted to include them in our society *if
> they would only act normal!*

> In their support for Johnson's Great Society, in their applause
> after *To Sir with Love*, our neighbors and relatives made
> clear their well-intentioned belief that the Negroes were
> fully capable of being just like white people—but then what
> was this? they asked themselves as they saw pictures on
> television. (Eugenides, 2003, p. 240)

As the climax of the narrative in the novel related to the riot and
the characters approaches, Calliope/Cal's father, Milton, confronts
an African American character, Morrison, who stands at the door
of Milton's store in the firestorm of the riot to buy cigarettes:

> As [Morrison] did, the riots, his frayed nerves, the smell of
> fire in the air, and the audacity of this man Morrison dodg-
> ing sniper fire for a pack of cigarettes all became too much
> for Milton. Suddenly he was waving his arms, indicating
> everything, and shouting through the door, "What's the
> matter with you people?"

> Morrison took only a moment. "The matter with us," he
> said, "is you." And then he was gone. (Eugenides, 2003, p.
> 246)

"The matter with us is you" becomes a paradoxical refrain for
Milton, Calliope/Cal explains, and these scenes of a novel blending often ignored U.S. history and fiction serve as a portal to the
"no excuses" ideology driving a significant portion of education

reform today.

Seeking Equity: Not "If," But "How" and "Why"

Under President Obama, the education reform agenda has intensified, rising on the foundation built by President George W. Bush and No Child Left Behind (NCLB). The tensions in the debate concerning the quality of U.S. public education and the reforms needed have created two broad camps that I have identified as "No Excuses" Reformers and Social Context Reformers:

> "No Excuses" Reformers insist that the source of success and failure lies in each child and each teacher, requiring only the adequate level of effort to rise out of the circumstances not of her/his making. …
>
> Social Context Reformers have concluded that the source of success and failure lies primarily in the social and political forces that govern our lives. (Thomas, Porfilio, Gorlewski, & Carr, 2014, p. 1)

Social Context Reformers tend to place social justice at the center of their views of why we must support public education, and how we need to reform that system to fulfill the promise of universal education. "No Excuses" Reformers have begun to claim their commitment to the free market is also a commitment to social justice. As well, "No Excuses" Reformers, led by Secretary of Education Arne Duncan (as well as Bill Gates and Michelle Rhee), hold the power in the debate, often branding Social Context Reformers as reactionaries.

Since "No Excuses" Reformers have the bully pulpit, key elements of the "no excuses" ideology drive government policies such as Race to the Top (RTTT). These same elements directly and indirectly reinforce non-public, private enterprise initiatives such as Teach For America (TFA) and Knowledge Is Power Program (KIPP) charter schools. Much of the stated focus of the "No Excuses" Reformers has become children living in poverty and children of color, while other marginalized groups have remained marginalized, such as special needs students and English language learners.

"No Excuses" Reformers claim to be seeking social justice for children living in poverty, and they frame that commitment within mantras such as "poverty is not destiny" and "poverty is not an excuse." Recently, I have discovered that "No Excuses" Reformers have added a new claim: progressive educators (their pejorative term for Social Context Reformers) are not helping impoverished and minority students; they are in fact the *cause* of those children's failure.

While engaging with a "No Excuses" Reformer in a discussion thread for an *Education Week* blog (Ravitch, 2012) and later on Twitter, I was confronted by the charge that Lisa Delpit had put people of "my ilk" (as I was characterized, suggesting falsely that I am a progressive) in their place. First, from Buck (2006):

> What I found most interesting was the fact that she high-lighted some scathing comments by other black teachers who seem to view so-called "progressive" education as a liberal racist ploy.

And more recently, a charge against Alfie Kohn's *Education Week* piece confronting the "pedagogy of poverty" stated that Delpit's work refutes Kohn's positions and supports the "no excuses" ideology: "[Delpit] eventually adopted more traditional approaches—the same approaches that most of her African American colleagues used. Probably including some techniques that high-performing charter schools like KIPP still use today" (Petrilli, 2011).

If the "No Excuses" Reformers are in fact presenting the true avenue to social justice, then Social Context Reformers are not simply offering a failed alternative, but they are, as the two commentaries above suggest, perpetuating inequity.

The problem, however, is that "No Excuses" Reformers are making two key errors. First, the debate about seeking equity is not about "if," but about "how" and "why" we address inequity in our schools as a confrontation to inequity in our society. Next, simply put, they are grossly misrepresenting Delpit's work in order to offer false evidence for their own corrosive ideology.

Not taken out of context, Delpit (1988) has established herself as a strong opponent of standardized testing, a key element of the "no excuses" ideology, and she has clearly refuted any claims that her work justifies traditional practices:

> I do not advocate a simplistic 'basic skills' approach for children outside of the culture of power. It would be (and has been) tragic to operate as if these children were incapable of critical and higher-order thinking and reasoning. Rather, I suggest that schools must provide these children the content that other families from a different cultural orientation provide at home. *This does not mean separating children according to family background* [emphasis added], but instead, ensuring that each classroom incorporate strategies appropriate for all the children in its confines.
>
> *And I do not advocate that it is the school's job to attempt to change the homes of poor and nonwhite children to match the homes of those in the culture of power* [emphasis added]. That may indeed be a form of cultural genocide....In fact, [poor parents] transmit another culture that children must learn at home in order to survive in their communities. (p. 286)

While the "No Excuses" Reformers mask their racist and classist assumptions (dramatized in the passages from *Middlesex* above) as teaching children from poverty and children of color middle-class codes, their masking helps avoid the central questions of "why" and "how" to achieve the emancipatory goals voiced by Delpit.

Unlike Buck and Petrilli, Monique Redeaux (2011) explains that Delpit rejects the deficit perspectives found among "No Excuses" Reformers (including self-proclaimed poverty expert Ruby Payne):

> At first glance, [Delpit's position] seems to be the message conveyed by Payne: poor students of color need to be explicitly taught the hidden rules or codes of the middle/upper class in order to be successful in school, work, etc. When

examined more closely, this could not be further from the truth. Both terms, the "culture of poverty" (Payne) and the "culture of power" (Delpit) locate the problem in culture—*but in different ways/places* [emphasis added]….[T]he "culture of power" perspective suggests that the middle/upper class hold the power and key to institutional success, partly through their monopolization of educational skills, and that they do all they can to make sure that they and their offspring maintain that power.

When Delpit began her work on 'other people's children' she predicted that her purpose would be misunderstood… However, what she was actually advocating when she referred to "skills-based instruction" was the "useful and usable knowledge that contributes to a student's ability to communicate effectively in standard, generally acceptable literary forms" and she proposed that this was best learned in meaningful contexts. In other words, Delpit argued that both technical skills and critical thinking are essential: a person of color who has no critical thinking skills becomes the "trainable, low-level functionary of the dominant society, simply the grease that keeps the institutions which orchestrate his or her oppression running smoothly."…

The key distinction between Delpit and Payne is the reason *why* [emphasis added] they believe students should be taught the "hidden rules."…Delpit…does not believe that students should passively adopt an alternate code simply because it is the "way things are," especially if they want to achieve a particular economic status. Instead, Delpit asserts that students need to know and understand the power realities of this country with the purpose of changing these realities. (n.p.)

"No Excuses" Reformers offer no excuses for the norms of middle-class American values that still ignore, allow, and perpetuate a wide range of inequities—racial, social, gender. For "No Excuses" Reformers, education is a tool of the elite to train the masses to conform to a world that maintains the current status quo.

As extensions of "no excuses" ideology and mechanisms for indoctrinating certain children to be "just like white people," TFA and KIPP are preying on and perpetuating inequity—not confronting the codes in hopes of realizing equity. Social Context Reformers view social justice as a revolutionary goal; thus, education is offering all children the same opportunity to come to know the world in order to change it.

Let's turn now to another work of fiction, the Showtime series *Shameless*. This American version of a British series set instead on the South Side of Chicago looks at the world of inequity and poverty through the Gallagher family. In Episode 5 of Season 2, Veronica, a neighbor of the Gallaghers, is caring, with her husband Ken, for Ethel, a foster child. Ethel is still a child, but has had a child while living in a polygamous relationship and a disturbingly sheltered life. Ethel begins to experience the complex real world, and part of that includes a budding relationship with a young African American who has fathered a child.

When Ethel is going to the park to meet this boy, Veronica tells her: "Anybody offers you candy, that's code for crack. Apple Jacks, Crunch 'n Munch, hotcakes, jellybeans, fries, caviar...all crack." And this is yet another powerful message about the nature of codes and the privilege and oppression inherent in those codes. While the "No Excuses" Reformers seek to further entrench the codes of middle-class America, they are misrepresenting both the norms of language (so-called standard English does Ethel less good than the idiom of the streets, for example) and the possibility that norms may need to be confronted and changed.

Social justice is, again, an act of revolution. "No Excuses" Reformers are seeking to conform *some* children (not theirs) to the norms that have given the powerful their status of privilege. Recall Delpit: "And I do not advocate that it is the school's job to attempt to change the homes of poor and nonwhite children to match the homes of those in the culture of power."

To apply Calliope/Cal's confession to today, "No Excuses" Reformers are sending the message that children of color and children in poverty will be embraced "if they would only act normal"—and that normal is for the "No Excuses" Reformers to decide, but not for other people's children to question.

Lisa Delpit's work does not put Social Context Reformers in their place (her message reinforces that argument), but "No Excuses" Reformers are in fact seeking to use schools to put *other people's children* in their place.

That is inexcusable.

3

Adrienne Rich: Artist of the Possible and Life Among the Ruins

In late November of 2003, I sat on the floor in a crowded luncheon just a few feet and slightly behind Adrienne Rich, who was speaking and reading her poetry at the annual convention of the National Council of Teachers of English, held that year in San Francisco. Appropriately, Rich was reading from her upcoming collection, *The School Among the Ruins*, and talking about teaching, teachers, and education. I was struck by many things that day, and eventually I wrote a poem to capture the moment (see below).

As a poet, teacher, reader, and human, I have been deeply and permanently moved and changed by the poetry and essays of Rich, from the genius of "Diving into the Wreck" and "Aunt Jennifer's Tigers," to the reconsideration of Emily Dickinson in "Vesuvius at Home: The Power of Emily Dickinson" (see *On Lies, Secrets, and Silence*), to her remarkable and soaring *Arts of the Possible*, that includes one of the most cited passages in my scholarly works:

> Universal public education has two possible—and contradictory—missions. One is the development of a literate, articulate, and well-informed citizenry so that the democratic process can continue to evolve and the promise of radical equality can be brought closer to realization. The

other is the perpetuation of a class system dividing an elite, nominally "gifted" few, tracked from an early age, from a very large underclass essentially to be written off as alienated from language and science, from poetry and politics, from history and hope—toward low-wage temporary jobs. The second is the direction our society has taken. The results are devastating in terms of the betrayal of a generation of youth. The loss to the whole of society is incalculable. (Rich, 2001, p. 162)

For Rich, the human condition is a fact of what is spoken and unspoken:

The study of silence has long engrossed me. The matrix of a poet's work consists not only of what is *there* to be absorbed and worked on, but also of what is missing, *desaparecido*, rendered unspeakable, thus unthinkable. (p. 150)

When I discovered that Rich had passed (Fox, 2012), I recognized that while she would no longer speak again to us, she would never be unspoken. With her work, Rich remains the artist of the possible.

Woman as Poet: Possibilities

The life and writing of Rich are testaments to and challenges against the hegemonies of gender, marriage, sexuality, and human agency. She lived many lives in her one life, a fact common for women trapped in the expectations of gender that often create burdens that are nearly impossible to carry.

Her early life included marriage and three sons, and then she lived a much different life after separating from her husband, a life often characterized by a sort of radical feminism that celebrated her lesbianism. Her life as a poet/writer paralleled this personal transformation, with Rich acknowledging that her early success as a poet was built on her embracing modernist traditions, leading to her "Aunt Jennifer's Tigers" being both, according to her, a rejection (somewhat unconsciously) and model of those traditions. The poet

Rich, however, became a radical as well, resulting in canon czars such as Harold Bloom marginalizing Rich as merely political—missing entirely Rich's powerful argument that political is all that poetry and a poet can be: "I take it that poetry—if it is poetry—is liberatory at its core" (Rich, 2001, p. 116).

Rich's poetry and her critical work on Dickinson were central parts of my teaching during my nearly two decades as an ELA high school teacher. In fact, one of the most important and influential units I eventually included in the quarter we explored poetry included Rich's work paired with the poetry of Sylvia Plath and Anne Sexton. Along with these poets, we viewed the film *Pleasantville*, framing the lives and poetry of Rich (1929-2012), Plath (1932-1963), and Sexton (1928-1974) against the Betty Parker (Joan Allen) character in the film, the TV mother trapped in the norms of 1950s American.

This unit asked students to consider the suicides of Plath and Sexton against the life and poetic transformations of Rich. We also discussed how the film portrayed Betty Parker, both as a model of the norms of 1950s America and the real person trapped under her make-up, and the oppressive roles of wife and mother (dramatizing the poetry of Rich's "Aunt Jennifer's Tigers": "The massive weight of Uncle's wedding band/ Sits heavily upon Aunt Jennifer's hand").

And for the words Rich brought to my classroom and my life, I am forever in her debt. She validated things I had dared to think but feared to speak. She reminds me daily of the humility that should be at my core, a paradoxical radical humility, a commitment to human dignity and agency that are both threatened by the mere fact of my being a man in a world and society that allows the norm of manhood to oppress and silence.

It is deeply sad to lose Adrienne Rich (2001), and profoundly uplifting to know all that remains forever from her words and her life:

> The possibilities that exist between two people, or among
> a group of people, are a kind of alchemy. They are the most

interesting thing in life. The liar is someone who keeps losing sight of these possibilities....

It isn't that to have an honorable relationship with you, I have to understand everything, or tell you everything at once, or that I can know, beforehand, everything I need to tell you. It means that most of the time I am eager, longing for the possibility of telling you. That these possibilities may seem frightening, but not destructive, to me....

The possibility of life between us. (pp. 39-40)

It cannot be coincidence that just a few days before Rich's death I sat in my office talking with one of my students; I pulled four books of Rich's from the shelf and recommended her to the student.

The morning after Rich's passing that same student walked into my office with a *New York Times* article on Rich. No, this could not be a coincidence, and yes, it must be the bittersweet symmetry of the universe that reminded me during my moments of sadness of the possibilities.

Life Among the Ruins: Seeking the Rational Among the Irrational

In her *The School Among the Ruins*, Rich (2002) confronts the intersection of school and violence, poems written in the time designated as the turn of a century (Benson, 2005). In the U.S., we are faced again and again with the incomprehensible intersection of children, teachers, schools, and unspeakable violence. Each time, it is ours to honor those taken from us by seeking the rational among the irrational.

Let us commit ourselves to a vigilance, to protecting these moments against the petty, against the call to heap irrational upon irrational, against allowing the needed confrontations and discussions to become too narrow. We must confront our culture of violence and the fetish with guns within that culture of violence, and not just gun control.

We must confront health care access and mental health care access, and not just mental illness.

We must confront our negative national discourse about teachers and schools—that misrepresents the sacred duties of those teachers and schools that are now memorialized in the names of innocent lives lost in an elementary school.

We must admit that we have been too quick to police children (Nolan, 2011), and too slow to protect, cherish, and serve those children—particularly some children, too often "other people's children."

To allow the gaze of blame to be focused too narrowly absolves the larger root causes to remain, to thrive, and to perpetuate further the ruins.

Words matter, yes, but actions speak louder than words.

How children matter, whose children matter—our commitments daily send messages.

The world we have created is the world we want, or at least the world we allow; as Kingsolver (1992) notes:

> In the United States, where people like to think that anyone can grow up to be President, we parents are left very much on our own when it comes to the little Presidents-in-training. Our social programs for children are the hands-down worst in the industrialized world, but apparently that is just what we want. (n.p.)

In a poem of mine, "the world (frantic)," I end with the following: *"the world was exactly as they expected/ exactly as they knew it to be/ and mostly not as it could have been/ or should have been."* To build that world out of the ruins requires action, action built on principles, in order to build monuments of peace and love against violence and destruction.

Poem

"upon hearing adrienne rich speak and read her poetry"

i cannot shake the rush
of my own maternal grandmother—
hair cropped short—
rush over me whenever
i see adrienne rich—

this time—in person—
i felt the hunger to cry
as i watched her—
cane in hand—shuffle on stage
like but not my grandmother—

my chest and eyes welled
again and again from her words—
speaking about teaching
the frailty of teaching
in America—*America*—

because she knows—
if "knows" means "tastes in the air"
if "knows" means "feels with her blood"—
because she knows
what no one can teach

this mother of us teachers
who lives that which cannot be taught—
the doubling over in pain
from other people's suffering
that is surely not of *this* America—

and if i told her
"adrienne, my lives have split
me into pieces, pieces"
she might cry right there
her eyes welled as mine

because it is that knowing
that makes us cry
at the slightest suffering
of any anyone who hurts
and struggles against this whip

called "living"

4

Maxine Greene and the "Frozen Sea Inside of Us"

The image of Franz Kafka that captures most clearly *Kafkan* for me is the one of Kafka himself coming to consciousness in the morning, numbed from the waist down after sitting in one spot writing all night. He, of course, was lost in his text in a way that is something like dreaming—a hybrid of consciousness and unconsciousness.

The text of Kafka that speaks most directly *about* Kafka for me is his January 1904 letter to Oskar Pollack:

> I think we ought to read only the kind of books that wound and stab us. If the book we're reading doesn't wake us up with a blow on the head, what are we reading it for? So that it will make us happy, as you write? Good Lord, we would be happy precisely if we had no books, and the kind of books that make us happy are the kind we could write ourselves if we had to. But we need the books that affect us like a disaster, that grieve us deeply, like the death of someone we loved more than ourselves, like being banished into forests far from everyone, like a suicide. A book must be the axe for the frozen sea inside us. (Popova, 2014)

And although Kafka is writing here specifically about fiction,

I think the core sentiment ("A book must be the axe for the frozen sea inside us") is the perfect entry point into why Maxine Greene's works remain more important than ever, her voice the *axe* against the *frozen sea* of relentless but misguided education reform.

Greene's *Releasing the Imagination*, a collection of essays, is one such book.

Releasing the Imagination: "Breaking with Old Quantitative Models"

Published in 1995, *Releasing the Imagination* speaks *from* the middle of the current 30-year cycle of accountability-based education reform, which is driven by standards and high-stakes testing. But the volume also speaks *to* the resilient nature of the fundamental source for why education reform remains mired in the same failed policy paradigm that is repackaged over and over:

> In many ways, school restructure does, indeed, mean break-ing with old quantitative models; but countering this break is an anxiety that is driving people into what John Dewey called "the quest for certainty" (1929)....In response to school changes, many parents yearn not merely for the predictable but also for the assurances that used to accom-pany children's mastery of the basics. (Greene, 1995, p. 18)

Threads running though Greene's work are powerfully weaved into this important recognition of the Siren's song of "certainty" that appears to be captured in quantitative data (think test scores as evidence of student learning and teacher quality). These threads include Greene's existential philosophical lens, her rich progres-sive commitment, and her ability to frame education within larger societal and cultural realities.

Greene (1995) continues her examination of *breakthroughs* by referring to the poetry of Wallace Stevens, Emily Dickinson, and Denise Leverton (again, the style that distinguishes Greene), which she incorporates seamlessly with the framing of Dewey and then Paulo Freire. By example and then explicitly, Greene is making a

case for setting aside the veneer of certainty presented by measurement and numbers, and adopting instead the ambiguity and
unexpected of art:

> In contradicting the established, or the given, art reaches
> beyond what is established and leads those who are willing
> to risk transformations to the shaping of social vision.

> …Dewey, in *Art as Experience*, talks about how important it
> is for people to plunge into subject matter in order to steep
> themselves in it, and this is probably more true of works of
> art than other subject matters….In our engagements with
> historical texts, too, with mathematical problems, scientific
> inquiries, and (not incidentally) the political and social
> realities we have constructed along with those around us,
> it is never enough simply to label, categorize, or recognize
> certain phenomena or events. There has to be a live, aware,
> reflective transaction if what presents itself to consciousness
> is to be realized.

> …The beholder, the percipient, the learner must approach
> from the vantage point of her or his lived situation, that is,
> in accord with a distinctive point of view and interest….
> Imagination may be a new way of decentering ourselves,
> of breaking out of the confinements of privatism and self-
> regard into a space where we can come face to face with
> others and call out, "Here we are." (pp. 30-31)

From A Nation at Risk and then No Child Left Behind as that
morphed into the Common Core movement, education reform has
remained focused on the exact measurement ("label, categorize, or
recognize") Greene warns against, while that reform has also con-
currently erased the arts from the lives and education of children,
and more often than not, from the lives and education of the most
marginalized children.

Along with the allure of quantifying as the pursuit of both
certainty and control, bureaucracy is also exposed as a recurring flaw of education reform. Greene (1995) recognizes that

"[c]ommunity cannot be produced simply through rational formulation nor through edict," (p. 39), adding:

> Community is not a question of which social contracts are the most reasonable for individuals to enter. It is a question of what might contribute to the pursuit of shared goods: what ways of being together, of attaining mutuality, of reaching toward some common world. (p. 39)

The bureaucracy of education reform built on recycling the accountability paradigm also fails because we remain committed, not to community and democracy, but to competition and market forces—charter schools and dismantling teachers unions and tenure, for example. Education reform is, in fact, not reform at all; education reform insures that public institutions, such as schools, maintain the status quo of society. As a result, students are being indoctrinated, not educated—as Greene (1995) confronts the trap teachers face:

> This brings me back to my argument that we teachers must make an intensified effort to break through the frames of custom and to touch the consciousness of those we teach. It is an argument stemming from a concern about noxious invisible clouds and cover-ups and false consciousness and helplessness. It has to do as well with our need to empower the young to deal with the threat and fear of holocaust, to know and understand enough to make significant choices as they grow. Surely, education today must be conceived as a model of opening the world to critical judgments by the young and their imaginative projections and, in time, to their transformative actions. (p. 56)

Education today, in this time of high-stakes accountability, may at best be preparing students to make choices between buying a Honda Accord or a Toyota Camry (which is no real choice at all), but *education today*, in this time of high-stakes accountability, is not empowering students to choose not to own or drive a car at all, nor empowering them to imagine another world, a better world.

Greene (1995) recognized that we are tragically paralyzed by the pursuit of certainty and the need to complete our tasks; as a result, we remain trapped like bugs in the amber of capitalism, never freeing ourselves to pursue democracy: "Dewey found that democracy is an ideal in the sense that it is always reaching toward some end that can finally never be achieved. Like community itself, it has to always be in the making" (p. 66).

And so we stand now, in the wake of Greene's death, and before us is the frozen sea of education reform. Greene's *Releasing the Imagination* is one of the axes waiting for us to take in hand, to break us free.

These essays, now about two decades old, serve as foundational explorations of all that is wrong with how we fail to re-imagine our schools and our commitments under the misnomer of "reform." In "Teaching for Openings" (Chapter Nine), Greene (1995) presents a tour de force for those of us who embrace the label "teacher," and it is here that I argue for the enduring importance of finally listening to Greene:

> Still, caught in the turmoils of interrogation, in what Buber called the pain, I am likely to feel the pull of my old search for certainty. *I find myself now and then yearning after the laws and norms and formulations, even though I know how many of them were constructed in the interests of those in power* [emphasis added]. Their appeal to me was not only due to the ways in which they provide barriers against relativism. It was also due to my marginality: I wanted so much to be accepted in the great world of wood-panelled libraries, authoritative intellectuals, sophisticated urban cafes....
>
> That means that what Elizabeth Fox-Genovese has called the elite culture must be transformed. This is the culture white male scholars tend to create....Our obligation today is to find ways of enabling the young to find their voices, to open their spaces, to reclaim their histories in all their variety and discontinuity. *Attention has to be paid to those on the margins* [emphasis added].... (pp. 114, 120)

As I write to implore us all to beware the roadbuilders, as I skimmed through Alice Walker's *The Color Purple* to find the truth I felt compelled to offer, I stood on Greene's shoulders, as I often do, trying in my very small way to pay attention to those on the margins. With the axe Greene provided me, I was able to begin breaking the frozen sea of my privilege.

In her death, then, we must return not only to Greene's (1995) words, but to the alternative she points to with those words: "Art offers life; it offers hope; it offers the prospect of discovery; it offers light. Resisting, we may make the teaching of the aesthetic experience our pedagogic creed" (p. 133).

5

On Howard Zinn

Howard Zinn would have turned 90 in 2012. I have to imagine after reading and re-reading most of Zinn's works that if Zinn were alive today, he would remain baffled at how America is a country antagonistic to unions and tenure, especially teachers' unions and tenure.

Zinn was a radical historian, activist, and in my opinion, most of all a teacher. And it is at the overlap of Zinn as historian/activist/teacher I find his *A People's History of the United States* an invaluable place to ask, "Why tenure and unions?"

As a life-long resident and worker in South Carolina, a right-to-work state, I want to clarify here that I am not now and have never been a member of a union, I never had my pay or any sort of public school tenure negotiated for me by a union, but I have been awarded tenure by my private university during my most recent decade as a professor.

Why Tenure and Unions?: On Democracy and Equity in the U.S.

The unique and powerful quality Zinn brought to history is that his volume is a *people's* history. Zinn confronts directly that the truth embedded in any history is shaped by *perspective*.

Traditionally, the so-called objective history students have been and are fed in formal schooling is from the *point of view of the winners*, but Zinn chose to examine the rise and growth of the U.S. from the point of view of the common person—what I will characterize as primarily the viewpoint of the *worker*. I am most concerned about the misleading political and public messages that the U.S. has somehow left behind the oppressive corporate world of the robber barons (see Zinn's Chapter 11) and the horrors fictionalized in Upton Sinclair's (2001) *The Jungle*. These idealistic beliefs are similar to Americans claiming we have achieved a meritocracy instead of the fact that Americans should still be working toward a meritocracy.

In the twenty-first century Americans appear to be anti-union and anti-tenure, again notably in terms of how that impacts teachers. This sentiment is disturbing to me as it signals an anti-*worker* sentiment in the U.S.—a country that claims to embrace ideals such as equity, democracy, and hard work. This contradiction is connected, I believe, to the exact problem confronted by Zinn as a historian: Americans' anti-worker sentiments (expressed in anti-union and anti-tenure sentiments) can be traced to who controls the public narrative—the CEO elite.

If the American public considers for a moment why unions and tenure exist (as well as what tenure means), most Americans would reject the CEO-skewed messages about both. The American worker (unlike many workers in other comparable countries throughout the world) remains shackled to working in ways that dictate any worker's essential humanity; *work in the U.S. is not a matter of just pay, but of health insurance and retirement—essential for basic human dignity*. The dramatic abuses of the meat packing industry in *The Jungle* may appear more extreme than working conditions in the twenty-first century U.S., but bosses and management still hold a powerful upper-hand over the American worker.

Unionization as a concept, then, came out of and remains an act against the inherent inequity and tyranny in the workplace when the powerful few control the working many. Unionization is an act of democracy, an act of equity. To reject unions is to reject democracy and equity. Making a case for *why unions* does not ignore that specific union policies have failed. *It is certainly legitimate to confront individual union policies and outcomes (I have and continue to do that myself), but this discussion is about the broad anti-union sentiment in the U.S. that reveals anti-worker sentiments.*

Tenure is more complicated, but certainly grows out of the same commitment to democracy and equity—especially for teachers. The tenure argument is often distorted because the term itself, "tenure," is misrepresented as "a job for life," and rarely distinguishes between tenure at the K-12 level and tenure at the college/university level. Tenure is an act of democracy and equity as well because it creates power for workers as a guarantee of *due process* and, for teachers, it secures a promise of *academic freedom*.

Are there failures in how unions and tenure have been and are implemented in America today? Yes. Should those failures be addressed? Yes. But the broad anti-union and anti-tenure agenda being promoted by the CEO elite and embraced by the American public is a corrosive rejection of equity and democracy. When unions and tenure are not fulfilling their obligations to equity and democracy, they both must be confronted.

But unions and tenure remain needed and even necessary mechanisms in America's search for equity and democracy—both of which are being eroded by the American elite that is indebted to and dependent on the inequity that drives American capitalism. Although speaking directly about Americans' embracing war, Zinn (2006) makes an important point for this discussion:

> We are penned in by the arrogant idea that this country is the center of the universe, exceptionally virtuous, admirable, superior.

> If we don't know history, then we are ready meat for carnivorous politicians and the intellectuals and journalists who supply the carving knives. I am not speaking of the history we learned in school, a history subservient to our political leaders, from the much-admired Founding Fathers

to the Presidents of recent years. I mean a history which is honest about the past. If we don't know that history, then any President can stand up to the battery of microphones, declare that we must go to war, and we will have no basis for challenging him. He will say that the nation is in danger, that democracy and liberty are at stake, and that we must therefore send ships and planes to destroy our new enemy, and we will have no reason to disbelieve him. (n.p.)

Without, then, the democratic and equity-based purposes for unions and tenure, the American public remains "ready meat for carnivorous politicians and the intellectuals and journalists who supply the carving knives."

Zinn also personified a message of rejecting neutrality, of democracy as activism. Writing about Sacco and Vanzetti, Zinn (2009) shares questions raised by Vanzetti, questions still relevant today against the knee-jerk and self-defeating anti-union and anti-tenure sentiments rising in the U.S.:

Yes, it was their anarchism, their love for humanity, which doomed them. When Vanzetti was arrested, he had a leaflet in his pocket advertising a meeting to take place in five days. It is a leaflet that could be distributed today, all over the world, as appropriate now as it was the day of their arrest. It read:

"You have fought all the wars. You have worked for all the capitalists. You have wandered over all the countries. Have you harvested the fruits of your labors, the price of your victories? Does the past comfort you? Does the present smile on you? Does the future promise you anything? Have you found a piece of land where you can live like a human being and die like a human being? On these questions, on this argument, and on this theme, the struggle for existence, Bartolomeo Vanzetti will speak." (n.p.)

Howard Zinn and the Failure of Standards Movements in Education

The Zinn Education Project notes, "Howard Zinn passed away three years ago, on January 27, 2010. At the time, writer and activist Naomi Klein spoke for many of us: 'We just lost our favorite teacher'" (Bigelow & Menkart, 2013). The life and work of Zinn represents the personification of confronting the world from roles of authority that have historically been positioned as neutral—historian, teacher. But as Zinn (1994) came to understand and then to confront and embody, neutral is not an option:

> When I became a teacher I could not possibly keep out of the classroom my own experiences. . . .Does not the very fact of that concealment teach something terrible—that you can separate the study of literature, history, philosophy, politics, the arts, from your own life, your deepest convictions about right and wrong?. . .In my teaching I never concealed my political views. . . .I made clear my abhorrence of any kind of *bullying*, whether by powerful nations over weaker ones, governments over their citizens, employers over employees, or by anyone, on the Right or the Left, who thinks they have a monopoly on the truth. . . .From that moment on, I was no longer a liberal, a believer in the self-correcting character of American democracy. I was a radical, believing that something fundamental was wrong in this country—not just the existence of poverty amidst great wealth, not just the horrible treatment of black people, but something rotten at the root. The situation required not just a new president or new laws, but an uprooting of the old order, the introduction of a new kind of society—cooperative, peaceful, egalitarian. (pp. 7, 173)

As the Common Core movement, as well as the concurrent new and expanded battery of high-stakes tests, seems inevitable (as some continue to debate), Zinn's radical stance as a historian and teacher offers a powerful window into why any standards movement is a failed process in education, particularly in universal public education designed to serve democracy and individual freedom.

Standards as Acquiring Some Authority's Mandates

Zinn as historian and teacher personified the act of *investigating* content. For Zinn, our obligation as teachers and students is to ask questions—notably questions about the sources of power—about not only the world around us, but also the narratives of the world around us, narratives cast about the past, narratives being cast about the present, and narratives envisioning the future.

Who was Christopher Columbus—in his own words, in the narratives built around him by centuries of historians, in the narratives of textbooks, and in the narratives of state-mandated curriculum? Why are there so many versions of Columbus, which ones are true (if any), and who benefits from these narratives?

Who was Martin Luther King Jr.—in his own words, in the narratives built around him by decades of historians, in the narratives of textbooks, and in the narratives of state-mandated curriculum? Why are there so many versions of King, which ones are true (if any), and who benefits from these narratives?

Narratives, whether they be history or mandated curriculum in the context of Common Core, are manufactured myths, and ultimately, manufactured myths are created by some authority to suit some goal, some goal that benefits the designer of the myth. And therein lies the ultimate failure of all standards movements.

A standards paradigm masks the locus of power. Some authority somewhere decides what knowledge matters, creates the accountability structure that makes that knowledge the goal of passive implementation (teachers) and compliant acquisition (students), and then creates a teaching and learning environment that can assume a neutral pose, while in fact replacing education with indoctrination. *Authentic education for democracy and individual freedom is a continual asking: What knowledge matters and why? It is a journey, an adventure, a perpetual gathering to confront, to challenge, to debate, and to serve the teacher and learner in their joint re-reading and re-writing of the world.*

Common Core, just as the dozens of standards movements before it, discounts the need to confront, to ask, and to re-imagine, because standards are an act of authoritarian mandates. Regardless of intent, standards always become mandates and what-is-tested-is-what-is-taught. "Who decides" is rendered unnecessary, and the curriculum becomes a faux-neutral set of content that teachers must implement and students must acquire so that the ultimate faux-neutral device can be implemented—high-stakes testing.

Like the "remarkable apparatus" in Franza Kafka's (2007) "In the Penal Colony," high-stakes testing ultimately becomes all that matters, "a mechanism of objectification" (Foucault, 1984), the inevitable abdication of authority and autonomy to a mechanism. What-is-tested-is-what-is-taught supersedes any possibility of asking "why?" or of examining "who decides?" and by what authority the decisions are made.

Kafka's (2007) nightmare allegory has been and will be replayed time and again, as adopting and implementing Common Core along with the high-stakes tests uncritically, passively, and with a pose of neutrality ("I am simply doing as I have been mandated as well as I can") feed the machine that consumes all who come near it, just as the Officer who implements the apparatus of punishment eventually acquiesces to it himself:

> The Traveller, by contrast, was very upset. Obviously the machine was breaking up. Its quiet operation had been an illusion. He felt as if he had to look after the Officer, now that the latter could no longer look after himself. But while the falling gear wheels were claiming all his attention, he had neglected to look at the rest of the machine. However, when he now bent over the Harrow, once the last gear wheel had left the Inscriber, he had a new, even more unpleasant surprise. The Harrow was not writing but only stabbing, and the Bed was not rolling the body, but lifting it, quivering, up into the needles. The Traveller wanted to reach in to stop the whole thing, if possible. This was not the torture the Officer

wished to attain; it was murder, pure and simple. (n.p.)

The American Character, Inscribed: "A Monopoly on the Truth"

While the education establishment, both progressives and conservatives, races to see who can implement Common Core the fastest, concurrent education reform initiatives such as charter schools and Teach for America help reinforce the worst elements of the standards and accountability movement. Embedded in the charter school commitment is a parallel pursuit of standards: Character education.

In the "no excuses" model, made popular in the Knowledge Is Power Program (KIPP) charter chain, the standard for character and "good behavior" is not something teachers and students explore, discover, and debate, but rules that must be implemented and followed.

For example, consider the "National Heritage Academies (NHA) and its approach to character and citizenship education," highlighted by Rick Hess (2013) at *Education Week*. Hess, by the way, notes, "I think I'm wholly behind what NHA is doing." What does a standardized approach to character and civic education look like?:

> "I pledge allegiance to the flag of the United States of America," chant the students of Ridge Park Elementary School in Grand Rapids, Michigan. "And to the Republic for which it stands . . ."
>
> In the back of the room, a dozen parents stand with their hands over their hearts. Some are US citizens by birth, others by naturalization, and some by aspiration. Their children recite: "One nation, under God, with liberty and justice for all."
>
> A National Heritage Academies (NHA) charter school, Ridge Park starts every day with the Pledge of Allegiance,

the Star-Spangled Banner, and the school creed: "I am a Ridge Park scholar. I strive to achieve academic excellence. I exemplify high moral character. I work diligently to prepare for the future . . ."

> Character education is ubiquitous and relentless at NHA schools. Each month is assigned a "moral focus" or virtue, which teachers are supposed to weave into their lessons and students write about from kindergarten through eighth grade. Signs in classrooms and hallways honor examples of virtue. (Jacobs, 2013, n.p.)

"Chant," "recite," "ubiquitous," "relentless," "troop"—these are the bedrocks of a standards-driven school environment, but this is indoctrination, not education—whether the standard is character or curriculum. And what sort of history curriculum does a character-driven model embrace? The cultural heritage work of E. D. Hirsch (Jacobs, 2013).

No, let's not confront the histories of the U.S., not here at NHA, because that may lead to the sorts of questions Zinn would ask: Who decides and why, and then who benefits from these narratives of character and history? [Hint: "National Heritage Academies, a for-profit charter management company, runs 74 schools in Michigan and eight other states, making it the second largest charter network in the country" (Jacobs, 2013).]

Further into Jacobs' (2013) description of NHA "America-centric" core curriculum, Martin Luther King Jr. is highlighted as an example for students of character. King as martyr for Hirsch's flawless U.S.A.? Consider:

> In fact, King *was* a radical. He believed that America needed a "radical redistribution of economic and political power." He challenged America's class system and its racial caste system. He was a strong ally of the nation's labor union movement. He was assassinated in April 1968 in Memphis, where he had gone to support a sanitation workers' strike. He opposed U.S. militarism and imperialism, especially

the country's misadventure in Vietnam. (Dreier, 2013, n.p.)

Do you suppose *this* is the King NHA students study and are encouraged to emulate? And it is here I will end with the ultimate caution about being neutral in regards to Common Core, charter schools, character education, and a whole host of education reform mandates and commitments that seem inevitable: The powerful control the narratives and those narratives control the rest of us—all for the profit of the powerful.

6

Many Closets, One Fear: How Not to Be Seen

This starts with caveats and clarifications so please be patient.

I am white, male, and heterosexual—by the coincidences of my birth, many of my defining characteristics place me in the norm of my culture and combine to bestow upon me through no merit on my part a great deal of privilege.

Below, then, I am making no claim that the closets I have suffered and that others suffer share some sort of ultimate *equivalence*, even though they share the crippling power of fear. I remain deeply angered at the scars of racism, sexism, and homophobia that linger in my country that claims to be a beacon of life, liberty, and the pursuit of happiness. I remain deeply angered at the scar of poverty that flourishes in that same country, wrapping its crass consumerism and capitalism in the flag in order to continue to ignore inequity.

But as a privileged person, I too understand the weight of the closet and the paralysis of fear, so I am venturing into this not as a pity party, not as navel gazing, and not to make some grand claim that I know what it is like to be the daily victim of racism, sexism, or homophobia, or what it is like to be homeless or hungry.

I don't.

This, however, is a place to offer a few words about the intersections that may at first not seem like intersections at all: NBA player Jason Collins coming out of the closet, the Boston Marathon bombing, Common Core, the Knowledge Is Power Program (KIPP) and other "no excuses" schools.

"Stones can make people docile and knowable," writes Foucault (1984). "The old simple schema of confinement and enclosure—thick walls, a heavy gate that prevent entering or leaving—began to be replaced by the calculation of openings, of filled and empty spaces, passages and transparencies" (p. 190). Here, Foucault is being literal, confronting the culture of control that is housed in social institutions such as hospitals, prisons, and schools. But I want to consider the enclosure of the metaphorical closet before coming back to the role of the brick-and-mortar school below.

My privilege built on gender, race, and sexuality (all elements of my being I have not chosen, but essentials of whom I am) has contributed to my existential angst of coming to recognize throughout my life the equally important aspects of my Self that are distinctly outside cultural norms. In my late 30s, I began to experience panic attacks, notably ones not directly associated with an event but attacks that were, as best as I can describe them, the manifestation of a war with myself. The attacks came upon me any time I tried to sleep, relax, and this was when my Normal Self let down the guard enough for the real and true me to begin to fight for the surface.

Again, I don't want to belabor my personal struggles, but I do want to emphasize that the human condition is fraught with closets of many kinds that are joined by *fear*.

My closeting has always been an existential one: I have never felt the sort of normal response to religion that others appear to embrace (a powerful closeting condition in the South), but even more profoundly, I recognize my worldview as completely out of kilter with almost all other humans. It has created for me an often overwhelming sense of alienation.

What often is left unspoken is that it is in the moments of conflict between who we truly are and who we are expected to be that we feel self-conscious, we imagine that all eyes are on us, judging us, recognizing us for who we truly are in order to banish us from the community. For me, it is the never-ending ritual of "Let us pray...," or that split second when someone says something and everyone else nods in agreement while I calculate the damage that would be done if I said my piece. Both of these seem trivial to me in the text I just typed, but the cumulative effect of this *daily*, I think, must not be discounted—particularly as it occurred in my childhood and youth.

Closets exist because humans come to recognize two forces—who we truly are and who the World around us demands that we *be*. If who we truly are doesn't match the demand, we often gather the stones to build our closets because above all else we are afraid of not being accepted, not being loved, not being cherished for who we truly are.

Even in our moments of such recognitions, we reach out for someone to join us:

> I'm Nobody! Who are you?
> Are you – Nobody – too?
> Then there's a pair of us!
>
> I'm Nobody! Who are you? (260)
> Emily Dickinson

The closet, then, is a place to hide, how not to be seen (less funny, of course, than a Monty Python skit). However, the human condition involves a drive not only to be seen, but also to be accepted, embraced. This has been profoundly demonstrated in Jason Collin's (2014) own words about his motivation for confronting his sexuality within the exponentially judgmental worlds of social and athletic homophobia, and the normative expectations for being fully a man.

This tension between being seen and not being seen is at the center of Foucault's (1984) culture of control: "This infinitely scrupulous concern with surveillance is expressed in the architecture by innumerable mechanisms....The perfect disciplinary apparatus would make it possible for a single gaze to see everything constantly" (p. 191).

Constant surveillance, then, achieves two ends: The power and coercion of normalizing (control, obedience), and the creation of anxiety and fear, where neither are warranted: "The perpetual penalty that traverses all points and supervises every instant in the disciplinary institutions compares, differentiates, hierarchizes, homogenizes, excludes. In short, it *normalizes*" (Foucault, 1984, p. 195).

The existential angst within the human condition, made more pronounced from within our many closets, confronts the concrete structures recognized by Foucault—hospitals, schools, prisons—but also now confronts a pervasive surveillance that was identified and then normalized itself because of the Boston Marathon bombing in 2013. The Brave New World of constant surveillance confronts us through smart phones, ubiquitous surveillance cameras, and the interconnectivity afforded through the Internet.

The normalizing came in the form of repeated comments from political leaders, law enforcement, and the media that constant surveillance had now shown itself as essential for our safety—from the (criminal) Other, the manifestation of the middle-class cocoon.

"Similarly," Foucault (1984) explains, "the school building was to be a mechanism for training" (p. 190). Building on Foucault's recognition of the structures within a culture of control, DeLeuze (1992) details:

> We are in a generalized crisis in relation to all the environments of enclosure—prison, hospital, factory, school, family....The administrations in charge never cease announcing supposedly necessary reforms: to reform schools....But everyone knows that these institutions are finished....These are the societies of control, which are in

the process of replacing the disciplinary societies....In the
disciplinary societies one was always starting again (from
school to the barracks, from the barracks to the factory),
while in the societies of control *one is never finished with
anything* [emphasis added]. (pp. 3, 5)

And now we come to the intersections among closeted exis-
tences, fear, constant surveillance and the Boston Marathon bombing, and Foucault's "age of infinite examination" that is education
reform built on accountability, standards, and high-stakes testing.

First let's zoom in to the life of the student, specifically the
student marginalized in her/his home and community and then
marginalized in her/his school. Foucault (1984) explains that "a
pupil's 'offense' is not only a minor infraction, but also an inability
to carry out his tasks" (p. 194), predating significantly the new
norm of "no excuses" school cultures captured by Sarah Carr's
(2013) look at post-Katrina New Orleans and the rise of KIPP and
similar charter schools:

> The reformers approach students they perceive as disad-
> vantaged in much the same way they do struggling teach-
> ers....[L]ow income children must be taught, explicitly and
> step-by-step, how to be good students. Staff at a growing
> number of "no-excuses" charter schools...are prescriptive
> about where new students look (they must "track" the
> speaker with their eyes), how they sit (upright, with both
> feet planted on the ground, hands folded in front of them),
> how they walk (silently and in a straight line, which is
> sometimes marked out for them by tape on the floor), how
> they express agreement (usually through snaps or "silent
> clapping" because it's less disruptive to the flow of class),
> and, most important, what they aspire to (college, college,
> college). This conditioning (or "calibration" or "accultura-
> tion"...) starts with the youngest of students. (pp. 42-43)

"The disciplinary mechanisms," Foucault (1984) explains,
"secreted a 'penalty of the norm,' which is irreducible in its principles and functioning to the traditional penalty of the law" (p.

196). Both Carr (2013) and Nolan (2011), in her ethnography of zero tolerance policies in urban high schools, shine a light on *how schools and the penal system have merged* in the U.S. for "other people's children" (Delpit, 2006)—creating both a school-to-prison pipeline and schools as prisons.

Common Core and the high-stakes tests designed to enforce those standards, then, are a logical extension of the broader purposes of school to control, an institution that "compares, differentiates, hierarchizes, homogenizes, excludes[,]...*normalizes*" through the mechanism of tests:

> The order that the disciplinary punishments must enforce is of a mixed nature: it is an "artificial" order, explicitly laid down by a law, a program, a set of regulations. But it is also an order defined by natural and observable processes: the duration of apprenticeship, the time taken to perform an exercise, the level of aptitude refer to a regularity that is also a rule. (Foucault, 1984, pp. 194-195)

Deleuze (1992) recognizes education is in a constant state of crisis, reform, and standardization, within which schools, teachers, and students can never finish the perpetual bureaucratic demands. Our Brave New World of standardization and "infinite examination" is one of international rankings, school rankings, teacher rankings, and student rankings—all of which assure that virtually everyone cannot possibly measure up; number two is perpetually the first loser. "The power of the Norm appears throughout the disciplines," adds Foucault (1984):

> The Normal is established as a principle of coercion in teaching with the introduction of a standardized education and the establishment of the *ecoles normales* (teachers' training college)....Like surveillance and with it, normalization becomes one of the great instruments of power at the end of the classical age. (p. 196)

A culture of control is the antithesis of a community.

A culture of control uses the normative gaze to breed conformity and to excise the Different, the Other from the herd.

A community reaches out, lends a hand, opens arms. A community is an invitation to the recognition of the humanity that joins all people despite the diversity among us individually. *Many closets, one fear*—this should speak to our hearts in a way that moves us beyond cultures and societies of control and towards a community. We should also come to see that our culture of control is built upon and perpetuated by a dehumanizing education mechanism grounded in surveillance and fear.

Just as fear is the wrong motivation for embracing the perpetual surveillance created by smart phones, cameras on every street corner, and the Internet, fear is the wrong motivation for how we build our schools. Ultimately, KIPP and other "no excuses" charter schools, Common Core, and the perpetual churn of education reform are the consequences of fear. Ceaseless school reform is irrational and heartless; it is building closets from the stones of test scores.

Ceaseless school reform creates schools and a society in which we all must find ways not to be seen, fearful that if we take the risk to stand as our true selves in that open field, we too will be shot down like a punch line in a comedy sketch.

7

Le Guin's "The Ones Who Walk Away from Omelas": Allegory of Privilege

"With a clamor of bells that set the swallows soaring, the Festival of Summer came to the city Omelas, bright-towered by the sea," opens Ursula K. Le Guin's (1975) "The Ones Who Walk Away from Omelas." The reader soon learns about a people and a land that leave the narrator filled with both a passion for telling a story and tension over the weight of that task:

> How can I tell you about the people of Omelas? They were not naive and happy children—though their children were, in fact, happy. They were mature, intelligent, passionate adults whose lives were not wretched. O miracle! but I wish I could describe it better. I wish I could convince you. (p. 278)

The narrator offers an assortment of glimpses into these joyous people and their Festival of Summer, and then adds:

> Do you believe? Do you accept the festival, the city, the joy? No? Then let me describe one more thing. (p. 280)

The "one more thing" is a child, imprisoned in a closet and its own filth—a fact the people of Omelas "explained to children when they are between eight and twelve, whenever they seem capable of understanding":

> They all know it is there, all the people of Omelas. Some of them have come to see it, others are content merely to know it is there. They all know that it has to be there. Some of them understand why, and some do not, but they all understand that their happiness, the beauty of their city, the tenderness of their friendships, the health of their children, the wisdom of their scholars, the skill of their makers, even the abundance of their harvest and the kindly weathers of their skies, depend wholly on this child's abominable misery. (Le Guin, 1975, p. 282)

And how do the people of Omelas respond to this fact of their privilege at the expense of the sacrificed child? Most come to live with it: "Their tears at the bitter injustice dry when they begin to perceive the terrible justice of reality, and to accept it" (Le Guin, 1975, p. 283). But a few, a few:

> They leave Omelas, they walk ahead into the darkness, and they do not come back. The place they go towards is a place even less imaginable to most of us than the city of happiness. I cannot describe it at all. It is possible that it does not exist. But they seem to know where they are going, the ones who walk away from Omelas. (p. 284)

Le Guin's sparse and disturbing allegory has everything that science fiction/ speculative fiction/ dystopian fiction can offer in such a short space—a shocking other-world, a promise of Utopia tinted by Dystopia, the stab of brutality and callousness, and ultimately the penetrating mirror turned on all of us, now. At its core, Le Guin's story is about the narcotic *privilege* as well as the reality that privilege always exists at someone else's expense. The horror of this allegory is that the sacrifice is a child, highlighting for the reader that privilege comes to some at the expense of others through no fault of the closeted lamb.

In the U.S., we cloak the reality of privilege with a meritocracy myth, and unlike the people of Omelas, we embrace both the myth and the cloaking—never even taking that painful step of opening the closet door to face ourselves. What's behind our door in the U.S.? Over 23% of our children living lives in poverty through no fault of their own (2103 data book, 2013).

While Le Guin's story ends with some hope that a few have both a soul and a mind strong enough to walk away from happiness built on the oppression of the innocent, I feel compelled to long for a different ending, one where a few, a few rise up against the monstrosity of oppression and inequity, to speak *and act against*, not merely acquiesce or walk away.

8

"The Poor Are Too Free"?: Unlocking the Middle-Class Code

Walking outside the Commander's compound in the "heart of Gilead," Offred (June) is reminded of her past, now swept away by the rise of Gilead, the theocracy at the center of Margaret Atwood's (1998) *The Handmaid's Tale*:

> Luke and I used to walk together, sometimes, along these streets. We used to talk about buying a house like one of these, an old big house, fixing it up. We would have a garden, swings for the children. We would have children. Although we knew it wasn't too likely we could ever afford it, it was something to talk about, a game for Sundays. Such freedom now seems almost weightless. (p. 23)

This idealized middle-class fantasy ignores that behind the weightless freedom often lurked the life-long burden of debt—the thirty-year mortgages, the monthly bills, the billowing cost of college-for-all. A motif of *freedom* weaves its way through Atwood's (2013) "dystopia from the female point of view – the world according to Julia, as it were" (n.p.), a work with George Orwell just below the surface.

To fulfill her role as a handmaid (fertile women designated to conceive with the Commanders), Offred (June) has been re-educated at the Rachel and Leah Center by the Aunts, women controlling women. The Aunts as the *teachers* for Gilead help the handmaids understand *freedom*:

> There is more than one kind of freedom, said Aunt Lydia. Freedom to and freedom from. In the days of anarchy, it was freedom to. Now you are being given freedom from. Don't underrate it….We were a society dying, said Aunt Lydia, of too much freedom. (Atwood, 1998, p. 24).

As Atwood (2012) explains,

> Gilead has utopian idealism flowing through its veins, coupled with a high-minded principle, its ever-present shadow, sublegal opportunism, and the propensity of the powerful to indulge in behind-the-scenes sensual delights forbidden to everyone else. But such locked-door escapades must remain hidden, for the regime floats as its raison d'être the notion that it is improving the conditions of life, both physical and moral; and like all such regimes, it depends on its true believers. (n.p.)

In the "no excuses" charter school movement, David Whitman (2008a) is a true believer, a voice for the "new" paternalism that shares a haunting parallel with the paternalism of Atwood's dystopia:

> By paternalistic I mean that each of the six schools is a highly prescriptive institution that teaches students not just how to think, but also how to act according to what are commonly termed traditional, middle-class values. These paternalistic schools go beyond just teaching values as abstractions: the schools tell students exactly how they are expected to behave, and their behavior is closely monitored, with real rewards for compliance and penalties for non-compliance….Paternalistic programs survive only because they typically enforce values that "clients already believe," Mead notes. But many paternalistic programs remain controversial because they seek to change the lifestyles of the

poor, immigrants, and minorities, rather than the lifestyles of middle-class and upper-class families. The paternalistic presumption implicit in the schools is that the poor lack the family and community support, cultural capital, and personal follow-through to live according to the middle-class values that they, too, espouse. (n.p.)

Another true believer, quoted by Whitman in his *Sweating the Small Stuff*, is Lawrence Mead: "'The problem of poverty or under-achievement is not that the poor lack freedom. The real problem is that the poor are too free'" (Whitman, 2008b, p. 36). (Note: While Whitman attributes this quote to Mead, those words do not appear in Mead's book. I discovered, however, the concept is not mislead-ing, only the direct quote attribution. In an email exchange with me, Mead clarifies that pages 21-23 of his *The New Paternalism* appear close to the ideas attributed in the misquoting.)

Now let's add all this up: President Barack Obama + Secretary of Education Arne Duncan + speechwriter David Whitman + "the poor are too free" = "no excuses" education policy.

People trapped in poverty, Whitman argues, are suffering from *too much freedom*; therefore, they must be given *freedom from* (like the handmaids). Our "new" paternalistic schools, then, are gifts of the middle-class code bestowed upon children living in poverty, disproportionately children who also are African American and Latino/a.

So just what are these impoverished children being given free-dom from? Natalie Hopkins (2013) has one suggestion:

It's a great question—one that gets to the heart of the ten-sions over "urban" school reform. What will our schools look like once they "succeed"? Will black girls stop playing hand games? Will black boys lose the urge to tap West Afri-can rhythms on their desks? Will children graduate bearing no trace of the poverty, riches, triumph, failure, and *culture* that form the complex kaleidoscope of blackness in this country?...From desegregation to today's "school choice" [such as charter schools], every single scheme has been designed to kill off the Negro soul—or at least provide an escape hatch from it. (n.p.)

As well, what are the consequences of these new urban schools policies?

Examining the rise of "no excuses" charter schools in post-Katrina New Orleans, Sarah Carr (2013) cites one teacher: "'The first week of school is all about compliance,' said Kaycee Eckhardt, one of the founding teachers" (p. 81). But Carr notes that Andre Perry (Founding Dean of Urban Education at Davenport University) "is troubled by the idea that children—and poor children of color most especially—need to be controlled. 'There's an insidious mistrust of children reflected in having them walk on lines or making them stay silent'" (p. 81).

Although "no excuses" charter schools are driven by a "new" paternalism that embraces a deficit view of children (Dudley-Marling, 2007), people in poverty and people of color remain committed to *freedom from*, despite the potential long-term outcomes:

> Sci Academy and other ["no excuses"] charter schools like it run a risk in creating such structured, disciplined environments where students receive motivation from external rewards and punishments. The approach can backfire in the long run if students do not know how to function once all the structure and incentives disappear and if they do not learn how to think for themselves....Despite the guiding ambition to send all their students through college, Sci's learning environment is the opposite of collegiate in many respects. (Carr, 2013, p. 189)

And here we find the ugly truth behind the claim that "no excuses" paternalism seeks to offer impoverished children of color the key to middle-class values: The people these students are being trained to be—as Hopkins unmasks—is not some middle-class ideal such as the one recalled by Offred (June), but the ideal that privileged people want for "other people's children"—controlled, passive, silent, obedient, *freedom from*—so that privileged children can maintain their *freedom to.*

As in Gilead, the privileged orchestrate a world in which they have *freedom to* build on the rest of us having *freedom from.* And this deficit view by a paternalistic state extends well beyond schools, as Deborah Meier (2013a) condemns in her quote of the day:

> "We are coming to find you and monitor every step you take. And we are going to learn about every bad friend you have. And you're going to get alienated from those friends because we are going to be all over you." Joanne Jaffe, of the New York City Police Department, on a program meant to steer juveniles away from crime.
>
> Joanne Jaffe may have heart of gold, but she, and the NYC Police Department, couldn't be further off the mark. This quotation and the story it goes with sent shivers up my spine. The idea that the kids will follow our advice if we treat them unfairly, interfere with their perfectly legal rights, harass them a bit more, is so far from reality that it truly is scary.

Meier seeks a different barometer for the standards we allow for "other people's children," however:

> That's why medicine rests on "do no harm"—and so does raising children. So I often rest my arguments on "would I do it to myself" and "would I do it to my own offspring?" And if so, why not?

In "A Report from Occupied Territory," James Baldwin (1966) confronted an "arrogant autonomy, which is guaranteed the police, not only in New York, *by the most powerful forces in American life*" and the corrosive deficit view of race it is built upon: "'Bad niggers,' in America, as elsewhere, have always been watched and have usually been killed." [Think of the Trayvon Martin, Jordan Davis, and Michael Brown shootings.] As an example, Baldwin adds:

> Here is the boy, Daniel Hamm, speaking—speaking of his

country, which has sworn to bring peace and freedom to so many millions. "They don't want us here. They don't want us—period! All they want us to do is work on these penny-ante jobs for them—and that's *it*. And beat our heads in whenever they feel like it. They don't want us on the street 'cause the World's Fair is coming. And they figure that all black people are hoodlums anyway, or bums, with no character of our own. So they put us off the streets, so their friends from Europe, Paris or Vietnam—wherever they come from—can come and see this supposed-to-be great city."

There is a very bitter prescience in what this boy—this "bad nigger"—is saying, and he was not born knowing it. *We taught it to him in seventeen years* [emphasis added]. He is draft age now, and if he were not in jail, would very probably be on his way to Southeast Asia. Many of his contemporaries are there, and the American Government and the American press are extremely proud of them. (n.p.)

Baldwin's (1966) central message appears relevant to the hall-ways of "no excuses" schools as well as the streets of urban America:

This is why those pious calls to "respect the law," always to be heard from prominent citizens each time the ghetto explodes, are so obscene. The law is meant to be my servant and not my master, still less my torturer and my murderer. To respect the law, in the context in which the American Negro finds himself, is simply to surrender his self-respect. (n.p.)

This surrender of self, of culture, of race can be found in the normalizing effect of zero tolerance policies (Nolan, 2011) that turn the school-to-prison pipeline into school-as-prison as well as the conversion of urban public schools into "no excuses" charter schools. "DuBois might have called our flight from blackness and fixation with standardized tests 'measuring one's soul by the tape of a world that looks on in an amused contempt and pity,'" explains Hopkins (2013), adding:

In order to move beyond the black/white, negative/positive binary that dominated DuBois' 20th century, we need to generate some new definitions. What does it mean to be educated? What is history? What is "culture" and how can our public institutions value it? We need new definitions for success – hopefully ones that don't deodorize the funk.

The middle-class code of "no excuses" school reform, it seems, is more about ensuring everyone else's *freedom from* to preserve for the few the *freedom to* remain privileged.

While privileged children sit in gifted classrooms and private academies that celebrate creativity and respect a child's innate zest for learning, a separate and unequal school system is being built on a "new" paternalism platform that hides issues of race and class behind code words like "middle class."

As Baldwin (1966) envisioned almost fifty years ago, if "no excuses" ideologies win, "the meek American Negroes—those who survive—shall enter the Great Society" (n.p.), but it will be one designed for them and not by them.

9

Whence Come *The Leftovers?*: Speculative Fiction and the Human Condition

Nora Durst finds herself at the intersection of something routinely normal for middle-class Americans living in the comfort of suburbia and distinctly otherworldly at the same time in Tom Perrotta's *The Leftovers*, his 2011 novel venturing into speculative/dystopian fiction (see *The Leftovers* series adaptation from HBO).

Visiting the mall with her sister during the Christmas season, Nora confronts the sudden disappearance of her entire family several years before on October 14, when millions of people also vanished in the Sudden Departure that prompts many to believe the world has finally experienced The Rapture:

> Her heart was still racing when she stepped inside, her face hot with pride and embarrassment. She'd just forced herself to make a solo circuit of the big Christmas tree on the main level, where all the parents and kids were waiting to meet Santa Claus. It was another holiday challenge, an attempt to face her fear head-on, to break her shameful habit of avoiding the sight of small children whenever possible. That wasn't the kind of person she wanted to be—shut

down, defensive, giving a wide berth to anything that might remind her of what she'd lost. A similar logic had inspired her to apply for the day-care job last year, but that had been too much, too soon. This was more controlled, a one-time-only, bite-the-bullet sort of thing. (Perrotta, 2011, p. 193)

This moment for a fictional woman who has lost her family, has lost *everything*, is the essence of Perrotta's mix of dark satire and moving authenticity about the human condition. But it also leads me to move beyond the book and consider what dystopian fiction, what speculative fiction offers readers that proves time and again to be so compelling.

Our Speculative World, "Off-to-the-Side"

Margaret Atwood has provided her readers four brilliant dys-topian/speculative works of fiction—which she often uses to argue against simplistic labels such as "science fiction": *The Handmaid's Tale, Oryx and Crake, The Year of the Flood*, and *MaddAddam*. In "Writing Utopia" (from *Writing with Intent*), Atwood (2005) clari-fies her distinction about genre, specifically about science fiction:

I define science fiction as fiction in which things happen that are not possible today—that depend, for instance, on advanced space travel, time travel, the discovery of green monsters on other planets or galaxies, or that contain various technologies we have not yet developed. But in *The Handmaid's Tale*, nothing happens that the human race has not already done at some time in the past, or that it is not doing now, perhaps in other countries, or for which it has not yet developed the technology. We've done it, we're doing it, or we could start doing it tomorrow. . . .So I think of *The Handmaid's Tale* not as science fiction but as speculative fiction; and, more particularly, as that negative form of Utopian fiction that has come to be known as the Dystopia. (pp. 92-93)

Atwood (2011) has also turned to considering science fiction, speculative fiction, and dystopian fiction more fully in her *In Other Worlds*, where she writes about Kazuo Ishiguro's *Never Let Me Go*:

> Ishiguro likes to experiment with literary hybrids, and to hijack popular forms for his own ends, and to set his novels against tenebrous historical backdrops....An Ishiguro novel is never about what it pretends to pretend to be about, and *Never Let Me Go* is true to form. (p. 168)

And Perrotta's dystopia can be described in much the same way; it isn't "about what it pretends to pretend to be about"—which may be just that *thing* that makes the hard-to-explain genres of science fiction, speculative fiction, and dystopian fiction so hard to explain.

"I Can't Look at Everything Hard Enough"

I found reading the passage about Nora quoted above nearly as overwhelming as the experience appears to be for Nora herself. I began to think about my own daughter, Jessica. Jessica, the three-year-old, is gone, disappeared, seemingly instantaneously, lost forever.

Jessica, the twelve-year-old, gone.

Jessica, the nineteen-year-old, gone.

My daughter is alive, at this writing in her twenties, married, and has birthed her first child, Skylar, a daughter. But the scene with Nora in Perrotta's world "off-to-the-side," as Atwood (2011) describes Ishiguro's dystopia in *Never Let Me Go*, is not about what *might* happen, is not a speculative work about the possibility of The Rapture.

Through the lens of my own layered life with those I love, I think Perrotta is offering his readers a timeless message, one found in Thornton Wilder's *Our Town*. As Perrotta explains about the relationship between *Our Town* and his novel:

> This was part of the challenge of *The Leftovers*, as I wrote

about characters left behind in the wake of the disappear-ances. The last moments of the disappeared people became supercharged with significance—even though that was not a special day, even though they disappeared while doing ordinary things. You might say the line from *Our Town*— "choose the least important day in your life. It will be important enough"—helped inform these histories, because I looked to simple, everyday moments. Nora's daughter spills some juice, so she goes into the kitchen for some paper towels—when her daughter disappears. Jill is in the room with an old friend of hers watching a YouTube video, and suddenly the friend is gone. So, cleaning a spill or watch-ing a dumb video: It's the through minutiae of everyday life these moments come alive. (Fassler, 2014, n.p.)

In Wilder's play, Emily grows from childhood, to falling in love, to marriage, and then to her own too-early death. By the final act, Emily views her life in replay from beyond and exclaims: "I can't look at everything hard enough." She then turns to the Stage Man-ager and asks, distraught: "Do any human beings ever realize life while they live it—every, every minute?" And the Stage Manager replies, "No—Saints and poets maybe—they do some" (Wilder, 2003, pp. 105, 108).

And this is the very real and starkly *True* center of Perrotta's pervasive dark satire and insightful authenticity as a novelist, star-ing at and then breathing life into the human condition, masked as fantastic events that are unimaginable, except for those who look at everything hard enough and pause to realize life every, every minute.

10

Review: *An Untamed State*, Roxane Gay

Toward the final pages of Roxane Gay's (2014) *An Untamed State*, the primary narrator, Mireille, admits about her response to the earthquake in Haiti in the wake of her own personal horror of being kidnapped and repeatedly raped and tortured over thirteen days of captivity: "We sent money instead and it was then I felt like a true American" (p. 345).

When Margaret Atwood writes about Canada, she is also writing about the U.S. When Atwood writes about women, she is also writing about men. And in both dualities, Atwood writes about the intersections (Thomas, 2007), Canada/U.S. and woman/man—as Classen and Howes (2014) explain:

> From Atwood's perspective, Canada has traditionally occupied, and internalized, the position of the female in relation to the dominant, male land to the south (Atwood 1982: 389), and so the figure of the female is well suited to represent the Canadian character. As Rosemary Sullivan writes in her biography of Atwood, within Canada "national identity and gender were both predicated on second-class status" (Sullivan 1998: 128).

In fact, in many of Atwood's poems and stories, the context

for the exploration of dualism and borders subtly shifts back and forth from the personal or the interpersonal to the national (Hutcheon 1988).

In Gay's (2014) novel, readers find a parallel to Atwood's dualities as Gay confronts both Haiti and the U.S. through a personal hell experienced by Mireille, who personifies some deeply ugly Truths: when poverty and privilege intersect, violence occurs; when males and females intersect, violence occurs; in both dynamics, as Mireille concludes, "Girl children are not safe in a world where there are men" (p. 344).

An Untamed State: Of Mind, Body, and Nation

My entry point to Gay's writing was "There is No 'E' in Zombi Which Means There Can Be No You Or We" (Gay, 2010). The story reached out from the computer screen and demanded that I find more by Gay to read so I ordered *An Untamed State* the same day after exploring Gay's web site. That first story struck me with Gay's use of voice, genre manipulation, and tone; I was lost during much of the story until the end, which pays off brilliantly.

My experience with the novel confirms my initial attraction to Gay's gifts, but the novel presents a paradox: The story is so brutal, it is nearly unreadable, unbearable, and the story is so brutal, I never wanted to put the book down until I reached the last word.

I am prone to placing books on my bookshelves in ways that honor how I feel about those books. I will slip *An Untamed State* beside Atwood's *The Handmaid's Tale* and Stieg Larsson's Millennium trilogy because at their cores these works are about what Mireille (again at the end of the novel and after the 2010 earthquake in Haiti) proclaims:

There was an earthquake....It was a new sorrow, a fresh break in an already broken place. The tents are still there, providing no shelter. Women are in even more danger. There is no water. There is no hope. My parents survived and for that I was grateful, in spite of myself. My father's buildings stood strong while the rest of the country fell. I imagine he is proud of his work, these standing monuments of his resolve. (Gay, 2014, p. 344)

The most powerful motifs of the novel are weaved into the passage above, exhibiting a simplicity that masks the weight the novel carries from the very title itself. "An Untamed State" speaks to Haiti as a country, especially as that contrasts with the U.S., and as privilege and poverty are dramatized in Mireille's parents (and their gated estate in Haiti), Mireille's captivity once kidnapped, and to the fragility of Mireille's mental and physical states.

"Forgive me for my father's sins"

Gay's narration mixes time and perspectives with both a suddenness and grace that left me as conflicted about the style, structure, and point of view as I was about the content, Mireille's kidnapping, the repeated scenes of rape and torture, and the tension Gay creates with her characters and her themes. For example, what am I to do when the kidnappers and rapists express valid confrontations about the violence of inequity?

Within the first few pages, the dominant motif is established, as Mireille offers the first flashback embedded in her coming to consciousness in captivity: "We sat on our lanai, illuminated by paper lanterns and candles, all of us drunk on the happiness of too much money and too much food and too much freedom" (Gay, 2014, p. 10). This passage echoes for me the opening of Chapter III in F. Scott Fitzgerald's (2004) *The Great Gatsby*:

There was music from my neighbor's house through the summer nights. In his blue gardens men and girls came and went like moths among the whisperings and the champagne and the stars. (p. 39)

But in Gay's novel, the opulence and decadence are framed against Mireille's story of being grotesquely tamed, her nightmare of awareness germinated in her native Haiti: "There are three Haitis—the country Americans know and the country Haitians know and the country I thought I knew" (p. 11).

Also in those first few chapters, I came to recognize that the chapter numbering was tallying—I, II, III, IIII, ...—a subtle technique that reveals the fact of Mireille's many states of captivity: captive to her father's privilege and arrogance; captive to her native Haiti; captive to her existence as a woman; captive to her life as a Haitian married to a pale American; captive for 13 days to kidnapping, rape, and torture; and then captive to her history for the entirety of her life.

An Untamed State is a compelling novel and deserves your time if you love to read well-crafted stories and characters, but the work is also a brave and piercing spotlight on the violence of this world bred by socioeconomic and gender inequity. Gay (2014) focuses those messages, in part, on Mireille's father:

> My father does not understand obstacles, doesn't believe they exist. He cannot even see obstacles. Failure was never going to be an option. He often says, "There is nothing a man cannot get through if he tries hard enough."
>
> He built skyscrapers....My father said, "There's no telling how high a man can reach if he's willing to look up into the sky and straight into the sun." (p. 32)

The father's discourse is steeped in the sort of rugged individualism mythology at the core of the U.S., is paternalistic and chauvinistic, and is ironic in its embracing of a concluding image of self-induced blindness.

As a Haitian embodying the Great American Myths, Mireille's father embodies the "no excuses" and "grit" ideologies found in current education reform discourse and policies in the U.S.:

> Growing up, my father told my siblings and me two things—
> I demand excellence and never forget you are Haitian first;
> your ancestors were free because they took control of their
> fate.. When he came home from work each night, he'd find
> us in our corners of the house and ask, "How we you excel-

lent today?"…If he disapproved, he'd remove his glasses and rub his forehead, so wearied by our small failures. He would say, "You can be better. You control your fate."…

It was easy for my father to overlook the country's painful truths because they did not apply to him, to us. He left the island with nothing and returned with everything—a wife, children, wealth. (Gay, 2014, pp. 35, 36-37)

In the wake of her father's arrogant idealism, however, is the living death of Mireille—reduced to a shell of herself, sated only by hunger like a Kafkan nightmare, and left always a captive, mostly of her being a woman and the unfortunate child of privilege in a violently untamed state.

Readers are not left only with these tragedies, although the counterweight to the consequences of the sins of the father don't quite equal out despite the novel's final word being "hope." Over the course of the novel, Mireille and her mother-in-law form a compact built on basic human kindness; in fact, the word "kindness" rises to the level of refrain throughout the last third of the novel. But it is a kindness shared by battered women risen from the ashes of a man's razed world.

The reader learns of Mireille's last moments with the Commander, the lead kidnapper who brutalizes her, in the final chapter of the novel when Mireille utters to him, "'Forgive me for my father's sins'" (Gay, 2014, p. 363).

Heavy with this novel, I put it down recognizing that like Tom and Daisy in *The Great Gatsby*, Mireille's father, a man of privilege, and Mireille's captor, a man of poverty, walk away from their carnage, but I fear Mireille's plea rings louder in my ears than in the ears of either of these men, these sinners.

11

Review: *Eleanor & Park*

I cried on the first page of *Eleanor & Park* by Rainbow Rowell (2013).

But to be perfectly honest, I am a crier, and that may not be my most compelling argument for this disturbingly beautiful novel. I agree, however, with this review:

> But I have never seen anything quite like "Eleanor & Park."…
>
> "Eleanor & Park" reminded me not just what it's like to be young and in love with a girl, but also what it's like to be young and in love with a book. (Green, 2013, n.p.)

Before discussing the novel more directly, I want to offer a few points of context. First, I am a strong advocate of young adult literature, but I must confess, I also tend to be disappointed by young adult literature. Too often, I believe, young adult novels ask too little of readers, slip into simplistic language and ideas, and drift into condescension. I must stress strongly here that *Eleanor & Park* is not one of those novels.

Second, quite by accident, I read *Eleanor & Park* immediately after reading Jeffrey Eugenides's (2003) *The Virgin Suicides*. I will examine this further below, but both novels are powerful works that ask the reader to consider the fragility of adolescence and the often-dangerous conditions in which adolescents and children live—both physically and psychologically dangerous.

And third, I knew I had fallen in love with *Eleanor & Park* when it immediately reminded me of *Notting Hill* (which oddly began running on cable just as I started reading Rowell's novel; karma, I suppose). Eleanor and Park are fearful, hesitant to wade into love, similar to William and Anna in the film. And the first page of the novel describes a broken Park, confirming William's fear:

> **William:** The thing is, with you I'm in real danger. It seems like a perfect situation, apart from that foul temper of yours, but my relatively inexperienced heart would I fear not recover if I was, once again, cast aside as I would absolutely expect to be. There's just too many pictures of you, too many films. You know, you'd go and I'd be... uh, well buggered basically. (Michell, 1999)

I cannot say more emphatically or directly that I believe everyone should read *Eleanor & Park*; it is equally a novel for adolescents and adults. And for that reason I cannot separate my reasons why you should read it, so I'll simply offer here my arguments for dedicating some of your reading life, your heart, and your tears to this novel.

Rowell beautifully and elegantly frames scene by scene the budding and doomed love between Eleanor and Park, two adolescents joined by qualities that Rowell examines without romanticizing, without condescending. Eleanor and Park represent and share both gender-based and universal characteristics: low self-esteem and self-consciousness related to body image; nerdom linked to comic books, music, social awkwardness and anxieties, and fashion; and navigating the painful transition from childhood to adulthood that includes hurdles related to peer groups, family dynamics, and social institutions such as school.

And while I anticipate everyone crying while reading this novel, I can assure you that spontaneous laughter comes about in an equal amount. Rowell (2013) is perceptive and empathetic as a writer, but she is also damned funny: "It was the nicest thing she could imagine. It made her want to have his babies and give him both her kidneys" (p. 93). Again, I think anyone who loves to read, who loves novels, will love *Eleanor & Park*, but I also have some more targeted suggestions.

If you are a parent (or expect to be some day) or a teacher (or expect to be some day), Rowell reminds us about the power—both positive and negative—of the adults in the lives of children and adolescents. As I noted above, *The Virgin Suicides* is a disturbing portrait of the tragic consequences of the misguided home, the overbearing parents.

While Eugenides's *The Virgin Suicides* is focused, Rowell invites the reader into two homes that serve as complex and nuanced narratives about how difficult parenting is—especially for Eleanor's family because of the weight of poverty and the frailties of her mother, joined with the inexcusable terror of her mother's second husband. Park's family is also complex, but there are moments of real kindness, change, and just-plain-real-life in Park's home that serve to put Eleanor's challenges in stark relief.

Rarely are things or people all evil or all good (think about Tina in the novel when you read), but the impact of parents on their children is central to why parents and teachers must read this novel.

And while the school is somewhat less defined or fully developed in the novel, school and teachers share another burden along with the parents. Yes, there is terror and cruelty in school for Eleanor, but there are moments of real tenderness and kindness (DeNice and Beebi are wonderful friends for Eleanor) that serve to avoid the typical portrayal of schools in young adult works (think *Ferris Bueller's Day Off*).

If You Love

"Damn, damn, damn," [Eleanor] said. "I never said why I like you, and now I have to go."

"That's okay," [Park] said.

"It's because you're kind," she said. "And because you get all my jokes…" (Rowell, 2013, p. 113)

My second targeted suggestion is nearly impossible to express so I am likely to wander.

When my daughter was a child, sleeping each night upstairs in a child's daybed, I would often tip-toe up the stairs and into her room to stand next to her sleeping like a stone. Like me, she radiates heat while sleeping, but my nighttime ventures were to take her tiny warm foot in my hand, squeezing it slightly, feeling the softest skin and the curve of her arch. That is the only other experience for me that compares to holding the hand of the one you love. And that is the only way I can come close to my broad second recommendation.

If you love holding hands, you should read this book.

If you have the sort of anxiety that creeps into self-loathing and the fear that you are unlovable, you should read this book.

If you believe in or want to believe in soul-mates, you should read this book.

If your heart breaks at the sign of human kindness, you should read this book.

If you love adolescents and realize that some of being an adolescent is always with us (and should be) and that some of being a child is always with us (and should be)—if you regret that for most people "down they forgot as up they grew," you should read this book: "She would never belong in Park's living room. She never felt like she belonged anywhere, except for when she was lying on her bed, pretending to be somewhere else" (Rowell, 2013, p. 127).

I suppose in the end what I want to say is that if you are fully aware of what it means to be a human and you are determined to cling to the dignity of being fully human for yourself and everyone else, you should read this book because it is a beautiful reminder, a powerful confirmation that creeps into you bone-deep, like the love you have for that one person who also resides there in your bones forever.

12

On Barbara Kingsolver

Made in America

"The woman in the gold bracelets tells her friend," begins a poem by Barbara Kingsolver (1998) from her collection *Another America/Otra America*. A careful reading notices "gold bracelets," suggesting more than affluence, opulence. The poem continues as the two women speak interchangeably about the fired domestic worker and the vase, both reduced to "one," and "worked" is repeated only about the broken vase, an object for decoration and a Christmas gift. "It" and "colors" also haunt the conversation. In this brief poetic scene, the callousness of two affluent women about the value of an ornament over a worker, one who apparently is not a native speaker of English, and as suggested by the Spanish/English versions of all the poems and the title of the collection, likely Latino/a, is couched in a larger context found in the poem's title, "What the Janitor Heard in the Elevator."

This flippant conversation is *overheard* by another worker, a janitor (who do you see as the "janitor"?), standing essentially unseen, unacknowledged beside these women (who do you see as these women?), trapped momentarily in an elevator. Kingsolver's stark and vivid poem captures, as does Kingsolver's entire collection, the existence of two Americas, a slogan trivialized by politicians and ignored like the janitor by much of the public in the U.S.

The two Americas include the few and affluent, mostly white, who have virtually all the power and, as the poem shows, a *voice* in the nation, and the remaining many, *disproportionately* middle-class, working-class, working poor, and poor as well as African American and, increasingly, Latino/a.

Let's consider for a moment what students may be asked to do if presented with this poem in a public high school in the U.S., specifically in this expanding era of accountability and the encroaching specter of Common Core and the concurrent new high-stakes tests. Based on my having been an educator during the entire past thirty years of the accountability era, I would suggest that this poem would be reduced to mechanistic analysis, in much the same way we have treated F. Scott Fitzgerald's *The Great Gatsby* for decades.

While many are rightfully concerned that the Common Core will significantly decrease the focus on fiction and poetry in schools, we have yet to address that even if we maintain great poetry and fiction in the education of our children, we do them or that literature little service to allow those works to be reduced only to their literary parts, mere interchangeable fodder for identifying lination, stanzas, diction, symbolism, narration, characterization, setting, and the endless nuts and bolts deemed worthy of dispassionate analysis in school.

How many generations of students, for example, have examined at length the symbolism of the green light at the end of Daisy's dock and Gatsby' yellow car? How many students have been guided through the technical precision of Fitzgerald's novel while never confronting his vivid challenge to the American Dream?

Have students been asked to look carefully at the corpses of Myrtle and George (the wrong kind of people, George a mere worker and Myrtle left like road kill in the middle of the road) as well as Gatsby (the wrong kind of rich) floating dead in his pool? Have students been asked why Tom and Daisy (the right kind of rich) go on vacation in the wake of these deaths, seemingly untarnished because of the Teflon coating of their affluence?

Have students been asked to consider carefully why Tom hits Myrtle but bends to Daisy's taunts?

These are distinctions of analysis—suggesting that Common Core and curriculum are trivial debates if we do not address *what* happens in the classroom and *for whom*.

Segregation by Design

The technical approach to literature that ignores critical literacy is a subset of the larger technical debate about education and education reform that focuses policy and public attention on the details of schooling (public versus charter and private schools, Common Core, high-stakes testing, value added methods of evaluating teachers) and ignores the *substance of schooling* like a janitor trapped in an elevator with two wealthy women.

The substance of schooling today is a stark contrast to the moment of cultural consciousness stretching from the early 1950s into the 1970s when *separate but equal* was confronted and rejected. As society in the U.S. wrestled with the integration of institutions, the cancer of segregation was merely shifted from separate schools to schools-within-schools:

- White and affluent students tend to sit in Advanced Placement, International Baccalaureate, and honors classes with experienced and qualified teachers and low student-teacher ratios.

- African American, Latino/a, and impoverished students tend to sit in remedial, test-prep, and tech-prep classes with new and unqualified teachers (in the twenty-first century that means often Teach for America recruits as temporary workers) and high student-teacher ratios.

In-school segregation has been driven by affluent parents,

who use their privilege to insure that their children get theirs, and damn the rest. But segregation by design has now been joined by two powerful and corrosive mechanisms—charter schools and segregated higher education access.

Charter schools have failed to achieve the academic miracles proponents have promised, but charter schools have exposed the most predictable outcome of school choice, segregation. As Sarah Carr (2013) has shown, New Orleans is a disturbing record of the charter schools flood, the role that disaster capitalism plays in destroying equity and opportunity for "the deliberately silenced, or the preferably unheard" (Roy, 2004), African Americans and people trapped in poverty.

While schools-within-schools and charter schools highlight K-12 segregation by design in the U.S., just as troubling is the entrenched privilege of affluence found in higher education, augmenting Matt Bruenig's (2013) conclusion: "you are better off being born rich *regardless of whether you go to college* than being born poor and getting a college degree." Carnevale and Strohl (2013) have identified the separate and unequal access to higher education that constitutes the full picture of segregation by design in the U.S.:

> The postsecondary system mimics the racial inequality it inherits from the K-12 education system, then magnifies and projects that inequality into the labor market and society at large....

> Whites have captured most of the enrollment growth at the 468 most selective and well-funded four-year colleges, while African Americans and Hispanics have captured most of the enrollment growth at the increasingly overcrowded and under-resourced open-access two- and four-year colleges....

> These racially polarized enrollment flows have led to an increasing overrepresentation of whites at the 468 most selective four-year colleges....

> At the same time, African Americans and Hispanics are

increasingly underrepresented at the most selective 468 four-year colleges....

At the same time, African Americans and Hispanics are increasingly underrepresented at the most selective 468 four-year colleges.... (pp. 3, 6, 10, 12)

The inequitable access to elite higher education mirrors the inequitable access to quality K-12 education (Thomas, 2012, May 15) and to experienced and qualified teachers (Peske & Haycock, 2006). Inequitable access, then, creates inequitable outcomes:

[H]igh-scoring African Americans and Hispanics are far more likely to drop out of college before completing a credential....

Among high-scoring students who attend college, whites are far more likely to complete a BA or higher compared to African Americans or Hispanics....

Each year, there are *111,000* high-scoring African-American and Hispanic students who either do not attend college or don't graduate.

About *62,000* of these students come from the bottom half of the family income distribution....

Racial inequality in the educational system, paired with low social and economic mobility in the United States, produces enormous differences in educational outcomes: Whites are twice as likely as African Americans and three times as likely as Hispanics to complete a BA or higher.... (Carnevale & Strohl, pp. 24, 26, 28, 37)

Despite the meritocracy myth at the heart of the American Dream, then, Carnevale and Strohl conclude: "In the United States, parents' education determines the educational attainment of their children" (p. 38).

The cruel irony of education in the U.S. includes that most privileged children will find themselves in classrooms where color imagery (the gold bracelet in Kingsolver's poem, the green dock light and yellow car in *The Great Gatsby*) will be the key to the already unlocked door leading to college and secure, high-paying jobs, while African American and Latino/a, as well as impoverished students, are shown a quite different door.

All the while, the colors that matter—black, brown, white, and green—remain invisible and unspoken under the veneer of the American Dream of meritocracy that is less credible than any work of fiction soon to be dropped from the school day.

Review: *Flight Behavior*, Barbara Kingsolver

A young woman in the Appalachian hills of the rural South finds herself pregnant far too young and marries her high school sweetheart, only to lose the child. Years later, living on the farm owned by her in-laws and now the mother of two children, she walks up a mountain on that land to a rendezvous with adultery.

The hike is taxing—she struggles without her glasses (left behind out of vanity) and with her incessant craving for a cigarette—but before she meets her would-be young lover, she encounters what appears to be the entire valley below her in flames. Except there is no fire, only a billow of orange spread out beneath her.

Is this a vision from God? Or a human-made disruption of nature? Or both?

Following *The Lacuna* (2009), a novelization of the relationship between artists Diego Rivera and Frida Kahlo in Mexico, Barbara Kingsolver explores the life of Dellarobia Turnbow in *Flight Behavior* (2012), as Kingsolver explains:

> I had been wanting to write about climate change for some years. One morning I imagined millions of butterflies settling in the treetops – a drastically altered natural phenomenon that people would not understand as dangerous, one that looks really beautiful but is in fact dreadful. I don't know how that vision came into my head as that is not

how this business usually works. Most every book I bring into the world is like birthing a baby, it's a lot of effort! So when it did, I thought: oh, this is a perfect starting point. (Kappala-Ramsamy, 2013)

Kingsolver's critical and popular reputations rest, still, on her tour-de-force *The Poisonwood Bible*—although Kingsolver praises *The Lacuna* as her most enduring (Kappala-Ramsamy, 2013). But she has published to date an impressive collection of novels, wonderful collections of essays, a collection of short stories, and a powerful bi-lingual collection of poems, *Another America* (see above). Throughout Kingsolver's writing, her most compelling gift is her attention to the craft of writing as it intersects with her politics. Barbara Kingsolver has a political agenda, but her messages remain beautifully housed in her gifts as a novelist, essayist, and poet.

As a Kingsolver fan while reading *Flight Behavior*, I was transported back to *Prodigal Summer*, my favorite Kingsolver novel, and *Animal Dreams* (Thomas, 2005). In this newest narrative, the characters are diverse and compelling. Kingsolver is never condescending or unkind when she creates characters with competing worldviews and backgrounds—even when the characters stand outside Kingsolver's own commitments.

Flight Behavior creates several complimentary tensions that rise out of what would seem to most readers a premise that is anything except compelling—the appearance of butterflies on a Tennessee farm. What drives the novel, however, is Dellarobia and her own external and internal tensions as a young mother and wife:

But being a stay-at-home mom was the loneliest kind of lonely, in which she was always and never by herself....

The ones that lived through winter lasted longer, a few months, by going into something like hibernation. "Diapause," he called it, a pause in the normal schedule of growing up, mating, and reproducing. Somewhere in midlife, the cold or darkness of winter put them all on hold, shutting down their sex drive until further notice.

Like life in an uninsulated house, she thought. Maybe like
marriage in general. (Kingsolver, 2012, pp. 59, 145)

As an occasional Kingsolver scholar (Thomas, 2005), I have
examined and recommended her work for the classroom. And
here is where I'd like to focus, emphasizing, of course, that I highly
recommend *Flight Behavior* to anyone who has enjoyed Kingsolver
before, as well as readers of fiction who are drawn to rich narratives,
engaging characters, and beautiful craft with language. Kingsolver
delivers. Further, *Flight Behavior* offers readers, teachers, and students a sort of double duty as a work of a novelist as a public intellectual and a narrative that forces readers and students to consider
the role of scholars and academics as they interact with the public
about large social issues.

Kingsolver has explained that at its core, this novel is about
climate change, but Kingsolver also notes:

Motherhood is so sentimentalised and romanticised in
our culture. It's practically against the law to say there are
moments in the day when you hate your children. Everyone
actually has those moments. So to create this mother, who
loves her children, of course, but is just so fed up of living
in a house with people who roll plastic trucks on the floor,
was a writing challenge. (Kappala-Ramsamy, 2013)

In other words, although Kingsolver has a clear agenda, a
political point to make about climate change, she also respects her
art form, her readers, and the characters she has created enough
to avoid allowing this novel to slip into mere preaching or to be
tarnished by simplistic representations. *Flight Behavior* personifies the often reductive and misleading climate change debate that
occurs in the U.S. over talk radio and among talking heads on TV.

Ironically, in Kingsolver's imagined world she captures the all-
too-real world of climate change as it intersects with the lives and
jobs of typical people, people bound to the land, people bound to
their faith, people bound to pasts they regret but cannot change or
escape. *Flight Behavior* soars when Kingsolver invites the reader

to witness the intersections of scholars with people without much formal learning, of different races and cultures, of believers and non-believers, of privilege and poverty (importantly, I believe, the working poor).

As a Southerner and an educator, I was nervous about how Kingsolver would portray Southerners, and I was very concerned in one scene when Dellarobia details her experience in high school with math and science, as well as her characterization of how schools continue to fail students. In that context of my own sensitivities, I can anticipate how scientists and climate change deniers may read the novel. And this is where I have my highest recommendation: Kingsolver treads on thin ice often in this novel and masterfully makes her way to the other side of the pond without falling through.

I don't expect any artist to be perfect, especially when artists venture into producing art with earnest political messages. In fact, I still cringe when I share with students Kingsolver's essay rejecting TV—a topic about which I disagree strongly with her. *Flight Behavior* may stumble (although I am hard-pressed to say so), but it definitely maintains its legs from the wonderful opening scene to the series of surprises and inevitable outcomes that tie together a beautifully weaved story that will not disappoint a wide range of readers who may choose this work for different reasons and with different worldviews.

Ultimately, there is no dichotomy between Kingsolver the scientist (she has degrees in biology) and Kingsolver the novelist—just as there is no dichotomy between science and faith in the novel. In the end, then, the novel itself is both embodiment and testament to the message Kingsolver makes clear: We are all one.

13

King's Next Shining Novel: More "True History of the Torrance Family"

Stephen King's career reminds me of the career of Kurt Vonnegut (Thomas, 2006) in three ways: (1) they suffered the negative consequences of being associated with writing *genre* fiction, (2) they are often devalued as being too popular to be credible "literary" authors, and (3) as many popular writers are, they are often associated with one work—King with *The Shining* and Vonnegut with *Slaughterhouse-Five*. King, as well, has been further marginalized by the stigma that being prolific means a writer can't possibly be high quality.

Doctor Sleep, Stephen King

With *Doctor Sleep*, then, King takes on some monumental challenges since this 2013 novel is a sequel of possibly his most treasured work, *The Shining*, from 1977. King (2013) confronts the task of writing a sequel, as well as the weight of the popular film adaptation, in a concluding Author's Note:

> Did I approach the book with trepidation? You better
> believe it. *The Shining* is one of those novels people always
> mention…when they talk about which of my books really
> scared the bejeezus out of them….

I like to think I'm still pretty good at what I do, but nothing can live up to the memory of a good scare, and I mean *nothing*, especially if administered to one who is young and impressionable....

And people change. The man who wrote *Doctor Sleep* is very different from the well-meaning alcoholic who wrote *The Shining*, but both remain interested in the same thing: telling a kick-ass story. (pp. 529-530)

Like many people, I was first drawn to King's *The Shining* after seeing the 1980 film adaptation made popular by Jack Nicholson's role. While I am certain I read the novel, I also realize I tend to recall more vividly the film version (the culturally iconic "Here's Johnny!" and "Redrum"), which King (2013) warns about in a parenthetical comment in his Author's Note: "If you have seen the movie but not read the novel, you should note that Doctor Sleep follows the latter, which is, in my opinion, the True History of the Torrance Family" (p. 530).

I should also add that I am no fan of King's primary genres, such as horror, and have not been an avid reader of King over the years. During a couple summers in the early 2000s when I was an instructor in a regional National Writing Project institute, we assigned King's *On Writing*, solidifying my argument that King remains a writing treasure as well as a writer's writer, one who informs what we know and understand about the craft of narrative.

In 2013, I had bought several King novels, deciding once and for all to spend more time with his work because an avid reader I trust deeply is a devoted King fan, but I had yet to find one that grabbed me. Then I came across Adam Roberts's (2013) "Best science fiction books of 2013," in which he praised *Doctor Sleep* along with Margaret Atwood's *MaddAddam*. Although not intended as a book review, I want to offer first that *Doctor Sleep* delivers on King's (2013) stated goal, "telling a kick-ass story" (p. 530).

Dan Torrance is a fully developed and compelling character as a haunted adult, and his new shining companion, Abra Stone, is equally engaging as a child character replicating but also expanding some of the power found in Danny as a child in *The Shining*. If you are looking for a novel worthy of your commitment as a "long-distance reader" (Robinson, 2014), this is more than worthy of your time and investment. But there are two aspects of the work I want to highlight beyond a recommendation.

First, as a regular and enthusiastic beer drinker who knows the horrors of alcoholism among men on my mother's side of the family, the most haunting aspect of the novel is the examination of alcoholism and the personal yet not idealistic dramatization of Alcoholics Anonymous. At over 500 pages in hardback, the book took several days to read and it bore into my thoughts deeply and pervasively, making me contemplative about even raising a pint of beer with a meal. The weight and terror associated with the life of alcoholism are rendered far more frightening in this work than the vampire-like threat of the "True Knot" tribe of people in *Doctor Sleep*. For readers, the damage done by alcoholism is real, and the damage done to humans in its wake, including children, haunts Dan and the reader as powerfully as the apparitions expected in a King-penned work of horror.

Many so-called types of genre fiction—such as science fiction, fantasy, and horror—incorporate social commentary through allegory. In *Doctor Sleep*, King does not hide his examination of alcoholism beneath a metaphorical veneer; instead he pairs the twin demons of alcoholism and the supernatural—resulting in a work that may be more disturbing in the real rather than the imagined.

The second powerful aspect of the work involves the relationship between being a child and also being vulnerable because of that mere status as well as because of the nearly debilitating fears that you are alone because you are different. Much of *Doctor Sleep* for me is about childhood, itself a scary thing. When Dan as a struggling adult crosses paths with Abra, their shared shining creates a compelling look at how any child and all humans must come to terms with the Self, even or especially when that Self feels or is dramatically unlike social norms or what appears to be normal: "'I'm okay,' [Abra] said. 'Really. I'm just glad not to be alone with this inside my head'" (King, 2013, p. 236). You don't have to have the shining to understand Abra's relief.

Even as Abra finds solace in her connection with Dan—and their shared shining—she remains a victim of her own anxieties, especially as she feels compelled to hide her differences from her parents in order to protect them. Abra also has a terrifying connection with a murdered boy—again speaking to both the fragility of being a child in a harsh adult world and the weight of isolation and bonds that are beyond any person's control. This connection is stunning and, like the focus on alcoholism, haunts the reader:

> *They cut him up and licked his blood and then they did something even worse to him* [emphasis in original]. In a world where something like that could happen, mooning over a boy band seemed worse than wrong. (King, 2013, p. 209)

Abra's story is more than the narrative of a paranormal girl; it is the story of the collision between childhood and adulthood, and the potential of that child*hood* and even child*ren* being left in the wake. Again, this very real element is somehow much more terrifying than the supernatural.

King's noting that he is a different man than the one who wrote *The Shining* informs the big picture about *Doctor Sleep* since this novel of horror has a compassionate and soothing narration to it—the gift of a master storyteller—that keeps the reader somewhere between Abra's anxiety and the eternal drift into slumber, both the daily ritual of sleep and the inevitable exit from this mortal coil. Yes, *Doctor Sleep* is "a kick-ass story," but it also much more; it will not soon leave you once you've returned to, or entered for the first time, the Torrance Family Album.

14

On Children and Childhood

children guessed (but only a few
and down they forgot as up they grew
"[anyone lived in a pretty how town]," e.e. cummings

In one of those early years of becoming and being a teacher, when I was still teaching in the exact room where I had been a student (a school building that would eventually be almost entirely destroyed by a fire set by children), it was the first day of school, and I was calling that first roll—a sort of silly but important ritual of schooling for teachers and students.

Toward the back of the room and slightly to my left sat a big young man, a white male student typical of this rural upstate South Carolina high school in my home town. Like me, he would accurately be considered in that context as a Redneck. Just about everyone knows everyone in my hometown, and we are very familiar with the common names of that town. So when I came to this young man's name—Billy Laughter (it rhymes with "slaughter")—I said "Billy *Laughter*" (rhyming the last name with "after").

Smiling, I scanned the room and then turned my eyes back to Billy; he was red-faced and on the edge of having a very bad first day, one that was likely going to result in his being punished for my having done a very stupid thing. I raised my hand, palm facing him, and said, "Billy, my mistake. I'm sorry. I was trying to be funny but it wasn't." And then I said his name correctly. Billy had suffered a life of people mangling his name, and he wasn't in any mood for my being clever on the first day of school.

Several years later, when I was teaching a U.S. history class as part of my usual load as a member and chair of the English department, while I was having students form small groups, two young white males bumped into each other, back to back, while moving their desks. I caught the moment out of the corner of my eye and had to rush over to deter the fight that was about to occur.

I wasn't surprised—this was typical of my small community, along with fights starting because "he/she looked at me wrong"— but soon after this, I saw a research study that explained how people in the South and North handled personal space differently. In the South, bumping into someone or looking at someone wrong is often interpreted as challenging someone's honor, requiring a response. People in the North, conditioned by mass transit and crowded cities (I suspect the study was as much about rural and urban, as about South and North), are not as apt to find acts of close proximity anything other than that. So setting aside the urge to examine the Redneck honor code, I want to add just one more event from my coaching life in those middle years of my teaching.

While running a drill at soccer practice, I heard a comment from a player in a group behind me. My mind heard a player with whom I had been having trouble. He was difficult in class and on the team, and worst of all, he was very disruptive at practice. I turned and, without hesitating, I announced, "You are out of here," pointing with my finger up the hill. Throwing him out of practice? No, I kicked him off the team. As the young man was walking up that hill, a timid player on the team said, "Coach, that was me."

I had just kicked a young man off the team who had, in fact, not said a thing.

The Ends Can Never Justify the Means

Once, I received an email from Alfie Kohn about his then-new book, *The Myth of the Spoiled Child*. Alfie was apologetic about self-promotion so I replied, thanked him for the book, and noted a book I was co-editing that appeared to be of a similar mind about children and childhood, *Pedagogies of Kindness and Respect: On the Lives and Education of Children*. I added that our perspectives on children—on how parents, teachers, and society *treat* children—appeared to be a *minority* view. I have been mulling, then, or more likely stewing about this for some time: What makes adults—even the ones who *choose* to spend their lives with children—so damned negative and hateful about those children? That, I must admit, is the source of my palpable anger at the "grit," "no excuses," and "zero tolerance" narratives and policies related to education in the U.S.

I grew up and live in the South where the default attitude toward children remains that they are to be seen and not heard, that a child's role is to do as she/he is told. If a child crosses those lines, then we must teach her/him a lesson, show her/him who is boss—rightfully, we are told, by hitting that child: spare the rod spoil the child. That Christ's love comes in the form of corporal punishment has never made any sort of sense to me, but I find that same deficit view of children is not some backwoods remnant of the ignorant South; it is the dominant perspective of children throughout the U.S.

Barbara Kingsolver (1992) explains in "Everybody's Somebody's Baby":

This is not the United States.

For several months I've been living in Spain, and while I have struggled with the customs office, jet lag, dinner at midnight and the subjunctive tense, my only genuine culture shock has reverberated from this earthquake of a fact: People here like kids. They don't just say so, they *do*....

With a mother's keen myopia, I would tell you, absolutely, my daughter is beautiful enough to stop traffic. But in Santa

Cruz de Tenerife, I have to confess, so is every other person under the height of one meter. Not just those who agree to be seen and not heard. When my daughter gets cranky in a restaurant (and really, what do you expect at midnight?), the waiters flirt and bring her little presents and nearby diners look on with that sweet, wistful gleam of eye that before now I have only seen aimed at the dessert tray. Children are the meringues and eclairs of this culture. Americans, it seems to me now, sometimes regard children as a sort of toxic-waste product: a necessary evil, maybe, but if it's not their own they don't want to see it or hear it or, God help us, smell it.

I just don't get it. (n.p.)

A child is not a small adult, not a blank slate to be filled with our "adult weariness" (LaBrant, 1949, p. 276), or a broken human who must be repaired (I won't belabor, but the whole Original Sin idea doesn't help and justifies the drive to use the rod).

But it is also certainly true that children are not angels, not pure creatures suited to be simply set free to find the world on their own. Seeing children through deficit or ideal lenses does not serve them, or anyone, well. And within the U.S. culture there is a schizophrenia—we worship young adulthood in popular media, but seem to hate children—that is multiplied exponentially by a lingering racism and classism that compounds the deficit view of childhood. Consider the research showing how people view children of color:

Asked to identify the age of a young boy that committed a felony, participants in a study routinely overestimated the age of black children far more than they did white kids. Worse: Cops did it, too....

The correlation between dehumanization and use of force becomes more significant when you consider that black boys are routinely estimated to be older than they are....

The less the black kids were seen as human, the less they were granted "the assumption that children are essentially innocent." And those officers who were more likely to dehumanize black suspects overlapped with those who used more force against them. (Bump, 2014; see Goff, et al., 2014)

In the enduring *finger-pointing* dominant in the U.S.—blaming the poor for their poverty, blaming racial minorities for the burdens of racism, blaming women for the weight of sexism—we maintain a gaze that blinds us to ourselves, allows us to ignore that in the gaze are reflections of the worst among us.

Why do the police sweep poor African American neighborhoods and not college campuses in search of illegal drugs (Alexander, 2012)? Why do we place police in the hallways of urban high schools serving mostly poor African American and Latino/a students, demanding "zero tolerance" (Nolan, 2011)? Why are "grit" narratives and "no excuses" policies almost exclusively targeting high-poverty, majority-minority schools, often charter schools with less public oversight?

When I raise these questions, I can rest assured I will inspire the same sort of nasty response I often encounter when cycling. A few motorists make their anger known when we are riding our bicycles, and I am convinced that while some are genuinely frustrated with our blocking temporarily the road, the real reason they are angry is that *we are enjoying ourselves as children do*. And nothing angers a bitter adult as much as the pleasures of a child.

Children are not empty vessels to be filled, blank hard drives upon which we save the data we decide they should have. Children are not flawed or wild, needing us neither to repair nor break them. And children are not to be coddled or worshipped. They are children, and they are all our children.

Yes, there are lessons to be taught, lessons to be learned. But those driven by deficit or idealized views are corrupted and corrupting lessons. Each and every child—as all adults—deserves to have her/his basic dignity respected, and as adults charged with the care of any child, our initial question before we do anything with or to a child must be about ourselves. In 31 years of teaching, I can still see and name the handful of students I mis-served, like Billy above. Those faces and names serve as my starting point: With any child, first do no harm.

The ends can never justify the means.

15

George Saunders's
Allegory of Scarcity and Slack

The stories themselves, *literally*, are powerful and engaging, otherwise George Orwell's *1984* and Arthur Miller's *The Crucible* would not have endured as literature that people read again and again—and possibly *should* read again and again. However, ultimately, *1984* is not about the future, especially since we have long since passed the future Orwell may have envisioned, and *The Crucible* is not about the past, although Miller built his play on the very real and troubling history of Puritan witch hunt hysteria. These works are about the complicated *present* of both authors' worlds as that speaks to the enduring realities of the human condition.

All of that may seem weighty stuff before stepping into a look at what appears to be a children's book, but the paragraphs above should be more than a hint that looks can be deceiving—and enlightening. *The Very Persistent Gappers of Frip*, written by George Saunders and wonderfully illustrated by Lane Smith (whose *It's a Book* I cannot recommend highly enough), is a fanciful and satirical tale that proves in the end to be an allegory of scarcity and slack—a perfect companion read to Ursula K. Le Guin's allegory of privilege, "The One's Who Walk Away from Omelas."

Realizing that the Human Heart Is Capable

"Ever had a burr in your sock?" sets the story in motion—one sentence centered on the page over a giant question mark (Saunders & Smith, 2000, p. 1). It is an opening worthy of a child and all of us who cling to the wonder of childhood. While Le Guin is often described as a science fiction writer, in her work I recognize the blurring of genres that joins science fiction, speculative fiction, and fantasy. It is that "other world" about which Le Guin and Margaret Atwood appear to argue (Atwood, 2011), and it is a stark but rich *other world* Saunders conjures and Lane pictures.

The story of Frip involves three houses for three families, all with children at the center. The houses are distinguished with primary colors—child-like blue, green, and red—but Lane's artwork adds the ominous to Saunders' seemingly simple narrative that is tinged with more than a bite of satire. The illustrations echo the haunting works about and for children found in Neil Gaiman and Tim Burton.

A child standing precariously close to the end of a slanted cliff over an angry ocean catches the eye on page 7, and then the crux of the story pulls you back to the text on the facing page:

> Frip was three leaning shacks by the sea. Frip was three tiny goat-yards into which eight times a day the children of the shacks would trudge with gapper-brushes and cloth gapper-sacks that tied at the top. After brushing the gappers off the goats, the children would walk to the cliff at the edge of town and empty their gapper-sacks into the sea. (Saunders & Smith, 2000, p. 6)

Gappers, orange burr-like creatures with many eyes and the size of a baseball, come to represent throughout the story the *power of the systemic inevitable*. The presence of the gappers determines the lot of the families (and their goats), but most of the people in the tale remain unable to see beyond their own fixed and mostly misguided worldviews.

When the gappers cling to the goats of all three families, there is an ironic appearance of equality among them. But when the fortune of one family shifts, the gappers fulfill their name by creating the gap: "So that night, instead of splitting into three groups, the gappers moved into one very large and impressive shrieking group directly into Capable's yard" (Saunders & Smith, 2000, p. 12). Before this shift in the gappers' behavior, of course, the three families are not equal because Capable is an only child living with her father and who has lost her mother. Capable works as all the children are expected to work (removing gappers in a daily Sisyphean nightmare of chores) and seeks to serve the needs of her grieving father, who along with his grief is a prisoner of nostalgia:

> "I myself was once an exhausted child brushing off gappers. It was lovely! The best years of my life. The way they fell to the sea from our bags! And anyway, what would you do with your time if there were no gappers?" (Saunders & Smith, 2000, p. 11)

This nostalgia, masking an unnecessarily burdensome childhood, is but one ideology weighing on Capable because as soon as the other two families are relieved of gappers on their goats, those families reveal themselves to be very much like the people of Le Guin's Omelas:

> "It's a miracle!" Mrs. Romo shouted next morning, when she came out and discovered that her yard was free of gappers. "This is wonderful! Capable, dear, you poor thing. The miracle didn't happen to you, did it? I feel so sorry for you. God has been good to us, by taking our gappers away. Why? I can't say. God knows what God is doing, I guess! I suppose we must somehow deserve it!" (Saunders & Smith, 2000, p. 17)

Capable becomes the sacrificed child, and despite her misfortune, the relieved families read the events as their *merit* (and of course the ugly implication that Capable and her father deserve the burden of the gappers).

What follows from this shift in fate is the central story of Frip, with Capable as our main character. The message becomes clear, and Saunders and Lane make the ride one you'll want to take again and again. If you are lucky, the book could become one of those read alouds requested by son or daughter, or by a classroom of children.

And while I will leave the rest of the story to you, I think it is necessary to note here that this allegory is both a cautionary tale about how we view children and childhood as well as a brilliant call to reconsider how we view education and education reform.

George Saunders's Allegory of Scarcity and Slack

The U.S., like the characters (except for Capable) in Saunders's story, is tragically blinded by a belief in cultural myths (Thomas, 2011, January 26) that have little basis in evidence. These myths include that we live and work in a meritocracy, that competition creates equity, that children need to be "taught a lesson" about the cold cruel world lest they become soft, and such. As a result of these beliefs, schools often reflect and perpetuate rather harsh environments for children—or to be more accurate, schools often reflect and perpetuate rather harsh environments for *other people's children* (Delpit, 2006), as Capable personifies.

Here, then, I want to make the case that *The Very Persistent Gappers of Frip* is a powerful allegory of scarcity and slack as examined by Sendhil Mullainathan and Eldar Shafir (2013) in their *Scarcity: Why Having Too Little Means So Much*. Mullainathan and Shafir describe how the conditions of poverty and scarcity so overburden people psychologically, mentally, and physically that their behavior is often misread in the form of stereotypes—poor people are lazy; poor people make bad decisions, deserving their poverty, etc. In Saunders's story, scarcity and its burden are animated as the gappers, and readers witness how the coincidence of the onslaught of the gappers changes the families involved. In other words, the behavior of people is *determined* by the environment, and *not by the inherent goodness or deficiencies of any individual.*

The Very Persistent Gappers of Frip goes further, however, by showing that one person's scarcity (Capable) allows another person slack—privilege is built on the back of others, and those conditions are mostly arbitrary. While Mullainathan and Shafir (2013) argue that the slack enjoyed by those living in relative privilege provides the sort of cognitive space needed to excel, Saunders speaks to more than the slack enjoyed by the two families relieved of gappers and the compounding scarcity suffered by Capable (her lot in life and the addition of the gappers):

- The families gifted slack remain trapped within the corrosive burden of competition and their inability to recognize the value of compassion and cooperation (Johnson, 2013).

- Capable represents a counter-narrative to claims that impoverished children lack "grit." As her name suggests, this child is more than capable, but the world appears determined to defeat her.

- Capable also embodies Lisa Delpit's (2006) confrontation of "other people's children"—that those with privilege (slack) are willing to allow a set of standards for other people's children (often living and learning in scarcity), standards they will not tolerate for their own children.

As I stated in the opening, allegory seeks to open our eyes by diversion, creating an *other world* that helps us see both the flaws with our *now* and the enduring failures of humans to embrace our basic humanity, a failure that Capable teeters on the edge of making herself but cannot:

And [Capable] soon found that it was not all that much fun being the sort of person who eats a big dinner in a warm house while others shiver on their roofs in the dark.

That is, it was fun at first, but then got gradually less fun, until it was really no fun at all. (Saunders & Smith, 2000, p. 70).

In the end, it is this sort of charity, this sort of recognition of the community of humanity, a call for the kindness found in Kurt Vonnegut's similar mix of dark humor, about which Saunders appears to suggest we are all capable.

16

Click, Clack, Moo: Why the 1% Always Win

As a high school English teacher for nearly two decades, I came to embrace a need to offer students a wide range of lenses for interacting with and learning from many different texts. But I also learned that coming to read and re-read, to write and re-write the world is both a powerful and disorienting experience for young people. So a strategy I now use and encourage other teachers to implement is reading and discussing children's literature and picture books, while expanding the critical lenses readers have in their toolbox.

My favorite book for this activity is *Click, Clack, Moo: Cows that Type*. This work by Doreen Cronin with art by Betsy Lewin (2000) presents a clever and humorous narrative about Farmer Brown and his suddenly recalcitrant cows who, having acquired a rickety typewriter, establish a strike that inspires the chickens to join and ends with the neutral ducks aiding the revolt. This story is ideal for asking teachers to consider the traditional approach to text in schools, New Criticism—a focus on text in isolation and on the craft in any story, such as characterization, plot, and theme—in contrast with Feminist and Marxist criticism, for example. One fall, while doing the activity with a young adult literature class, I came against yet a new reading of Cronin and Lewin's work: Why the 1% always win.

The U.S. Public Likes Farmer Brown

As we explored *Click, Clack, Moo* in that course, the adult members of the class told me they *like* Farmer Brown, with one student characterizing the striking farm animals as "mean." And here is where I felt the need to consider how this children's book helps us all confront the Occupy Wall Street movement or the rise in antagonism toward teachers, tenure, and unions as well as why the 1% continue to own the 99%.

One important element of the story is that the cows and chickens are *female* workers under the authority of the *male* Farmer Brown. These female workers produce for the farmer and remain compliant until the cows acquire the typewriter—both a powerful tool of literacy since the cows and chickens cannot effectively strike until they gain access to language and a representation of access to technology. We should note that the cows and chickens produce typewritten notes that show they find an old *manual* typewriter, unlike the cleaner type produced by Farmer Brown on an *electric* typewriter, a representation of the inequity of access to technology among classes.

The cows and chickens, in effect, unionize and strike. Here, some members of my classes often fail to notice the unionization, but tend to side with the farmer even when we acknowledge the protest as unionizing—particularly bristling at the duck, as a neutral party, using its access to the negotiation to acquire a diving board for the duck pond.

Like the 1%, Farmer Brown is incensed that the cows and chickens demand the basic necessities for comfort, electric blankets, but he eventually secures a compromise, agreeing to give the barn animals the requested electric blankets for the return of the typewriter. The story ends with the obvious next step that the duck uses the typewriter to trade for the diving board.

What tends to be missed in this story is that *Farmer Brown ultimately wins*; in fact, the barn animals appear to be eager to abandon their one access to power, the typewriter, for mere material items—the electric blankets as a comfort many would see as a basic right and the diving board as frivolous entertainment.

The 1% have the 99% right where Farmer Brown has the barn animals—mesmerized by the pursuit of materialism and entertainment. Consider the eager hordes of consumers lined up to buy the then-new iPhone each different generation. *Just give us our iPhones and we'll be quiet, we'll work longer and harder for the opportunity to buy what the 1% tell us we want.* And when the 1% and their compliant media inform us that the top 20% pays 64% of taxes, we slip back to our barns with our tails between our legs, shamed.

Instead, we should be noting that, yes, the top 20% income earners pay 64% of taxes because they make 59% of income (Domhoff, 2008/2013). We, the 99% who tend to remain silent and compliant, wait patiently for the next generation of technology to occupy our time, our lives reduced to work and amassing the ever-changing and outdated things that become passé as the next-thing lures us further and further into our sheep lives.

Yes, if we remain eager to trade our voices for things, the 1% will always be the winners. When we learn to treasure voice over things, however, the chickens may come home to roost.

17

Our Dystopia Is Now: *The Circle* (Eggers) and *Feed* (Anderson)

For twenty-first century readers and students, George Orwell's dystopian novel *1984* poses, I think, a temporal paradox. Orwell's "other world" appears simultaneously a horrifying totalitarian future possibility for humanity, as well as a technological mutt of what someone in the past speculated about the future (consider the pneumatic tubes).

As I read *The Circle* by Dave Eggers, I began to imagine that my experience with this novel, published and read in 2013, was repeating what readers during the late 1940s and early 1950s (especially British readers) may have felt turning the pages of Orwell's Big Brother nightmare, a Kafkan dark satire of their lived England. My reading experience with *The Circle* has at least two problematic elements.

First, I read about a third of the novel before I lost interest and picked up *Feed* by M.T. Anderson (2012), which I read completely before returning to and finishing *The Circle*. And second, I never felt fully engaged with *The Circle* because I couldn't shake the feeling that the novel details that our dystopia is *now*. Both *The Circle* and *Feed* provide readers with a genre carnival of sorts—dystopia fiction, young adult fiction, science fiction, and speculative fiction. But

I struggled with *The Circle* in ways that I did not with *Feed*, despite my usual measured disappointment with many young adult novels.

Since Adam Bessie (2013) has explored the importance of *Feed*, especially as it informs education reform, I want to examine more closely *The Circle* in the context of *Feed* as well as my struggles to engage fully with Eggers's important novel. Just past the middle of *The Circle*, I began to see that Eggers's dystopia is a contemporary *1984*. When the main character, Mae, serves the will of the Circle by producing three slogan—Secrets Are Lies, Sharing Is Caring, Privacy Is Theft —Orwell's "War Is Peace, Freedom Is Slavery, Ignorance Is Strength" echoed in my mind's ear.

I feel compelled to place *The Circle*, then, within a dystopian tradition including *1984* and Margaret Atwood's *The Handmaid's Tale*—speculative works that weave contemporary social satire (albeit very dark satire) with imaginative logical extensions of *what if* that hold up one possible future for humankind. While *The Circle* reminds me of *1984* and *The Handmaid's Tale*—including the slogans above alluding to *1984* and elements of zealotry along with totalitarianism's dependency on currency manipulation (Atwood's prescience about debit cards) shared with *The Handmaid's Tale*—Eggers's other world is not removed nearly as far from the reader as in Orwell's and Atwood's novels.

Since I use and know a great deal about Google, Twitter, and Facebook, the Circle as a speculative logical extension of our real-world social media feels less speculative than *our dystopia is now*. For the privileged in the second decade of the twenty-first century and those on the edge of privilege wanting in, smartphones, tablets, and computers *connected through the Internet* have blurred almost every aspect of the human condition—social with professional, entertainment with commerce, etc.

We don't flinch when Google completes our typing as we search the web or when Gmail reads our emails in order to push product banners. We reduce our conversations to 140 letters with glee and among hundreds, even thousands of people we have never met in person. We *retweet, favorite,* and *like* (verbing all the way) while double posting on Twitter and Facebook—even clicking "like" under a Facebook post about the death of a dog, or a grandmother.

So when Eggers introduces the more fantastical elements of the novel, and there are some, I remained fixated on my lack of compassion for Mae and my inability to shake the feeling that Eggers is simply cataloguing the world that the privileged have created, the lived world of the contemporary privileged. I must add that *The Circle* and *Feed* focus on main characters who are compliant "insiders" of the dystopia, and that both have sacrificial radical characters. I found Mae in *The Circle* really hard to embrace, but I did feel compelled by Titus in *Feed*. I had the same bland response to the radical in *The Circle*, while caring deeply for *Feed*'s Violet, my favorite character of the two novels.

I suspect my view so far of *The Circle* may feel like less than a ringing endorsement; however, I do believe *The Circle* is a *1984* for our time, an important and insightful work. Let me, then, offer a few reasons why. At its essence, *The Circle* is the fictionalizing of concepts explored in Michel Foucault (1984) and Gilles Deleuze (1992): surveillance, "infinite examination," "societies of control." While Foucault and Deleuze are inaccessible in many ways for the general public, Eggers's other world, even as close as it is to now, is stark in its clarity. At times, *The Circle* reads with the same sort of dispassionate *camera* feel that Ernest Hemingway uses in "Hills Like White Elephants." In both works, there lies the danger that readers will fail to confront what has been placed before them—that the dispassion will read as endorsement or at least could be embraced by the readers.

Often true of any artwork, Eggers allows readers to close *The Circle* in much the same mindset as Mae (Book III is a mere three-pages long in its twist-style ending). As with *Feed*, *The Circle* also speaks directly to education reform, particularly as that overlaps with our current era of mass incarceration (Thomas, 2013, May 17):

- With fervor, the possibility of the Circle's role in education is championed—and the discussion sounds eerily close to home:

"That's the idea," Jackie said. "…[S]oon we'll be able to know at any given moment where our sons and daughters stand against the rest of American students, and then against the world's students."

"That sounds very helpful," Mae said. "And would eliminate a lot of doubt and stress out there."… "And it'll be updated how often?"

"Oh, daily. Once we get full participation from all schools and districts, we'll be able to keep daily rankings, with every test, every pop quiz incorporated instantly. And of course these can be broken up between public and private, regional, and the rankings can be merged, weighted, and analyzed to see trends among various other factors—socioeconomic, race, ethnicity, everything." (Eggers, 2013, p. 341)

- In possibly the most disturbing section of the novel, the Circle is characterized as a potential law enforcement tool that can erase crime and racial profiling, by color-coding everyone on the ubiquitous monitors invented by the Circle: "The three men you see in orange and red are repeat offenders" (Eggers, 2013, p. 418). This plan, however, works under the assumption that previous arrests are fair, themselves not the result of race or class bias.

In the end, *The Circle* is a warning shot about the end of privacy and universal surveillance. If readers feel uncomfortable while reading with their smartphone dinging nearby, it is likely because our dystopia is now, and *The Circle* is a nearly 500-page pamphlet saying, "Welcome to the Machine" (Pink Floyd).

18

On Isaac Asimov

The U.S. is a belief culture (Thomas, 2011, January 26). The public in the U.S. rejects evolution and climate change while also clinging to barbaric practices such as corporal punishment and grade retention of children—all because of belief and all without regard to abundant evidence to the contrary. Scientists and science fiction writers, then, often find themselves highly critical of a failure of reason and evidence. One of the more powerful examples of that frustration is Isaac Asimov, and his tagging the U.S. a "cult of ignorance."

Contemporary Education Reform and "A Cult of Ignorance"

Writing in *Newsweek* in the cusp of America's shift into the Reagan era of conservatism that included the roots of the current education reform movement built on accountability, standards, and high-stakes testing, Isaac Asimov (1980) declared the U.S. "a cult of ignorance," explaining:

> There is a cult of ignorance in the United States, and there always has been. The strain of anti-intellectualism has been a constant thread winding its way through our political and cultural life, nurtured by the false notion that democracy

means that "my ignorance is just as good as your knowledge." (p. 19)

While science fiction (SF), a genre within which Asimov is legendary, is often misread as *prediction*—SF is often allegorical or a critical and satirical commentary on the contemporary world, more so than predictive—Asimov's brief essay is eerily prescient about the most recent education reform movement and the discourse surrounding it.

As Reagan ascended to the presidency in the U.S., Asimov noticed a clear line being drawn by politicians between them as spokespeople *for* and *with* the public versus intellectuals, academics, and experts of all kinds. One shift Asimov observed was a move away from the 1960s "Don't trust anyone over 30" to a new conservative "Don't trust the experts." In America, it seems, economic elitism was desirable but intellectual elitism was to be avoided at all costs.

Asimov noted both the central importance of a powerful, independent, and critical media along with the inherent problem of how well equipped the public is to gain from such a media (if one exists). While I find his concern for Americans' literacy too flippant and suffering (ironically) from his own blind spot as an expert writer who likely was far less expert in the broader field of literacy and literacy instruction (his advanced degrees were in chemistry), Asimov (1980) did make a credible though garbled call for*critical literacy* among an American public that is functionally literate:

> [T]he American public, by and large, in their distrust of experts and in their contempt for pointy-headed professors, can't and don't read.

> To be sure, the average American can sign his name more or less legibly, and can make out the sports headline—but how many non-elitist Americans can, without undue difficulty, read as many as a thousand consecutive words of small print, some of which may be trisyllabic? (p. 19)

[Note: Asimov's immediate school bashing based on test

scores suggests he, too, was a victim of careless attention to the facts.]

Asimov (1980) eventually raised an important question about the right to know among a free people, the role of the media, and the need for an educated public in a free and democratic society:

> I contend that the slogan "America's right to know" is a meaningless one when we have an ignorant population, and that the function of a free press is virtually zero when hardly anyone can read....

> I believe that every human being with a physically normal brain can learn a great deal and can be surprisingly intellectual. I believe that what we badly need is social approval of learning and social rewards for learning.

> We can *all* be members of the intellectual elite and then, and only then, will a phrase like "America's right to know" and, indeed, any true concept of democracy, have any meaning. (p. 19)

As we time-travel forward thirty-plus years, we can appreciate that Asimov has offered the current education reform template as well as the tremendous hurdle facing teachers, researchers, and scholars seeking to raise their voices of expertise and experience against a political and public commitment to a cult of ignorance: Don't trust experts, but do trust politicians, celebrities, and billionaires. Asimov's essay, with only a few edits, could easily be written today and aimed squarely at the education reform movement. Secretary of Education Arne Duncan, Bill Gates, and Michelle Rhee warn the American public *not* to listen to the experts—teachers, researchers, and scholars.

That discourse remains robust as long as the media both report and perpetuate that political message and as long as formal education remains primarily bureaucratic, ensuring that schools fail to foster critical literacy while the consumer culture, feeding on entertainment, keeps the public so busy and distracted that few bother to consider the danger that ignoring experts poses to both freedom and democracy. The political and economic elites benefit themselves from marginalizing and demonizing educators and the educated (the expert). The political and economic elites also benefit indirectly and directly from keeping universal public education in the most reduced form possible, exactly what accountability, standards, and high-stakes testing ensure.

The education reform movement's commitments to Common Core State Standards, national high-stakes tests, teacher evaluation linked to those tests, and chain-store type charter schools are not quests for a better educated American public, but strategies for further entrenching the U.S. in the cult of ignorance Asimov unmasked over three decades ago.

The Rise of the Dogmatic Scholar: "A Cult of Ignorance" pt. 2

> *By oft repeating an untruth, men come to believe it them-*
> *selves.*
> *Thomas Jefferson, letter to John Melish, Jan. 13, 1812*

> *The moment a person forms a theory, his imagination*
> *sees, in every object, only the traits which favor that*
> *theory.*
> *Thomas Jefferson to Charles Thompson, 1787*

My university sits in the socially and politically conservative South, and our students tend toward a conservative political and world-view as well. The most powerful student organizations are self-identified as conservative as well as being awash in power and funding, some from outside the university. One conservative student organization, supported and funded by a network of such organizations spreading throughout campuses across the U.S., has for years dominated the Cultural Life Program of the university, a series of events students must attend as part of graduation requirements.

Several years ago, this organization brought Ann Coulter to campus, and when I mentioned my own concerns about her credibility during class, a student quickly defended Coulter by saying, "But she has footnotes in her book." Coulter's confrontational conservatism speaks to the world-views of many of our students and the greater public of South Carolina, and thus she seems credible even without footnotes. The student's defense highlights a key element in the rise of the dogmatic scholar that has its roots in the 1980s, a period identified by Isaac Asimov (1980) as "a cult of ignorance" guided by a new ethic, "Don't trust the experts."

April of 2013 was the thirty-year anniversary of *A Nation at Risk*, a political and popular turning point for America's perception of not only public education but also education reform as well as the discourse surrounding both. John Holton (2003) and Gerald Bracey (2003) have since then detailed that the report was also, in Bracey's words over a decade ago on the cusp of No Child Left Behind, "false":

> It has been 20 years, though, since *A Nation at Risk* appeared. It is clear that it was false then and is false now. Today, the laments are old and tired – and still false. "Test Scores Lag as School Spending Soars" trumpeted the headline of a 2002 press release from the American Legislative Exchange Council. Ho hum. The various special interest groups in education need another treatise to rally round. And now they have one. It's called No Child Left Behind. It's a weapon of mass destruction, and the target is the public school system. Today, our public schools are truly at risk. (p. 621)

What was "false" about *A Nation at Risk*? First, Holton (2003), as an insider, exposed that Ronald Reagan himself directed the commission to ensure his agenda for public schools:

> We met with President Reagan at the White House, who at first was jovial, charming, and full of funny stories, but then turned serious when he gave us our marching orders. He told us that our report should focus on five fundamental points that would bring excellence to education: Bring God

back into the classroom. Encourage tuition tax credits for families using private schools. Support vouchers. Leave the primary responsibility for education to parents. And please abolish that abomination, the Department of Education. Or, at least, don't ask to waste more federal money on education — "we have put in more only to wind up with less." Just discover excellent schools to serve as models for all the others. As we left, I detected no visible dismay in our group. I wondered if we were all equally stunned. (quoted from electronic version, n.p.)

Second, Bracey (2003) noted that despite the report claiming to depend on research and data, only one trend line out of nine suggested anything negative, and the commission focused on that one trend line in order to comply with the political pressure aimed at the committee. And third, *A Nation at Risk,* as a political document parading as scholarship, received not only a pass from the media but also a rush to benefit from the bad news by many stakeholders, as Bracey explained:

Alas, nothing else is new and, indeed, we must recognize that good news about public schools serves no one's reform agenda – even if it does make teachers, students, parents, and administrators feel a little better. Conservatives want vouchers and tuition tax credits; liberals want more resources for schools; free marketers want to privatize the schools and make money; fundamentalists want to teach religion and not worry about the First Amendment; Catholic schools want to stanch their student hemorrhage; home schooling advocates want just that; and various groups no doubt just want to be with "their own kind." All groups believe that they will improve their chances of getting what they want if they pummel the publics. (p. 621)

A Nation at Risk, the process involved to create the report, the uncritical media endorsement of the report, and the public and academic embracing of the report's claims represent a seminal moment in the rise of the dogmatic scholar, one foreshadowed by Asimov and personified by Coulter.

For example, a debate between Diane Ravitch and Patrick Wolf highlights how the dogmatic scholar looks today. Mercedes Schneider (2013) examines that debate by first addressing Wolf's credentials, Endowed Chair in School Choice, Education Reform, University of Arkansas. Both Schneider and Ravitch (2013) raise concerns about the conflict of interests when a scholar holds a chair in a department that is heavily funded by school choice advocates. As Schneider explains about Wolf's complaint that Ravitch attacked him personally: "Whereas she does not personally attack Wolf, Ravitch certainly clearly exposes Wolf's conflict of interest in evaluating a program obviously supported by his funders." I agree with Ravitch that this conflict of interest is noteworthy for its undeniable potential in shaping study reporting and outcomes.

At the root of this debate is the unmasking of the dogmatic scholar and the concurrent rise of conservative advocacy taking on the appearance of scholarship despite the historical claims among conservatives that pointy-headed intellectuals shouldn't be trusted (again, see Asimov [1982]). Coulter's book has footnotes to appear scholarly, and free market think tanks have increasingly embraced a formula that is both deeply deceiving and powerfully effective:

1. hire fellows with advanced degrees, preferably PhDs;

2. generate reports that include a great deal of data, statistics, and charts/graphs;

3. create scholarly but attractive PDFs of the reports accessible for free through the think tank web sites;

4. aggressively promote the reports through press releases; and

5. circumvent entirely the peer-review process—in fact, conservative think tanks actively demonize the peer-review process.

The dogmatic scholar differs from the traditional university-based scholar in several important ways. The university-based scholar and the promise of academia rest on some basic concepts, including the wall between undue influence and independent thought that tenure affords, combined with the self-policing effect of peer-review. While traditional scholarship, tenure, and peer-review are not without problems, this essential paradigm does allow for (although it cannot guarantee) rich and vibrant knowledge bases to evolve for the sake of knowledge, unaffected by the allure of profit or the influence of inexpert authority. As an example, tenure stands between university boards of trustees and faculty to ensure academic freedom.

As a critical educator and scholar, however, I do reject the traditional view that scholars must be apolitical and must assume some objective stance. In fact, I believe that scholars must be activists. Therefore, my concern about the rise of the dogmatic scholar is not the activism or advocacy, but two key failures found among dogmatic scholarship: (1) masking advocacy as objective, typically behind the use of statistics and charts/graphs; and (2) committing to an ideology despite the weight of evidence to the contrary. Activist scholars such as Howard Zinn and his confrontational work as a historian demonstrate the power of taking a public intellectual stance that is both ideologically grounded (social justice) and informed by scholarship.

The dogmatic scholarship typically found in think tanks, but increasingly occurring in externally funded schools, departments, and institutes within universities and colleges (such as Wolf's role at the University of Arkansas) is typified by a school choice report funded by the Wisconsin Policy Research Institute (WPRI), which is explicitly a free market advocacy think tank. "Fixing the Milwaukee Public Schools: The Limits of Parent-Driven Reform" by David Dodenhoff (2007) was released by WPRI with George Lightbourn, representing the institute, lamenting: "The report you are reading did not yield the results I had hoped for."

Further, despite the evidence of the research commissioned by WPRI, Lightbourn issued a commentary and explained: "So that there is no misunderstanding, WPRI is unhesitant in supporting school choice. School choice is working and should be improved and expanded. School choice is good for Milwaukee's children"

(McAdams, 2007). While Lightbourn's commentary raises some concerns about the data, the key message is "evidence be damned, WPRI remains committed to school choice!"

The problem, then, with the rise of the dogmatic scholar is that several contradictions lie underneath the movement. Conservative America has persistently marginalized and demonized the Left as biased, while embracing not only the possibility of objectivity but also the necessity for objectivity, especially among educators, scholars, and researchers—consider the uproar over climate change science. Yet, conservatives are the base of dogmatic scholars and those who embrace dogmatic scholars (or popular versions such as Coulter), despite dogmatic scholars being themselves advocates masquerading as objective and academic. Further, the dogmatic scholar is failing in the exact ways some traditional scholarship fails—by allowing the influence of funding and profit to skew the pursuit of knowledge. In fact, since dogmatic scholarship is often driven by market ideology, the influence of funding and profit is common.

The impact of dogmatic scholarship on education reform has been staggering, resulting in a common pattern found among researchers and think tanks committed to reviewing educational research such as Bruce Baker, Matthew Di Carlo, and the National Education Policy Center: The reports coming from dogmatic scholars produce impressive data sets, but misleading, incomplete, or contradictory claims and recommendations (see, for example, Baker [2012] on the highly publicized Chetty, Friedman, and Rock-off study). The reports coming from dogmatic scholars, notably school choice research, tend to replicate the comments coming from WPRI about Milwaukee school choice: *The claims and recommendations are decided before and in spite of the evidence of the data.*

In fact, school choice research has revealed a pattern of making a series of ever-changing claims simply to keep the debate alive, and thus the choice agenda vibrant. In the popular and enduring evolution debate, for example, Intelligent Design as a faux science endorses "teach the debate" to lend credibility to their claims and to gain equal footing with the scientific process without actually conforming to that process. Do Ravitch and Wolf, then, have the right to debate? Of course. Their debate is likely a potentially powerful mechanism for examining education reform. Does Wolf have a right to advocate for school choice? Again, I believe he does. The problem, however, with both Wolf's agenda and the debate is that Wolf wants to hide behind a mask of objectivity and has taken a "holier than thou" stance to marginalize Ravitch's credible concerns about school choice research.

In the end, the dogmatic scholar fails for the same reason dogma does—because neither can be questioned. All credible scholarship is rendered more valuable by the light of questions, so I will end with a simple solution offered by Julian Vasquez Heilig, Ph.D. to Wolf's complaint:

> Dr. Patrick, Please hurry and de-identify the data you used in your papers and provide it to independent researchers. I have the ability to critique the methodological rigor and quality of your actual research. I am very very much looking forward to it. (Wolf, 2013)

Among researchers, no claim is any more credible than the data the claim rests on. As long as dogmatic scholars ignore and hide the data, their work will be questioned in ways that also include questioning their motives.

The job of the scholar is not to be objective, but to be transparent—admitting that evidence-based stances provide context for claims and recommendations. Dogmatic scholars refuse to be transparent, and their weakness is their entrenched dishonesty. In short, all scholars likely should heed the opening comments of this section by Jefferson.

19

On Kurt Vonnegut

Kurt Vonnegut made a few powerful routines the foundation of his fiction and nonfiction. Along with his dark humor, part of his allure included a playful twisting of genres. For example, Vonnegut pushed back against being labeled a science fiction (SF) writer while writing novel after novel about the end of the world—a standard of SF. Ultimately, also typical of the best SF writers, Vonnegut exposed the greatest weaknesses of the human condition, often failures repeatedly self-imposed.

"Eager to Recreate the Same Old Nightmare": Revisiting Vonnegut's *Player Piano*

Few people could have imagined the acceleration of corporate influence that occurred in the years following the 2008 economic downturn in the U.S. that was associated with the activities of major banks and corporations as well as the election of Barack Obama, who was repeatedly demonized as a socialist. More shocking, possibly, has been the corporate influence on the public discourse about universal public education, driven by Secretary of Education Arne Duncan and promoted through celebrity tours by billionaire Bill Gates, ex-chancellor Michelle Rhee, and "Superman" Geoffrey Canada.

Adam Bessie (2010) has speculated about the logical progression of the current accountability era built on tests—which is destined to hold teachers accountable for their students' test scores despite the evidence that teachers account for only about 10-20% of student achievement—to the elimination of teaching as a profession. And Stephen Krashen (2011) believes that the corporate takeover of schools is at the center of the new reformers' misinformation tour. For Anthony Cody (2013), the future is a disturbing dystopia. While Bessie's, Krashen's, and Cody's commentaries may sound like alarmist stances–possibly even the stuff of fiction—I believe we all should have seen this coming for decades.

The SF genre has always been one of my favorites, and within that genre, I am particularly fond of dystopian fiction, such as Margaret Atwood's brilliant *The Handmaid's Tale*, *Oryx and Crake*, and *The Year of the Flood*. Like Atwood, Vonnegut spoke and often wrote about rejecting the SF label for his work (See Chapter 1 of *Wampeters, Foma & Granfalloons*), but Vonnegut's genius includes his gift for delivering social commentary and satire wrapped in narratives that *seemed* to be set in the future, *seemed* to be a distorted world that we could never possibly experience.

In 1952, Kurt Vonnegut published *Player Piano*, offering what most believed was a biting satire of corporate America from his own experience of working at GE. A review of the novel describes Vonnegut's vision of our brave new world:

> The important difference lies in the fact that Mr. Vonnegut's oligarchs are not capitalists but engineers. In the future as he envisages it, the machines have completed their triumph, dispossessing not only the manual laborers but the white collar workers as well. Consequently the carefully selected, highly trained individuals who design and control the machines are the only people who have anything to do. Other people, the great majority, can either go into the Reconstruction and Reclamation Corps, which is devoted to boondoggling, or join the army, which has no real function in a machine-dominated world-society. (Hicks, 1952)

Yes, in Vonnegut's dystopia, computers are at the center of a society itself run like a machine, with everyone labeled with his or her IQ and designated for the career he or she can pursue—although we should note that women's roles were even more constrained than men's, reflecting the mid-twentieth century sexism in the U.S. Where corporations end and the government begins is difficult to identify in this society that is simply a slightly exaggeration of the life Vonnegut had witnessed while working at GE before abandoning corporate America to be a full-time writer.

For me, however, Vonnegut's *Player Piano* is as much a warning about the role of testing and labeling people in our education system as it is a red flag about the dangers of the oligarchy that we have become. Today, with billionaire Bill Gates speaking not only for corporate America but also for reforming public education, how far off was Vonnegut's vision? In the first decade of the twenty-first century, how different is Vonnegut's world to what we have today, as income inequity and the pooling of wealth accelerate (Noah, 2010)?

We have witnessed where political loyalty lies during the taxpayer funded bailouts as corporate America collapsed at the end of George W. Bush's presidency. With corporate America saved and most Americans ignored, the next logical step is to transform public education by increasingly imposing the corporate business model that has been crippling the education system since the misinformation out of Ronald Reagan's presidency grabbed headlines with the release of A Nation at Risk. If Vonnegut had written this storyline, at least we could have been guaranteed some laughter. But this brave new world of public education is much grimmer—like George Orwell's *1984*.

Our artists can see and understand when many of the rest of us are simply overwhelmed by our lives. In *Player Piano*, we see how successfully corporate life disorients and overwhelms workers in order to keep those workers under control. And in the relationship between the main character Paul and his wife Anita, we watch the power of corporate life—and the weight of testing and reducing humans to numbers—being magnified by the rise of computers when Paul makes a plea to his wife:

"No, no. You've got something the tests and machines will never be able to measure: you're artistic. That's one of the tragedies of our times, that no machine has ever been built that can recognize that quality, appreciate it, foster it, sympathize with it." (Vonnegut, 1952, p. 178)

In the novel, Paul's quest and the momentary rise of a few rebels appear to be no match for corporate control. Today, I have to say I am no more optimistic than Vonnegut.

When Secretary Duncan (2010) offers misleading claims about international test scores and bemoans the state of public schools for failing to provide us with a world-class workforce, and almost no one raises a voice in protest (except those of us within the field of education, who are then demonized for protesting [Michie, 2011]), I am tempted to think that we are simply getting what we deserve—like Paul at the end of *Player Piano*: "And that left Paul. 'To a better world,' he started to say, but he cut the toast short, thinking of the people of Ilium, already eager to recreate the same old nightmare" (Vonnegut, 1952, p. 340).

On Foma and Mendacity: Letting the Cat Out of the Bag

Kurt Vonnegut's (1963) *Cat's Cradle* and Tennessee Williams's (2004) *Cat on a Hot Tin Roof* may seem at first blush to share only the use of "cat" in their titles, but both works are masterful examinations of something central to the human condition: the lie. But Vonnegut's foma at the heart of Bokononism and Big Daddy's railing against mendacity present contrasting dramatizations of "lying and liars," as Brick and Big Daddy wrestle with "one of them five dollar words" (Williams, 2004, p. 108). *Mendacity* is the darkest of lies because it corrupts and ultimately destroys relationships and even lives. For Big Daddy, mendacity is inevitable, central to the human condition: "I've lived with mendacity!—Why can't you live with it? Hell, you got to live with it, there's nothing else to live with except mendacity, is there?" (Williams, p. 111).

While Vonnegut's (1963) novel is also dark—and typically satirical—*foma* is offered as "harmless lies," as Julian Castle explains to the narrator:

"Well, when it became evident that no governmental or economic reform was going to make the people much less miserable, the religion became the one real instrument of hope. Truth was the enemy of the people, because the truth was so terrible, so Bokonon made it his business to provide the people with better and better lies." (p. 172)

Although different consequences result from the mendacity of *Cat on a Hot Tin Roof* and the foma of *Cat's Cradle*, all lies share one important characteristic: They are almost impossible to confront, and once confronted, they create a great deal of pain.

As a parent, I came face to face with letting the cat out of the bag when my daughter first unmasked the foma of the Tooth Fairy, and then connected that realization with Santa Claus. After I confessed to the truth—trying as I did to make a case about "harmless lies"—my daughter cut right to the heart of the matter, asking, "Why did y'all lie to me?"

The thinnest margins between mendacity and foma, I think, are found in our cultural myths—the fatal flaw of confusing the *ideals we aspire to* as a people with *conditions already achieved*. Many of those aspirations have tipped into mendacity, poisoning the possibility of those ideals—especially in the foundational promises of public institutions. Here, then, are those ideals that could have served us well as *aspiration*, but now work as *mendacity* and thus *against* our best intensions:

- *Capitalism and Choice.* The realization is now becoming hard to ignore, that capitalism (the free market) is incompatible with equity (see, for example, Thomas Piketty [2014]). Also, choice as a concept central to freedom is far more complicated than expressed in our public discourse. Both capitalism and choice have worked against cultural aspirations for equity, but those failures may be better explained by the reason they have failed: *idealizing* capitalism and choice while failing to commit fully to the power of the Commons (publicly funded institutions) to establish the context within which capitalism and choice could serve equity well.

- *Meritocracy*. In the U.S., possibly the greatest lie that results from confusing an aspiration with an achieved condition is the argument that we live in a meritocracy. The evidence suggests that we currently do not have a meritocracy—see how being born rich and not attending college trumps being born poor but completing college (Bruenig, 2013). Even more disturbing, we are unlikely to achieve a meritocracy; for example, see why "[e]qual opportunity cannot actually be achieved" (Fishkin, 2014).

- *Education as the Key to Equity*. Equally misleading as claims about the U.S. being a meritocracy (or that we are a post-racial country) are the assertions that education is the one true way to overcome social ills and how any individual can lift her/himself out of poverty. However, education has not changed and does *not*, in fact, change society; *rarely* lifts people out of the circumstances of their births; and serves as a marker for privilege—thus creating the illusion that education is a force for change, as Reardon (2013) explains:

  > Here's a fact that may not surprise you: the children of the rich perform better in school, on average, than children from middle-class or poor families. Students growing up in richer families have better grades and higher standardized test scores, on average, than poorer students; they also have higher rates of participation in extracurricular activities and school leadership positions, higher graduation rates and higher rates of college enrollment and completion.

Whether you think it deeply unjust, lamentable but inevitable, or obvious and unproblematic, this is hardly news. It is true in most societies and has been true in the United States for at least as long as we have thought to ask the question and had sufficient data to verify the answer.

What is news is that in the United States over the last few decades these differences in educational success between high- and lower-income students have grown substantially.... (n.p.)

- *Education Must Be Reformed.* One key to seeing the mendacity of cultural claims is recognizing how often those claims are contradictory. Many who champion the idealized and misleading belief that education is central to social and personal achievement also have historically and currently declared education a failure, concluding that education must be reformed. That reform is monolithic: Greater and greater accountability built on *new* standards and *new* testing. The concept of *having high standards*, however, proves to be as misleading as claims of the U.S. being a meritocracy because thirty years of standards-based education reform have revealed there is no correlation between the existence or quality of standards and student achievement (Mathis, 2012). Also, throughout more than 60 years of lamenting the international test score rankings of the U.S., we have no evidence of a correlation between those international rankings and any country's economic robustness or competitiveness (Strauss, 2010).

When my daughter allowed the evidence about the Tooth Fairy to lead her to a conclusion that made her at least uncomfortable if not disillusioned, she had to begin re-evaluating her perception of the world, a perception that included the nature of truth and the role of her parents in her navigating that world. That may sound dramatic about a conversation including the Tooth Fairy, but for a child, the intentions of foma have the same stinging consequences as the cynicism of mendacity. For adults, it seems, burying ourselves in the opiate of foma (Aldous Huxley's soma) allows us to ignore the bitter pill of mendacity. As aspirations, the bulleted concepts above remain important for a free people, but as mendacity, they have and will continue to ensure that *inequity cannot be achieved*.

Many readers miss the powerful theme of optimism that runs through Vonnegut's works; he maintains a genuine and compelling hope among the ruins for the capacity of humans to be kind. The bitterness and fatalism of Williams's Big Daddy, however, seem for now a more accurate assessment of the current human condition. More difficult to confront than either mendacity or foma, it appears, is the hard truth that the human pursuit of equity must come *before* merit can matter, and that in order to achieve that possibility, the human condition must commit to a spirit of community and collaboration, not competition.

Regretfully, most in power are apt to continue to not let that cat out of the bag.

Snow Blind: "Trapped in the Amber of This Moment"

What is wrong with the following claims?

- The rich and successful are rich and successful because of their work ethic.

- The poor are poor because they fail to take advantage of the American Dream.

- Women are paid less than men because they choose fields/careers that pay less and choose family over career.

- Prisons are overwhelmingly populated by African Americans because they are trapped in the cycle of poverty.

- Work hard and be nice.

- Education, especially college, is the main path for rising above the conditions of any person's home or community.

Before I examine the answer, consider this enduring claim:

- In 1492, Columbus sailed the ocean blue, and thus, Columbus discovered America. [The original poem ends "The first American? No, not quite./ But Columbus was brave, and he was bright."]

And how about this blast from the past: "Dewey Defeats Truman." As Lienhard (1997) explains:

Gallup brought science to that process. Richard Smith tells how, by the time Landon challenged Roosevelt, the prestigious *Literary Digest* magazine was America's leading pollster. The *Digest* featured a regular poll called "America Speaks." It drew samples from phone books and auto registrations. Gallup knew that such samples were biased toward people with means....

Then, in 1948, Gallup blew the Truman-Dewey prediction. How? His mistake was to quit polling two weeks before the election with fourteen percent of the electorate still undecided. After that humiliation, Gallup went back to analyze his error. He emerged with the maxim, "Undecided voters side with the incumbent." (n.p.)

By now, then, you'd think polling would have reached some higher and clearer process for predicting presidential outcomes, but instead, we had the Nate Silver element (O'Hara, 2012), yet another case about how the science of polling has flaws, human flaws.

Even, it seems, as science inspects itself—acknowledging and addressing confirmation bias, for example—we are always "trapped in the amber of this moment" (Vonnegut, 1991, p. 77) since the human condition is itself necessarily a subjective experience. And now, in order to answer my initial question, I want to turn to history. While history as a discipline is distinct from the hard sciences, both are dependent on evidence and then the conclusions drawn from that evidence—conclusions I call narratives (more on that below). Consider Howard Zinn (1995) on Christopher Columbus:

> My viewpoint, in telling the history of the United States, is different: that we must not accept the memory of states as our own. Nations are not communities and never have been. The history of any country, presented as the history of a family, conceals fierce conflicts of interest (sometimes exploding, most often repressed) between conquerors and conquered, masters and slaves, capitalists and workers, dominators and dominated in race and sex. And in such a world of conflict, a world of victims and executioners, it is the job of thinking people, as Albert Camus suggested, not to be on the side of the executioners.

> Thus, in that inevitable taking of sides which comes from selection and emphasis in history, I prefer to try to tell the story of the discovery of America from the viewpoint of the Arawaks, of the Constitution from the standpoint of the slaves, of Andrew Jackson as seen by the Cherokees, of the Civil War as seen by the New York Irish, of the Mexican war as seen by the deserting soldiers of Scott's army, of the rise of industrialism as seen by the young women in the Lowell textile mills, of the Spanish-American war as seen by the Cubans, the conquest of the Philippines as seen by black soldiers on Luzon, the Gilded Age as seen by southern farmers, the First World War as seen by socialists, the Second World War as seen by pacifists, the New Deal as seen by blacks in Harlem, the postwar American empire as seen by peons in Latin America. And so on, to the limited extent that any one person, however he or she strains, can "see" history from the standpoint of others. (pp. 9-10)

In other words, *shaping narratives bound by evidence* does not insure that those narratives are pure and certainly does not insure that those narratives are above bias or absent the urge to mold them in order to secure someone's agenda (likely someone in power).

Misleading narratives around Columbus or "I cannot tell a lie" George Washington—and the whitewashing of Steve Jobs to promote the "grit" narrative (compare the Jobs lesson [Smith, 2014] to the original 1492 poem about Columbus)—are not problematic because of the evidence, but because of the lens through which the narratives are shaped and by whom those narratives are created and in whose interest.

Consider Billy Pilgrim in a telepathic conversation with a Tralfamadorian in Vonnegut's (1991) *Slaughterhouse Five*:

> "Welcome aboard, Mr. Pilgrim," said the loudspeaker. "Any questions?"
>
> Billy licked his lips, thought a while, inquired at last: "Why me?"
>
> "That is a very *Earthling* question to ask, Mr. Pilgrim. Why *you*? Why *us* for that matter? Why *anything*? Because this moment simply *is*. Have you ever seen bugs trapped in amber?"
>
> "Yes." Billy, in fact, had a paperweight in his office which was a blob of polished amber with three ladybugs embedded in it.
>
> "Well, here we are, Mr. Pilgrim, trapped in the amber of this moment. There is no *why*." (pp. 76-77)

And that brings me to the "grit" debate, one in which advocates point to *scientific research* and prestigious grants. From that evidence, we have three contexts of narratives: disciplinary narratives (Angela Duckworth, Carolyn Dweck), popular narratives (Paul Tough, Jay Mathews), and political narratives (Arne Duncan, Michelle Rhee)—all of which are trapped like bugs in amber, or as I prefer to suggest, that "grit" narrative advocacy is *snow blind*.

If evidence and the narratives surrounding the evidence appear to support a privileged agenda, and since the privileged have a larger megaphone in a culture, then that evidence and narrative are disproportionately likely to gain momentum—regardless of how accurate they are in the context of the oppressed or marginalized—consider again history and the Zinn points above. And that inability by the privileged to see beyond their privilege is, I think, a state of being snow blind.

Thus, my answer to the initial question at the beginning is that those claims as narratives built on evidence are ideological distortions of the evidence. The "grit" narrative is similar to the *education equals income* argument that falls apart when analyzed: Education is a marker for privilege (since privilege leads to advanced education) just as "grit" qualities are markers for privilege.

Systemic Inequity v. Rugged Individualism

In *Slaughterhouse Five*, Howard W. Campbell (previously the main character in Vonnegut's *Mother Night*) is quoted:

> *America is the wealthiest nation on Earth, but its people are mainly poor, and poor Americans are urged to hate themselves....*

> *Americans, like human beings everywhere, believe many things that are obviously untrue....The most destructive untruth is that it is very easy for any American to make money. They will not acknowledge how in fact hard money is to come by, and, therefore, those who have no money blame an blame and blame themselves. This inward blame has been a treasure for the rich and powerful, who have had to do less for their poor, publicly and privately, than any other ruling class since, say, Napoleonic times.* (pp. 128, 129)

Snow blind and bugs trapped in amber, the privileged by their privilege and the impoverished by the blinding but misleading promise of the American Dream—the narratives become the product of *those who shape them* and for their benefit. The evidence, the artifacts, and the data all become irrelevant.

Let me end with Vonnegut's *Cat's Cradle*. John and Mona in

Cat's Cradle discuss *Boko-maru* (a sacred foot ceremony) and their culturally-bound and conflicting perceptions of love:

"Mona?"

"Yes?"

"Is—is there anyone else in your life?"

She was puzzled. "Many," she said at last.

"That you *love*?"

"I love everyone."

"As—as much as me?"

"Yes." She seemed to have no idea that this might bother me....

"I suppose you—you perform—you do what we just did—with other people?"

"*Boko-maru*?"

"*Boko-maru*."

"Of course."

"I don't want you to do it with anybody but me from now on," I declared.

Tears filled her eyes. She adored her promiscuity; was angered that I should try to make her feel shame. "I make people happy. Love is good, not bad."

"As your husband, I'll want all your love for myself."

She stared at me with widening eyes. "A *sin-wat*!"

"What was that?"

"A *sin-wat*!" she cried. "A man who wants all of somebody's love. That's very bad."

(Vonnegut, 1963, pp. 207-208)

John is trapped in the amber of the moment, and his patriarchal and possessive love leaves him snow blind to Mona's perspective. He either cannot see, or refuses to see.

So I have made a decision—one shared by Zinn, expressed by Eugene V. Debbs, and reflected in the research on poverty (Mullainathan & Shafir, 2013)—that the *perspectives of the marginalized must be honored in the context of systemic inequities*. This is a position of humility and a recognition that any human arrogance—whether it be scientific or not—is likely to lead to the sort of pettiness captured in Woody Allen's *Sleeper*. Both the satire aimed at the foolish dietary beliefs of the past and the incredulity of the scientists in the film's present ("You mean there was no deep fat…?") expose that, despite the scientists recognizing the misguided stances of the past, they remain trapped in their own certainty. Both the "grit" narrative and the "grit" research fail that litmus test. They both *speak from and to* a cultural norm that privileges individual characteristics (rugged individualism) as if they are indistinguishable from the systemic context of privilege—again, a claim refuted by Mullainathan and Shafir, but that narrative doesn't serve the privileged, and thus, isn't embraced as the "grit" narrative is.

"*Many novelties have come from America,*" the cited monograph in *Slaughterhouse-Five* from Howard Campbell notes, adding: "*The most startling of these, a thing without precedent, is a mass of undignified poor. They do not love one another because they do not love themselves*" (Vonnegut, 1991, p. 130). The human intellect is a wonderful thing, and thus we must pursue our efforts to understand the world and the human condition—a thing we call science. But as humans, it is not our right to somehow remove our basic humanity from that process (the folly of objectivity), but to choose carefully just how we shape the narratives from the evidence we gather.

I am then compelled to manipulate Einstein. His "Science without religion is lame, religion without science is blind," I think, is a call for the necessity of human kindness, decency, and compassion in the shaping of our narratives (Randerson, 2008). The "grit" narrative does no such thing. It is a snow blind story that is also deaf to the basic human dignity shared among all people:

> Your Honor, years ago I recognized my kinship with all living beings, and I made up my mind that I was not one bit better than the meanest on earth. I said then, and I say now, that while there is a lower class, I am in it, and while there is a criminal element I am of it, and while there is a soul in prison, I am not free. (Debs, 1918)

Kurt Vonnegut's Children's Crusade: Kindness

In his *Paris Review* interview, Haruki Murakami explained:

> I liked to read Kurt Vonnegut and Richard Brautigan while I was a college student. They had a sense of humor, and at the same time what they were writing about was serious. I like those kind of books. The first time I read Vonnegut and Brautigan I was shocked to find that there were such books! It was like discovering the New World. (Wray, 2004)

Murakami identified something essential in Vonnegut, a tension created by blending humor with serious themes and topics as well as Vonnegut's ability to shuffle non-fiction and fiction in his novels like a seasoned magician.

In fact, Gregory D. Sumner (2011) catalogues the gradual emergence of Vonnegut as a thinly fictionalized character in his own novels, notably by his most celebrated work, *Slaughterhouse-Five*: "The opening chapter of *Slaughterhouse-Five* annihilates the boundary between fiction and autobiography, inviting us into Vonnegut's uncertainty about just what he has written. It is a dance, rather than an exercise in cold objectivity" (p. 126). From this narrative ambiguity of genre, Vonnegut is often characterized as post-modern. And while there may be some waffling about details or accuracy, Vonnegut is quite certain—uncharacteristic for actual post-modern writers—about some foundational *ethics*, although even then he makes his most sacred pronouncements in the most challenging ways.

Vonnegut reveled in playing the free-thinker and atheist as he also referenced Jesus—a common routine in his speeches—and his persona in his speeches and non-fiction was certainly as much fabrication as Vonnegut. But the novels and their blend of memoir and fiction create and sustain the most tension. *Slaughterhouse-Five* presented Vonnegut a nearly insurmountable task of maintaining his joke-based writing pattern against the great human tragedy of World War II. This attempt to write a novel about being a POW during the fire-bombing of Dresden, in fact, becomes the opening chapter of the novel that doesn't genuinely start until Chapter 2. And in this first chapter, while visiting a fellow veteran of WWII and his friend Bernard V. O'Hare, Vonnegut (1991) is confronted by O'Hare's wife Mary, who is angry about Vonnegut's considering writing a novel about his war experience:

> "You were just babies then!" [Mary] said.
>
> "What?" I said.
>
> "You were just babies in the war—like the ones upstairs!"
>
> I nodded that this was true. We had been foolish virgins in the war, right at the end of childhood....
>
> So I held up my right hand and I made her a promise:...
>
> "I tell you what," I said, "I'll call it 'The Children's Crusade.'"
>
> She was my friend after that. (pp. 14-15)

Several years before his Dresden novel garnered him fame, Vonnegut had offered what I think is his central children's crusade: a paean to kindness, *God Bless You, Mr. Rosewater*. The titular character of the novel, Eliot Rosewater, implores:

> "Go over to her shack, I guess. Sprinkle some water on the babies, say, 'Hello, babies. Welcome to Earth. It's hot in the summer and cold in the winter. It's round and wet and crowded. At the outside, babies, you've got about a hundred years here. There's only one rule that I know of, babies—:

"'God damn it, you've got to be kind.'" (Vonnegut, 1964, p. 129)

On November 11 of any year, the day of Vonnegut's birth, while we who love his work raise our eyes to the heavens and hope he is in fact Resting In Peace, we might honor him by heeding those words, crafted in the glorious blasphemy that makes Vonnegut, Vonnegut.

Charter Schools, the Invisible Hand, and Gutless Political Leadership

Billy Pilgrim becomes unstuck in time in Vonnegut's *Slaughterhouse-Five*. Billy's experience introduces readers to Tralfamadorians:

> The creatures were friendly, and they could see in four dimensions. They pitied Earthlings for being able to see only three. They had many wonderful things to teach Earthlings, especially about time....

> The Tralfamadorians can look at all the different moments just the way we can look at a stretch of the Rocky Mountains, for instance. They can see how permanent all the moments are, and they can look at any moment that interests them. It is just an illusion we have here on Earth that one moment follows another one, like beads on a string, and that once a moment is gone it is gone forever. (Vonnegut, 1991, pp. 26, 27)

One of the most memorable moments of Billy becoming unstuck in time is his watching a war movie backwards. Viewed in reverse, the film becomes a narrative of renewal, of peace, as fighter planes "sucked bullets and shell fragments from some of the planes and crewmen," and "[t]he bombers opened their bomb bay doors, exerted a miraculous magnetism which shrunk fires, gathered them into cylindrical steel containers, and lifted the containers into the bellies of the planes" (Vonnegut, 1991, p. 74).

In the spirit of folding time back onto itself to give us clarity of sight, let's become unstuck in time while viewing American Indian Charter Schools. Like Billy watching a war film, we start now and move backward.

Jill Tucker (2013) reports that American Indian Charter Schools have had their charter revoked by the Oakland Unified School District:

> The American Indian charter schools, which enroll 1,200 students in grades K-12, are among the highest-scoring in the state on standardized tests.

> Yet Oakland district officials said they had a duty to the public to close the schools given the inability of the schools' management to rein in the misuse of taxpayer money....

> "In this situation, it is clear that academic performance is not enough to either overlook or excuse the mismanagement of public funds and the unwillingness from the board of directors to respond in ways that would satisfactorily address the legitimate concerns raised by OUSD," said Jed Wallace, president and CEO of the California Charter Schools Association, in a letter to the board in support of the revocation. (n.p.)

Mitchell Landsberg (2009) explains—in a provocatively titled "Spitting in the Eye of Mainstream Education"—about American Indian Charter Schools:

> Conservatives, including columnist George Will, adore the American Indian schools, which they see as models of a "new paternalism" that could close the gap between the haves and have-nots in American education. Not surprisingly, many Bay Area liberals have a hard time embracing an educational philosophy that proudly proclaims that it "does not preach or subscribe to the demagoguery of tolerance."

> It would be easy to dismiss American Indian as one of the nuttier offshoots of the fast-growing charter school movement, which allows schools to receive public funding but

operate outside of day-to-day district oversight. But the schools command attention for one very simple reason: By standard measures, they are among the very best in California....

"What we're doing is so easy," said Ben Chavis, the man who created the school's success and personifies its ethos, especially in its more outrageous manifestations. (One example: He tends to call all nonwhite students, including African Americans, "darkies.") Although he retired in 2007, Chavis remains a presence at the school. (n.p.)

Focusing on American Indian Charter Schools among five other "no excuses" schools adopting a new paternalism, David Whitman (2008a) praises the accomplishments and possibilities of these schools:

Yet above all, these schools share a trait that has been largely ignored by education researchers: They are paternalistic institutions. By paternalistic I mean that each of the six schools is a highly prescriptive institution that teaches students not just how to think, but also how to act according to what are commonly termed traditional, middle-class values. These paternalistic schools go beyond just teaching values as abstractions: the schools tell students exactly how they are expected to behave, and their behavior is closely monitored, with real rewards for compliance and penalties for noncompliance. Unlike the often-forbidding paternalistic institutions of the past, these schools are prescriptive yet warm; teachers and principals, who sometimes serve in loco parentis, are both authoritative and caring figures. Teachers laugh with and cajole students, in addition to frequently directing them to stay on task.

The new breed of paternalistic schools appears to be the single most effective way of closing the achievement gap. No other school model or policy reform in urban secondary schools seems to come close to having such a dramatic impact on the performance of inner-city students. Done right, paternalistic schooling provides a novel way to remake inner-city education in the years ahead....

Done well, paternalistic schooling would constitute a major stride toward reducing the achievement gap and the lingering disgrace of racial inequality in urban America. (n.p.)

Backward or forward, this story is ugly. "No excuses" and the new paternalism themselves are classist and racist—ways in which the middle class and affluent allow "other people's children" (Delpit, 2006) to be treated, but not their own—yet the larger faith in the Invisible Hand is the ugliest part of the narrative. Idealizing parental choice (Thomas, 2012) narrowly and choice broadly is the foundation upon which both political parties stand. Why is the Invisible Hand of the Free Market so appealing to political leaders?

The answer is simple: Abdicating political leadership to the market absolves our leaders from making any real (or ethical) decisions, absolves them from doing anything except sitting back and watching the cards fall where they may. And thus the charter school movement, with its school-choice light, allows progressives to tap into their closeted libertarian (Thomas, 2013, March 6). Experimenting with impoverished children, African American children, Latino/a children, English Language Learners, and special needs children—this is the acceptable playground for the Invisible Hand.

Political leaders bask in the glory of capitalism because the free market requires no moral conviction, no ethical stands, no genuine decision making based on careful consideration of foundational commitments to democracy and human dignity and agency. Capitalism allows Nero to sit and fiddle while Rome burns. If the fire needs putting out, and someone can monetize that, the market will take care of it, right?

Political leadership has ignored and marginalized children in poverty for decades, notably in the schools we provide in high-poverty, majority-minority communities. The school-choice light commitment to charter schools is a coward's way out of facing that reality and doing something about it.

So it goes.

20

College Athletes' Academic Cheating a Harbinger of a Failed System

Margaret Atwood's (1998) narrator, Offred (June), characterizes her situation in the dystopian speculative world of *The Handmaid's Tale*:

> Apart from the details, this could be a college guest room, for the less distinguished visitors; or a room in a rooming house, of former times, for ladies in reduced circumstances. This is what we are now. The circumstances have been reduced; for those of us who still have circumstances....
>
> In reduced circumstances you have to believe all kinds of things. I believe in thought transference now, vibrations in the ether, that sort of junk. I never used to....
>
> In reduced circumstances the desire to live attaches itself to strange objects. I would like a pet: a bird, say, or a cat. A familiar. Anything at all familiar. A rat would do, in a pinch, but there's no chance of that. (pp. 8, 105, 111)

In her "reduced circumstances" as a handmaid—her entire existence focusing on becoming pregnant by a Commander to whom she is assigned, potentially a *series of three* before she is cast aside as infertile and thus useless—Offred's (June's) fantasies about her

Commander turn murderous:

> I think about how I could take the back of the toilet apart, the toilet in my own bathroom, on a bath night, quickly and quietly, so Cora outside on the chair would not hear me. I could get the sharp lever out and hide it in my sleeve, and smuggle it into the Commander's study, the next time, because after a request like that there's always a next time, whether you say yes or no. I think about how I could approach the Commander, to kiss him, here alone, and take off his jacket, as if to allow or invite something further, some approach to true love, and put my arms around him and slip the lever out from the sleeve and drive the sharp end into him suddenly, between his ribs. I think about the blood coming out of him, hot as soup, sexual, over my hand. (Atwood, 1998, pp. 139-140)

The novel reveals no evidence that June in her life in "former times" has been anything other than a relatively typical young woman with a family and a normal life. Atwood asks readers to consider her reduced circumstances—ones she does not create, ones she has no power to change alone—and how they shape the individuals in this disturbing Brave New World.

Atwood's reduced circumstances are a narrative and fictional examination through a novelist's perspective, a thought experiment replicated in the graphic novels and TV series *The Walking Dead*. As the comic book creator Robert Kirkman (2006) explains: "I want to explore how people deal with the extreme situations and how these events *change* them. I'm in this for the long haul" (n.p.). Research on human behavior has revealed, as well, that the same human behaves differently as the situations around change between "scarcity" and "slack" (Mullainathan & Shafir, 2013). The "reduced circumstances" of *The Handmaid's Tale*, then, is a state of "scarcity," and poverty is one of the most common types of scarcity:

> Still, one prevailing view explains the strong correlation between poverty and failure by saying failure causes poverty.

> Our data suggest *causality runs at least as strongly in the other direction* [emphasis added]: that poverty—the scarcity mindset—causes failure. (Mullainathan & Shafir, pp. 148, 155)

Yet, popular perceptions of people trapped in poverty ignore the influence of social forces (scarcity):

> Given that we hold highly negative stereotypes about the poor, essentially defined by a failure (they are poor!), it is natural to attribute personal failure to them....Accidents of birth—such as what continent you are born on—have a large effect on your chance of being poor....The failures of the poor are part and parcel of the misfortune of being poor in the first place. Under these conditions, we all would have (and have!) failed. (Mullainathan & Shafir, pp. 154, 155, 161)

We are faced with a perplexing problem that sets up a clash between a powerful cultural ideal (the rugged individual and the allure of individual accountability) against a compelling research base that suggests individual behavior is at least as likely to represent systemic conditions, and not individual qualities—either those that are fixed or those can be learned, such as "grit."

Although they may seem unrelated narrowly, two academic cheating phenomena are ideal examples of this perplexing problem—attempting to tease out individual culpability from systemic forces. One consequence of the high-stakes era of accountability in public education has been the seemingly endless accounts of cheating on high-stakes testing; the most notorious being the DC eraser-gate under the reign of Michelle Rhee (Strauss, 2013, April 12), but also scandals such as the one in Atlanta public schools (Judd & Torres, 2010).

Academic cheating by college athletes has also been exposed at the University of North Carolina (Adelson, 2014). But college athletes cheating to remain eligible is not anything new; for example, Florida State University has received similar criticism for ignoring or covering up the academic deficiencies of athletes in the past (Florio, 2009). It is at this point—the academic cheating and dodging of college athletes—that I want to focus on the concept of "reduced circumstances" and "scarcity" in order to consider where the source of these outcomes lie.

A few additional points inform this consideration.

First, college athletes at Northwestern University sought to form a union so that they could gain some degree of autonomy over their circumstances as college athletes—circumstances dictated by the NCAA (Bennett, 2014). This move by athletes themselves appears to match a call by Andre Perry (2014, January 6), his being specifically about graduation rates:

> Black athletes have no choice but to play a major role in their own success. They must take full advantage of the scholarships afforded to them in spite of the climate. But some athletes have to pay a political price to force institutions to cater to black males' academic talents. Graduation is a team effort, but black athletes must flex their political muscle to pave a way from the stadiums in January to the graduation stages in May. (n.p.)

Perry's argument is one that focuses on individual agency and the athletes' ability to rise above "the climate."

However, David Zirin (2014), discussing a Meet the Press examination of the NCAA and the circumstances of college athletes, seeks a systemic focus:

> Yet far more glaring than the content of the discussion was what the discussion was missing. This is not surprising given the parties sitting around the table, but there was zero discussion about how institutionalized racism animates the amassed wealth of the NCAA, the top college coaches and the power conferences. It does not take Cornel West to point out that the revenue producing sports of basketball and football are overwhelmingly populated by African-American athletes. The population of the United States that is most desperate for an escape out of poverty

is the population that has gotten the rawest possible deal from an NCAA, which is actively benefiting from this state of affairs....

The issue of the NCAA is a racial justice issue. (n.p.)

The public and the media, I believe, have already sided with blaming the athletes as well as blaming a failure of leadership and accountability among coaches and university administration, including presidents.

For example, the media have rushed to identify a student paper (a bare paragraph) as an example of the cheating at UNC, a claim later refuted by the whistleblower in the scandal, Mary Willingham. That rush and misrepresentation highlight where the accusatory gaze is likely to remain—on the student athlete as culpable, on the coaches, professors, and universities. As Zirin (2014) asks, what will be missing?

Few will consider that the academic scandal among student athletes at UNC—like the cheating scandals on high-stakes tests in public schools—is powerful evidence of a flawed system, one that places young people in "reduced circumstances" that then change their behavior. As I have argued before from a position of my own experiences as a teacher and scholastic coach and as someone who advocates for student athletes, school-based athletics in the U.S. corrupts both sport and academics. *The entire scholastic sports dynamic is the essential problem.*

There simply is no natural relationship between athletics and academics, and by creating a context in which young people are coerced into academics by linking their participation in athletics to their classroom achievement, we are devaluing both athletics and academics. So I see a solution to the tension between Perry's call for athlete agency and Zirin's call for confronting systemic racism: We must *address the conditions first* so that we can clearly see to what extent individuals can and should be held accountable.

It seems simple enough, but if student athletes were not required to achieve certain academic outcomes (attendance, grades, graduation), then there would be no need to cheat. Hold athletes accountable for that which is athletic, and then hold students accountable for that which is academic. But don't continue to conflate the two artificially because we want to create the appearance that we believe academics matter more than athletics—*we don't and they aren't.*

In conditions of scarcity—demanding of anyone outcomes over which that person has no control or no hope of accomplishing without a change in systemic conditions (such as academic outcomes an athlete is not prepared or able to accomplish or closing an achievement gap between populations of students)—the same person behaves differently than if that person were in a condition of abundance or privilege, "slack" (Mullainathan & Shafir, 2013).

Let's return to *The Walking Dead*, a world created by Kirkman, in which "extreme situations…change" people. By killing others as a preventative measure, Carol has already demonstrated her ability to take extreme measures in "reduced circumstances" (season 4 episode 2, "Under My Skin" [Gonzalez, 2013]). In season 4 episode 14, "Look at the Flowers" (Gonzalez, 2014), Carol parallels Margaret Attwood's Offred (June):

> If you thought Carol had a zero-tolerance attitude when she killed and burned two bodies back at the prison to stop the spread of a deadly virus, tonight she went truly sub-zero. The insanity began when little Lizzie stabbed and killed her sister Mika to prove that she would come back to life, leaving Carol to knife Mika's brain to stop her from coming back as a zombie. She and Tyreese then had to decide what to do with Lizzie, with Carol saying that, "We can't sleep with her and Judith under the same roof. She can't be around other people." And with that, Carol walked Lizzie outside, told her to "look at the flowers," and then put a bullet in her brain. (Ross, 2014, n.p.)

Two children die, one at the hands of Carol, and that scene reminded me immediately of John Steinbeck's *Of Mice and Men*, when George shoots his best friend Lenny.

After Lenny has killed Curley's wife and run away to the hiding spot he and George have already designated, George finds Lenny:

> George had been listening to the distant sounds. For a moment he was business-like. "Look acrost the river, Lennie, an' I'll tell you so you can almost see it." (Steinbeck, 1993, p. 103)

George and Lenny are hired hands, workers, pursuing their own American Dream. That pursuit has been difficult, including George trying to overcome Lenny having the mind of a child guiding the powerful and large body of a man. And it is in this final scene that George, like Carol, finds himself in reduced circumstances. While Lenny gazes across the river, George tells the same story he's told hundreds of times, about the farm they will buy and the rabbits Lenny will tend as his own, and then:

> And George raised the gun and steadied it, and he brought the muzzle of it close to the back of Lennie's head. The hand shook violently, but his face set and his hand steadied. He pulled the trigger. The crash of the shot rolled up the hills and rolled down again. Lennie jarred, and then settled slowly forward to the sand, and he lay without quivering. (Steinbeck, 1993, p. 105)

Cultural assumptions are powerful lenses for judging outcomes. If we assume the "dumb jock" stereotype to be true, we point our fingers at the student athletes as cheaters and allow our gaze never to consider that the entire system is failing those student athletes.

If we assume people in poverty are lazy and use that as a mask for lingering racist stereotypes of African American and Latino/a students and people, then we can point our fingers and say they simply aren't trying hard enough; they need "grit." And we fail to recognize and confront the pervasive racism, classism, and sexism that constitute the reduced circumstances of their lives.

Of course, college athletes should not be cheating to maintain their academic status and therefore their access to participating in sports, but it may be important to consider who is responsible for putting them in that situation to begin with—and who benefits most from maintaining that system.

21

Time as Capital: The Rise of the Frantic Class

Imagine a world where time is capital.

This is the dystopian future of 2161 brought to film by Andrew Niccol's *In Time* (2011)—triggering some powerful parallels to *Logan's Run* (both the original novel from 1967 and the film adaptation in 1976). Both *Logan's Run* and *In Time* expose the human condition in terms of age and mortality—in the first, life ends at 30, and in the latter, people stop aging at 25, but at a price, which involves time.

Science fiction (SF) as a genre presents us with allegory in the form of other worlds, as Margaret Atwood (2011) both argues and speculates, but the most engaging aspect of SF for me as a fan and teacher is when SF unmasks universal and contemporary realities by presenting those other worlds. One of the recurring messages of SF is the crippling inequity that continues to plague human societies, such as the haunting and sparse Ursula Le Guin's "The Ones Who Walk Away from Omelas" that forces readers to admit that privilege exists on the backs of the innocent and oppressed (see Chapter 7 above).

The world of *In Time* presents an apparent meritocracy in which all people are given life until they reach 25, when they stop aging but when an embedded clock starts ticking, forcing everyone to earn time in order to live. This deal with the devil positions all labor as literally necessary in order for people to stay alive and puts banks, who control the sale of time, at the center of who survives.

The Frantic Distraction of Surviving

Americans' faith in a meritocracy is often expressed in claims of the U.S. being a post-racial society as well as a classless society. Like Suzanne Collins's Hunger Games trilogy, *In Time* highlights class distinctions as people are segregated in Time Zones. Eventually, the narrative brings together the two main characters, Will Salas from the ghetto and Sylvia Weis from the affluent zone, New Greenwich. Due to both personal tragedy and a huge gift of time from a stranger, Will confronts the norms of this dystopia while being hunted by a Timekeeper (a time policeman), Raymond Leon. One scene, I think, deserves closer consideration.

When Will travels from the ghetto through several Time Zones (incrementally costing him more and more time) to New Greenwich, he steps out of the cab and immediately begins jogging, a habit common in the ghettos since almost everyone is living, literally, from paycheck to paycheck (or under the weight of time loans, loan sharks, or pawn shops) until he notices that in New Greenwich people are eerily casual. This distinction comes up again when he is eating breakfast and the waitress notices that he isn't from affluent New Greenwich because he does everything fast. People in the ghettos, who can reasonably be called the working class and the working poor, lead lives that are so frantic that no one has the time to confront the inequity of the society, and because of the segregated society, these frantic workers have little insight into the lives of privilege, the casual lives that Will witnesses for himself and the viewer.

Also worth closer consideration is the role of the Timekeeper, Leon, who presents a truly complex character who functions under a code of ethics that is perfectly ethical within the norms of the culture, but is ultimately self-defeating and dehumanizing. Timekeepers enforce the laws, primarily couched in time as capital, but because of their close proximity to crime, they carry with them only small quantities of time, thus leading frantic lives themselves very similar to the working class/poor they help both keep in line and frantic.

Ultimately, Will exposes truths that challenge the norms of this society, truths that are in fact just as relevant to the world we now inhabit:

- Will discovers that time is not a limited commodity; there is plenty of "time capital," but the privileged create scarcity to keep the masses frantic and distracted.

- Timekeepers as a police force are unmasked as not seekers of justice (Leon admits this directly), but as agents of the privileged.

- The moving target of the free market is exposed as not so much "free," but an arbitrary mechanism that puts most people in a life situation much like caged gerbils on running wheels. Interest rates and prices incrementally increase daily as the workers accumulate time. The system is designed to keep workers trapped in their roles as workers.

- And privilege, as Le Guin's (1975) story shows, is always at the expense of others, captured by this exchange from *In Time*:

  Sylvia Weis: Will, if you get a lot of time, are you really gonna give it away?

  Will Salas: I've only ever had a day. How much do you need? How can you live with yourself watching people die right next to you?

  Sylvia Weis: You don't watch. You close your eyes. I can help you get all the time you want. (Niccol,

2011)

While the details may be exaggerated, the lessons learned by Will are disturbingly relevant to contemporary U.S. citizens because they not only inform us as workers, but also highlight that education reform is more concerned with producing workers than providing all children with equity, liberation, and autonomy.

Frantic Students, Frantic Workers: The Rise of the Frantic Class

The *frantic state of being* among the working class and working poor of *In Time* is a perceptive dramatization of the American worker, increasingly stripped of rights as unions are dismantled and as the essentials of human dignity (income, health care, retirement) are further tied to being employed (Parramore, 2012). But the allegorical messages of *In Time* also speak to how and why current education reform claims and policies are designed to appease the corporate need for frantic workers. One characterization of U.S. public education today is well represented in this dystopian world—frantic.

Current corporate education reform is built on implementing national standards that are designed to continue the historical call to incrementally increase both expectations and outcomes —the target for success in education has always been a moving target. This ensures that students, teachers, and schools are always under duress, always falling short, always so frantic that no one can pause to question, challenge, or do anything other than comply.

Imagine a world where time is capital, where all of any person's time is spent earning time in a fruitless cycle of acquisition, of seeking to comply with the mandates that not one of the masses has chosen for herself/himself.

But you don't have to imagine this.

This frantic world of *In Time* is the frantic existence of the American worker, and this frantic world is being fed by the corporate takeover of public schools, where accountability, standards and testing have reduced teachers and students to gerbils on running wheels. Today, workers, students, and teachers are the frantic class; like Will, we don't have time:

> **Will Salas:** I don't have time. I don't have time to worry about how it happened. It is what it is. We're genetically engineered to stop aging at 25. The trouble is, we live only one more year, unless we can get more time. Time is now the currency. We earn it and spend it. The rich can live forever. And the rest of us? I just want to wake up with more time on my hand than hours in the day. (Niccol, 2011)

The rising frantic class is necessary for the privileged few, the 1% controlling both manufactured austerity and the perpetually moving targets of success. While universal public education was created to feed the promise of the American Dream, the current corporate takeover of public schools is driving the American Nightmare of the frantic class.

We don't need a movie to see that.

Related Poem

"the world (frantic)"

> *"No, Mum. You're not stupid. But life is unfair."* Lisbeth Salander, *The Girl with the Dragon Tattoo*, Stieg Larsson

the world was exactly as they expected
       exactly as they knew it to be

and mostly not as it could have been
       or should have been

spring was pretty much spring
and summer was pretty much summer

as was winter and tumbling fall

dawn was always dawn
and day was always day

as was dusk and certainly night

and while children starved
and women bled, battered and bruised

some men pondered over $5000 suits
and a different shirt and tie each day

all in all everyone frantically did everything they could
and of course they did nothing at all

*the world was exactly as they expected
            exactly as they knew it to be*

*and mostly not as it could have been
            or should have been*

22

Gravity: The Unbearable Lightness of Being a Woman

In the film *Gravity*, Ryan Stone (Sandra Bullock) fulfills what appears to be a prerequisite for women in films: She undresses alone. As a science fiction film fan, I immediately thought of Sigourney Weaver in *Alien*, who also often filled the movie screen alone and barely clothed.

At the end of *Gravity*, when Ryan Stone crawls out of the water, again in her underwear, I was by then struck by her cropped hair and the camera's apparent fascination with her (Bullock's) physique, both of which can be fairly described as man-like—not unlike her name:

Matt Kowalski: What kind of name is Ryan for a girl?

Ryan Stone: Dad wanted a boy. (Cuaron, 2013)

While I found *Gravity* to be a powerful and well-crafted film— stunning cinematography, stellar acting, tight and compelling narrative—I am less enamored by the rugged individualism theme and the need to frame Stone as a (wo)man. The triumph of Stone is one grounded entirely in her conforming to male norms, much of which is portrayed in her androgynous body, boyish haircut, and man's name. Even the "Stone" of her last name erases the emotional core of the character that could have been celebrated more fully than the weightless tear scene.

Instead of *Gravity*, the film possibly should have been titled *Oxygen* or *Breathe*, but *Gravity* ultimately does capture the weight of the male gaze and the weight of the male norm that anchor the motifs and theme of the film—regretfully, not elements celebrating Stone as a woman, but ones that reduce her to the same tired messages coming from Hollywood about the Great White Masculine Hope. While the film appears to downplay Matt Kowalski (George Clooney), the quintessential man's man in film and life and Stone's cavalier Obi-Wan Kenobi, always there (even in delusion) to make sure she bucks up, his secondary role proves to be a distraction because Stone must assume the qualities Kowalski would have played if the roles were reversed. Lest we forget, Clooney strips alone in films as well (notably in *The American*).

The larger message found in *Gravity* is the inability of mainstream films to celebrate women as women. Consider the superhero makeover of Katniss in the Hunger Games films, as revealed in the second film's poster for Catching Fire—Katniss in archer's pose surrounded by fire. And Lisbeth Salander in the U.S. film version of *The Girl with the Dragon Tattoo*, notably her Batman-esque scenes in leather and on her motorcycle as well as her snarled, "There will be blood."

The Unbearable Lightness of Being a Woman

In early July 2014, I was in the delivery room while my only daughter gave birth to my first granddaughter. That experience was surrounded by the professional brilliance of a nursing staff (all women) who provided my daughter the medical and emotional support that made a difficult and painful experience far less difficult than it could have been. As a father, I was helpless, watching, worrying.

Once my granddaughter was born, and the baby and mother were healthy and safe, I could not stop considering how this day had held up to everyone the unbearable lightness of being a woman. Yes, childbirth is a solitary thing, and maybe even heroic, but it is nothing like the rugged individualism myth since childbirth is communal and life-affirming, while rugged individualism is competitive and conquering. To the contrary, we should be celebrating the essential qualities of women: the selflessness, the endurance, and that which we call "maternal." But the nurses as well—with their professionalism and care—demonstrated a woman's world, their pay and their status secondary to the doctor (a man).

Just the day before the birth of my granddaughter, Nikki Lee (2014) wrote "Ride like a girl," a blog exploring how riding a bicycle captures something like being a woman daily—vulnerability, being blamed even when a victim. Lee ends with:

> These are just a few of the thousand little environmental microaggressions that you don't have to deal with when you're sitting behind the wheel of a car. Any individual one isn't a big deal, and plenty of cyclists don't pay active attention to them at all. After a while you just kind of deal with it, because listing out these small annoyances mostly serves to make you feel bad.
>
> At the end of the day, you can always hang up your helmet and declare bike commuting "a great idea and all, but just not worth it".
>
> What if you didn't have a choice? (n.p.)

And that brings me back to *Gravity*, where filmmakers do have choices, and audiences have choices.

Objectifying and reducing women to the male gaze appears to be the choice we are bound to, a gravity of another kind.

23

On Ray Bradbury

Writing that highlights the importance of writing, and books that reveal the power of books—in the work of Ray Bradbury we find messages about the very human element of language and how that faculty is ultimately about power. Bradbury's *Fahrenheit 451* itself is powerful, but the work has also proven to be enduring, a model of the value found in science fiction formed as both dark criticism and a dire warning about *any now* and also *any what may be*. As the 60th anniversary of the novel passed, humanity appeared unwilling to see much of what Bradbury saw six decades ago.

Fahrenheit 451 60 Years Later: "Why do we need the things in books?"

"Sometimes writers write about a world that does not yet exist," Neil Gaiman begins his Introduction to the 60th Anniversary Edition of Ray Bradbury's *Fahrenheit 451*, continuing:

> This is a book of warning. It is a reminder that what we have is valuable, and that sometimes we take what we value for granted....

> People think—wrongly—that speculative fiction is about predicting the future, but it isn't; or if it is, it tends to do a rotten job of it....

What speculative fiction is really good at is not the future but the present—taking an aspect of it that troubles or is dangerous, and extending and extrapolating that aspect into something that allows the people of that time to see what they are doing from a different angle and from a different place. It's cautionary.

Fahrenheit 451 is speculative fiction. It's an "If this goes on…" story. Ray Bradbury was writing about his present, which is our past. (Bradbury, 2013, pp. xi-xii)

Like Margaret Atwood's *In Other Worlds*, Gaiman's clarification about the purposes of science fiction/speculative fiction builds a foundation for reading (or re-reading) *Fahrenheit 451* as well as for considering why Bradbury's novel on book burning endures.

Over sixty years ago in October 1953, *Fahrenheit 451* was published. The novel reads as an eerie crystal ball—despite Gaiman's caution: the pervasive Seashells like iPod earbuds, wall-sized monitors and reality TV. Yet, upon re-reading this anniversary edition, I am less interested in Bradbury's prescience about technology and its role in isolating humans from each other, and reminded—as Gaiman suggests—of what matters. The enduring flame of *Fahrenheit 451* is in fact perfectly stoked by Gaiman:

A young reader finding this book today, or the day after tomorrow, is going to have to imagine first a past, and then a future that belongs to that past.

But still, the heart of the book remains untouched, and the questions Bradbury raises remain as valid and important.

Why do we need the things in books?…Why should we read them? Why should we care?…

Ideas—written ideas—are special….

This is a book about caring for things. It's a love letter to books, but I think, just as much, it's a love letter to people…. (Bradbury, 2013, pp. xv-xvi)

Yes, Gaiman is a writer's writer so he is naturally suited to understand Bradbury, as well as marvel at the magic of *Fahrenheit 451*. But there is more.

This anniversary edition includes not only Gaiman's new Introduction but also a concluding section—History, Context, and Criticism. The opening piece by Jonathan R. Eller explains, "Bradbury virtually lived in the public libraries of his time" (Bradbury, 2013, p. 168). And later in a transcript of an audio-introduction, Bradbury adds:

> When I left high school, I began to go to the library every day of my life for five, ten, fifteen years. So the library was my nesting place, it was my birthing place, it was my growing place. And my books are full of libraries and librarians and book people, and booksellers. So my love of books is so intense that I finally have done—what? I have written a book about a man falling in love with books. (p. 196)

Here, I think, another important connection between Gaiman and Bradbury highlights why *Fahrenheit 451* endures: Both men are readers, readers who love the idea of books, who love specific books, and who recognize the human dignity represented by the *free access to books*. Like Bradbury, Gaiman (2013) has a life-long love affair with libraries:

> But libraries are about Freedom. Freedom to read, freedom of ideas, freedom of communication. They are about education (which is not a process that finishes the day we leave school or university), about entertainment, about making safe spaces, and about access to information. (n.p.)

For those of us who share this love of books and the "[f]reedom to read, freedom of ideas, freedom of communication," that *Fahrenheit 451* endures is both wonderful and chilling.

If the novel had been first published October 2013, I suspect it could have just as easily been applauded as a stark mirror of our present disguised as a futuristic dystopia:

"Jesus God," said Montag…."Why doesn't someone want to talk about it! We've started and won two atomic wars since 2022! Is it because we're having so much fun at home we've forgotten the world? Is it because we're so rich and the rest of the world's so poor and we just don't care if they are? I've heard rumors; the world is starving, but we're well fed. Is it true, the world works hard and we play? Is that why we're hated so much?" (Bradbury, 2013, pp. 69-70)

And then Montag recalls a brief encounter with an old man:

The old man admitted to being a retired English professor who had been thrown out upon the world forty years ago when the last liberal arts college shut for lack of students and patronage. (Bradbury, pp. 70-71)

Fahrenheit 451 ends with Montag as a criminal on the run who finds himself on the outskirts of the town among refugees, mostly outcast professors. If a reader picks up Bradbury's novel today, and then turns to his/ her iPad to read the online blog The Answer Sheet at *The Washington Post*, she may read this:

The discussion of why the humanities matter has picked up steam since *The New York Times* published a piece last week suggesting that even some top institutions are increasingly anxious about the proliferation of STEM (science, technology, engineering and math) majors.

Meanwhile, they report a declining interest in topics like French literature.

Only eight percent of students now major in the humanities, according to the American Academy of Arts & Sciences, down from a peak of more than 17 percent in 1967. The trend *is* worrisome, and plenty of college presidents have come to the defense of the humanities; views of all kinds have since been published….

Tolstoy endured. Will the liberal arts? (Willen, 2013, n.p.)

From Aldous Huxley to Ray Bradbury to Neil Gaiman—and countless authors and readers alike along the way—*Fahrenheit 451* should leave us all with Shakespeare ringing in our ears:

> **Miranda:** O wonder!
> How many goodly creatures are there here!
> How beauteous mankind is! O brave new world,
> That has such people in't.
>
> (William Shakespeare, *The Tempest*, Act V, Scene I, ll. 203–206)

Fahrenheit 451 remains a warning we need to heed, but once again likely won't. Be careful what brave new world we allow to happen when we aren't paying attention.

Setting Free the Books: On Stepping Aside as Teaching

While film critics have offered mostly negative reviews of *This Is 40*, I have watched all and then parts of the film multiple times during its run on cable TV because I am drawn to the scenes that include the children (who in real life are writer/director Judd Apatow's children with lead actress Leslie Mann). In one scene, the older daughter, Sadie (Maude Apatow), charges into the kitchen and unleashes a profanity-laced diatribe onto her parents. Many years ago, my daughter did the same to my wife and me, and when the two of us burst into laughter, my daughter stomped upstairs to her room, doubly infuriated at our response.

Maybe *This Is 40* isn't a good film, but as I write this, I am in my 50s and my daughter is in her mid-20s, having given birth to her first child in 2014. She and I are quietly emerging from many dark years between us, so I admit to viewing films and reading books through a sort of middle-aged nostalgia that allows me to appreciate things I probably didn't recognize when I should have. The dark years and incessant tensions between my daughter and me often included yelling, first by me and then by my daughter, who enjoyed accusing me of being bi-polar. Today, I recognize that throughout my life I have fumbled almost all of my close relationships because I have struggled with nearly paralyzing anxiety, combined with a proclivity toward feeling things deeply, feeling things *too* deeply.

As a result, my love has often manifested itself as all-consuming, overwhelming, suffocating. My only child, then, had little choice but to rebel, to seek freedom from the tidal wave that was my love. She is now an adult—working, married, and a parent herself. I have been forced in many ways to set aside the worst parts of how I tend to respond to loving another, and thus, we are re-building now how a father and daughter can be.

While I have struggled with personal love relationships, I have had two other loves that provide different contexts, ones that have confronted me with challenges as well—my love of books and my love for my students. Because of these three arenas of my life, my *life loving*, I am in the midst of a journey as a teacher that involves stepping aside as teaching.

On Stepping Aside as Teaching

The film *The Words* presents a multi-layered narrative about writers and their relationships with people as well as words. One story examines a writer that Clay Hammond (Dennis Quaid) creates in his eponymous novel in the film; Hammond explains to Daniella, "You have to choose between life and fiction. The two are very close but they never actually touch. They are two very, very different things" (Klugman & Sternthal, 2012). In Hammond's novel, the novel published by Rory Jansen (Bradley Cooper) but actually written by The Old Man (Jeremy Irons) explores a writer who comes to love the words more than the woman who has inspired him to write the words.

I think the film speaks to what happens when anyone begins to covet the extension of what one loves, even when that displaced urge corrupts the original love. And thus, this film speaks to parents, lovers, and teachers who are all bound by their passions as being essential to who they are. This brings me to books and teaching—two of my greatest loves—and a foundational question about how books matter in my teaching.

Since I have been an English and writing teacher for most of my 30-plus years of teaching, books are the lifeblood of my classroom. But I have always been deeply conflicted about the use of books when teaching. Traditional practices such as assigning required books and meticulously analyzing books—from the historical dominance of New Criticism in English courses to the more recent obsession with close reading in the Common Core—have always felt to me as if the inherent dignity of books was being violated.

I feel much the same way about how traditional teacher-centered instructional and discipline practices deny students autonomy and even their own dignity. Because I have always sought ways in which I can remain true to my love of books and my students, then, I have struggled in formal educational settings. My only recourse has been to create classes where both my students and the books we read are honored over me and my role as an authority (or realistically as *the* authority) in the classroom. In other words, I have come to view *stepping aside* as teaching, much as I have learned to view *stepping aside* as parenting.

Setting Free the Books

I have discussed above Ray Bradbury's *Fahrenheit 451*, fascinated by both the enduring power of the novel and Bradbury's own love affair with books. In the 60th anniversary edition of the novel, Bradbury (2013) in the text of an audio introduction explains: "I'm a library-educated person; I've never made it to college" (p. 196). Bradbury's love of books as a learner, a reader, and a writer creates for me even greater tension in my roles as reader, writer, and *teacher*—especially in the context of Charles Bingham, Antew Dejene, Alma Krilic, and Emily Sadowski's (2012) "Can the Taught Book Speak?" The authors address three questions:

First, what does the banning, and the unbanning of books

have to do with teaching? Second, what is the nature of a book, and do we honor the nature of books when we teach them? And third, is it possible for educators to let books speak for themselves? (p. 199)

Throughout the discussion, the role of the teacher—I would add the corrupting role of the teacher—is confronted:

> If a book is banned because it is dangerous as a written text, then a book could only be unbanned by letting loose the dangerous potential of such a written text. A book is only unbanned when it is let loose to be read by anyone, anywhere, any time. It is unbanned when it can be read in public *or* in private, aloud *or* in silence, and finally, and perhaps most importantly, without "a parent to protect" the book. When one teaches a banned book, one falls short of unbanning the book on a number of counts, but primarily on the last count. When one teaches a banned book, one does something different from unbanning the book. One parents the book. One stands against Plato's fear of writing to be sure, but one also sides *with* that same fear. One lets the book be read, but one makes sure there is a parent present at the reading. (Bingham, et al., 2012, p. 201)

Teaching a book, then, is the same as parenting that book—both the teaching and parenting here characterized as *intrusive* in the ways I have experienced and discussed above as both teacher and parent: "What Derrida thus reminds us is that the very act of teaching is always a parasitical act" (Bingham, et al., p. 202).

Teaching and parenting as necessarily "parasitical" and destructive parallels the way writers and their love of words above people is destructive in *The Words*:

> This figure of the teacher vis-à-vis the book might be formulated as follows: A teacher teaches a book. However, the teacher is not fully a teacher unless the book is not fully a book. That is to say, a teacher needs a book, but she needs a particular kind of book: a book in chains, a banned book, a

book that does not speak for itself. If a teacher were to teach a free book, a book unfettered by place, space, or human voice, then the teacher would not be a teacher. A teacher without a book to call her own —without a book to chain in some way, shape, or form — ceases to be, as a teacher.

To put this another way, as soon as a teacher teaches a book, then the book ceases to be a book. (Bingham, et al., 2012, p. 203)

As Bradbury's own experiences of reading in libraries and not attending college show, the book is its own reason for being. Bingham, et al., explain:

A book, after all, is meant to be free. A book is written. It is written to be read. A book is a book precisely because it is meant to be read, and to be read by anyone....This bookness of the book signifies something important for educators. Namely, it is not in the nature of a book to be taught. Why? Because a book is, itself, language. It is language that speaks. If the book was not language, if it did not speak, then it would not be a book. A book is not intended to be interpreted into speech. A book does not require that people come to consensus about what it says. A book is itself consensus. It already says something before any consensus. There is no book that requires or expects a teacher, just as there is no speaking person who requires or expects a teacher. A book speaks in and of itself. It speaks without the need of parasites, chains, or megaphones. (p. 203)

So what are we to do, we who are lovers of books and teachers?

Simply stated, the problem is this: the taught book cannot speak. Indeed, the solution to this problem would seem simple now that the problem has been identified. The problem would be solved if teachers were to leave books alone. (Bingham, et al., p. 206)

At the intersection of love, books, students, and teaching, I have come to recognize the importance of setting free the books by seeking ways in which I can practice *stepping aside as teaching*. Just as I had to understand that loving my daughter required me to leave her alone, I must leave books and my students alone—and thus the highest form of respect, the highest form of trust, the highest form of love.

The risks are high in this practice because so few adults trust children, and so few adults trust books. And in our paternalistic culture, *parenting* is viewed as both necessary and good—not intrusive and corrupting—in fact, we see books as potentially corrupting and childhood freedom as corrupting. Ultimately, *stepping aside as teaching* is a paradox likely to be perceived as not teaching at all—by students, parents, colleagues, and the public.

But risk we must, in the name of those things we love.

24

On Neil Gaiman

Popular and critically acclaimed, Neil Gaiman's work spans a wide range of genres and media—comic books and graphic novels, children's books, novels, TV scripts. His sporadic appearances on Twitter and his blog also feed his popularity and offer insight into his life as both a person and a writer. I imagine Gaiman cannot help writing just as he cannot help reading—in other words, writing and reading are integral parts of who he is as well as how he has come to be. Like Ray Bradbury, and many writers, Gaiman reflects in his works and his messages a love for the written word, the value of books, notably in the lives of children.

Neil Gaiman Should Be U.S. Secretary of Education: "Things can be different"

Some people view the world differently than others.

Some people view education and schools differently than others.

Some people view children, books, and libraries differently than others.

And then there is Neil Gaiman.

I have been a staunch defender of public education, writing

often against the negative consequences of Common Core (especially as related to literacy instruction) and doggedly resisting noneducators as leaders of the education reform movement. Despite my resistance to what I consider misguided reform as well as my skepticism about innovation and market forces, I have conceded a compromise on Common Core—using the movement to end high-stakes accountability as well as the massive money grab surrounding that movement —along with a clarification about that compromise. The response to that compromise has been underwhelming.

However, I am now willing to offer another compromise; this time about the qualifications for who should be our leaders in education reform. While I still call for the removal of Arne Duncan as Secretary of Education, I am recommending Neil Gaiman as the next Secretary of Education in the U.S.—and suggesting that this office be his for life. I am basing this new compromise on a speech presented by Gaiman (2013) for the Reading Agency in London (Brown, 2013). I must admit that it isn't entirely fair to judge Gaiman on a speech he wrote himself as that compares to the speeches *written for him* that Duncan then delivers. It also isn't quite fair to judge the positions of a beloved author against the pandering of a life-long political appointee. Certainly, Duncan is beholden to different constituencies than Gaiman. But judge I have, and here are my conclusions.

Gaiman's qualifications for Secretary of Education must begin with what his London speech does not include: no discussion of "grit," no chants of "no excuses," no praising of innovation or bowing to the brave new world of technology, no calls for new standards, no urgency about new high-stakes tests. Instead, Gaiman (2013) offers a genuine and compelling argument for the essential value in books, the power of fiction, and the sacred nature of libraries. Unlike typical political discourse, Gaiman confesses upfront his prejudices:

And I am biased, obviously and enormously: I'm an author, often an author of fiction. I write for children and for adults. For about 30 years I have been earning my living though my words, mostly by making things up and writing them down. It is obviously in my interest for people to read, for them to read fiction, for libraries and librarians to exist and help foster a love of reading and places in which reading can occur.

So I'm biased as a writer. But I am much, much more biased as a reader. And I am even more biased as a British citizen. (n.p.)

Immediately, Gaiman (2013) shows his political acuity by noting the importance of investing in literacy as one strategy for decreasing the rise in prisons in the U.S.:

I was once in New York, and I listened to a talk about the building of private prisons – a huge growth industry in America. The prison industry needs to plan its future growth – how many cells are they going to need? How many prisoners are there going to be, 15 years from now? And they found they could predict it very easily, using a pretty simple algorithm, based on asking what percentage of 10 and 11-year-olds couldn't read. And certainly couldn't read for pleasure.

It's not one to one: you can't say that a literate society has no criminality. But there are very real correlations. (n.p.)

Gaiman even understands the difference between causation and correlation—a dramatic advantage over U.S. Secretaries of Education in the past two administrations.

But Gaiman (2013) shines best when he speaks about and to the essential value in reading, recognizing what the field of literacy has known for a century, at least—that children are drawn to reading by being offered an abundance of books and by being allowed to read by choice:

The simplest way to make sure that we raise literate children is to teach them to read, and to show them that reading is a pleasurable activity. And that means, at its simplest, finding books that they enjoy, giving them access to those books, and letting them read them.

I don't think there is such a thing as a bad book for children. Every now and again it becomes fashionable among some adults to point at a subset of children's books, a genre, perhaps, or an author, and to declare them bad books, books that children should be stopped from reading. I've seen it happen over and over; Enid Blyton was declared a bad author, so was RL Stine, so were dozens of others. Comics have been decried as fostering illiteracy.

It's tosh. It's snobbery and it's foolishness. There are no bad authors for children, that children like and want to read and seek out, because every child is different. (n.p.)

We may be able to imagine, also, how Gaiman would react to Common Core and its chief "architect," David Coleman:

And not everyone has the same taste as you.

Well-meaning adults can easily destroy a child's love of reading: stop them reading what they enjoy, or give them worthy-but-dull books that you like, the 21st-century equivalents of Victorian "improving" literature. You'll wind up with a generation convinced that reading is uncool and worse, unpleasant. (n.p.)

After an impassioned and thoughtful argument about science fiction (SF)—even China is on board with SF!—Gaiman (2013) turns to the power of libraries:

Another way to destroy a child's love of reading, of course, is to make sure there are no books of any kind around. And to give them nowhere to read those books. I was lucky....

They were good librarians. They liked books and they liked the books being read. They taught me how to order books from other libraries on inter-library loans. They had no snobbery about anything I read. They just seemed to like that there was this wide-eyed little boy who loved to read, and would talk to me about the books I was reading, they would find me other books in a series, they would help. They treated me as another reader – nothing less or more – which meant they treated me with respect. I was not used to being treated with respect as an eight-year-old. (n.p.)

No, it seems, education reform should not be about new standards or new high-stakes tests—but about preserving and expanding children's access to books. Education reform, it seems, isn't buried inside the promise of new technology either, Gaiman notes:

I do not believe that all books will or should migrate onto screens: as Douglas Adams once pointed out to me, more than 20 years before the Kindle turned up, a physical book is like a shark. Sharks are old: there were sharks in the ocean before the dinosaurs. And the reason there are still sharks around is that sharks are better at being sharks than anything else is. Physical books are tough, hard to destroy, bath-resistant, solar-operated, feel good in your hand: they are good at being books, and there will always be a place for them. They belong in libraries, just as libraries have already become places you can go to get access to ebooks, and audiobooks and DVDs and web content. (n.p.)

Gaiman (2013), we must stress, is not being merely fanciful; he acknowledges the role of literacy in the world economy and the value in preparing younger generations for that world economy. But his commitments are distinct from the current calls for market forces and innovation. In fact, Gaiman celebrates a different "I" word:

We all – adults and children, writers and readers – have an obligation to daydream. We have an obligation to imagine. It is easy to pretend that nobody can change anything, that we are in a world in which society is huge and the individual is less than nothing: an atom in a wall, a grain of rice in a rice field. But the truth is, individuals change their world over and over, individuals make the future, and they do it by imagining that things can be different.

Look around you: I mean it. Pause, for a moment and look around the room that you are in. I'm going to point out something so obvious that it tends to be forgotten. It's this: that everything you can see, including the walls, was, at some point, imagined. Someone decided it was easier to sit on a chair than on the ground and imagined the chair. Someone had to imagine a way that I could talk to you in London right now without us all getting rained on. This room and the things in it, and all the other things in this building, this city, exist because, over and over and over, people imagined things. (n.p.)

Along with "imagination," Gaiman also speaks about our commitment to beauty and our shared democratic responsibilities. Fostering literacy in our children, he argues, is an obligation: "This is not a matter of party politics. This is a matter of common humanity."

Ultimately, Gaiman's speech has inspired me to move outside my previous commitments to demanding that education reform be led by educators only. He has inspired me to imagine, and now I can join Gaiman (2013) in this belief: "You're also finding out something as you read vitally important for making your way in the world. And it's this: The world doesn't have to be like this. Things can be different" (n.p.).

Gaiman, Prisons, Literacy, and the Problems with Satire

Regarding my recommendation above that Gaiman become the U.S. Secretary of Education, Ken Libby took me to task on Twitter for, among other things, Gaiman's (2013) comment about prisons and literacy. I also received a friendly and much appreciated email from Chris Boynick addressing the same issue, noting that it is an urban legend that prisons use child literacy to predict prison needs (Graves, 2010; Sanders, 2013).

Boynick sent that same information to Neil Gaiman who responded on Twitter with: "@CBoynick Interesting. The person who told me that was head of education for New York city."

So let me make a few clarifications addressing all this:

1. My suggesting Gaiman for Secretary of Education above is *satire* (and to be honest, that should put all complaints to rest). I don't really endorse or want Gaiman as Secretary, although I think Gaiman is brilliant—as one Gaiman fan noted, we don't want to detract from his life as a writer! My real point is the calamity that is those who have served at Secretaries of Education—especially in the George W. Bush and Barack Obama administrations.

2. Nonetheless, Gaiman only relays a fact: He *did* hear this stated as a truth. So maybe we can level some blame at his believing this, but apparently a person with some authority who should have known the truth did state this in front of Gaiman.

3. Has Gaiman, then, been a victim (like many of us) of an urban legend? It appears so.

4. But, does Gaiman then make some outlandish or flawed claim based on misinformation? Not at all. In fact, I highlighted that Gaiman (2013) immediately made a nuanced claim: "It's not one to one: you can't say that a literate society has no criminality. But there are very real correlations." And that claim helps him move into a series of powerful and valid points. I should emphasize that most politicians and political appointees start with misinformation and then make ridiculous and flawed proposals. On that comparison, Gaiman wins.

And for good measure, I suggest Joe Ventura (2013), who addresses the urban legend, concluding with an important point relevant to this non-issue about Gaiman's speech and my original blog about it:

Perhaps it's best to call this a distortion of the truth. While there isn't evidence of State Departments of Corrections using third- (or second- or fourth-) grade reading scores to predict the number of prison beds they'll need in the next decade (one spokesperson called the claim "crap"), there is an undeniable connection between literacy skills and incarceration rates....

So, while prison planners do not use third grade reading scores to determine the number of prison beds they'll need in the decade to come, there is a connection between literacy rates, high school dropout rates, and crime. While we should file this claim as an urban legend, let's recognize why it resonates with us: *it speaks to the important ways that poor reading skills are connected with unfavorable life outcomes.* (n.p.)

With that, I rest my case: Gaiman's speech is overwhelmingly on target, moving, and brilliant, and he deserves a bit of space for a small error of fact, and the current Secretary of Education is incompetent.

This leads me to wonder: Why so much concern about one detail in an author's speech and my satirical blog, but so little concern for the incompetence of the Secretary of Education and the entire education agenda at the USDOE?

Gaiman's Mythical Folding of Childhood into Adulthood

I stumbled into the novels of Neil Gaiman—invariably identified with "for adults" by reviewers and critics (Connelly, 2013)—in a way that, upon looking back, the intersection now seems inevitable, not stumbling at all. Browsing as I often do along the center aisle of Barnes and Noble, over several visits I picked up *American Gods*, a hefty novel labeled by the publisher as the tenth anniversary edition. I have always tended to shun enormous novels, in part as a result of my teacher-self recognizing how often students struggle with big books, but I also found myself both avoiding Gaiman's most celebrated work and always taking it into my hands each time I saw it. In the way that books can, *American Gods* kept calling out to me, as the author's preferred text edition did after I read the original version.

The day I acquiesced to Gaiman the novelist—I had always known him as a comic book/graphic novel writer—I experienced a second disorientation: The publisher labels *American Gods* "science fiction." Not long after slipping with glee into Gaiman's other worlds, I had a similar experience with Haruki Murakami, whose *1Q84* is also marked "science fiction." Before Gaiman and Murakami, I counted myself among those dedicated to science fiction but stubbornly opposed to fantasy. No Hobbits for me! And Harry Potter? No way.

Gaiman represents my crisis of genre that would carry through into Murakami's universe(s). I could not find a thing in *American Gods* I would call science fiction, but I also felt "fantasy" failed the work. The best I could ever do was think of Gaiman's narrative as "contemporary mythology"—not Leda and the swan, but the gods right now in my time of existence. Regardless, of course, all that mattered for me was that I loved Gaiman's novels "for adults" and joined millions awaiting his most recent, *The Ocean at the End of the Lane*.

On Childhood and Adulthood

The best works of fiction reach into my chest, grab my heart, and squeeze until I cry because I love the characters in ways that I often fail to satisfy in this real world. In Sandra Cisneros's (2004) "Eleven," I experience that feeling every time I read it aloud to my students, and the central moment when I love eleven-year-old Rachel the deepest is also the most harrowing: "Because she's older and the teacher, she's right and I'm not" (p. 42).

"Eleven" is a sad and wonderful narrative of school and childhood crashing into adulthood. And that story, especially that passage, leapt to mind as I reached the middle of Gaiman's (2013) *Ocean*:

> Ursula Monkton smiled, and the lightnings wreathed and writhed about her. She was power incarnate, standing in the crackling air. She was the storm, she was the lightning, she was the adult world with all its power and all its secrets and all its foolish casual cruelty....

> Ursula Monkton was an adult. It did not matter, at that moment, that she was every monster, every witch, every nightmare made flesh. She was also an adult, and when adults fight children, adults always win. (pp. 86-87)

Gaiman's sleight of hand, his gift of contemporary mythology, achieves the sort of folding over into itself expressed by Kurt Vonnegut's (1991) Tralfamadorian view of time as "a stretch of the Rocky Mountains" (p. 27).

Ocean explores many things, but for me, Gaiman folds childhood into adulthood with a craft and care that makes the short novel speak to the collective, and far too often closed, heart of being fully human. Ursula Monkton as adulthood's "foolish casual cruelty" chills me to the bone in the way that the insensitivity of the teacher in Cisneros's story leaves me angry with adults.

The magic of Gaiman's *Ocean* is the seamless alchemy of turning adulthood into childhood by creating a narrative in which an adult approaching middle age recalls—and narrates for the reader like an Ancient Mariner or Marlow's journey into the heart of darkness or Harold Crick listening to his life as narration—his own childhood confrontation with adulthood.

Ocean is often adult as only a seven-year-old can express it: His father's adultery signaled by his lifting Ursula's skirt from behind is both essentially innocent and stunningly graphic: "I was not sure what I was looking at....He was hugging her from behind. Her midi skirt was hiked up around her waist" (Gaiman, 2013, p. 79).

There are many assorted terrors in this novel, ones that remain with me in a vividness unlike any terrors I have experienced in real life. But the most disturbing message Gaiman offers is about this real world. Ursula Monkton is a twist on the Evil Stepmother or Wicked Witch archetype, and the Hempstock family—three females like generational Muses or fairies (Russian nesting dolls, of sorts, personified)—offers a triumphant message of the possibilities of kindness and other-world guardian angels. While Gaiman doesn't stoop to simplistic idealizing of females, men haunt the world of childhood throughout the novel—although I think more as the embodiment of a belittling human compulsion toward harshness aimed at children than any direct indictment of men. Ursula, the father, and the opal miner share the specter of "adulthood," not gender.

Why, I am compelled to ask, are adults so angry and unforgiving with children, with childhood? Like the teacher in "Eleven" and the adult world in *Ocean*, the assistant principal in *Uncle Buck* represents not only adult antagonism for children, for childhood, but also how that drives the schooling of children. While Cisneros's math teacher's insensitivity to Rachel, John Hughs's warted assistant principal, and Gaiman's Ursula Monkton all speak as vivid creations of the imagination, the terrors of childhood remain quite real—and too often those terrors are connected with adults, and far too often those terrors are connected with schools.

When I set down *Ocean* after finishing this wonderful journey that reached into my chest, grabbed my heart, and squeezed until I cried because I love the characters in ways that I often fail to satisfy in this real world, I found myself thinking of the political, media, and public fascination with a very real-world Evil Stepmother, a Wicked Witch, an Assistant Principal Anita Hogarth: The Time cover of Michelle Rhee, imposing and holding a broom. No child asks to be brought into this world, and there remains no excuse for adults looming in quick and relentless judgment and anger over children.

Why must a child look to the other world for a hand held in unwavering kindness? Shouldn't the very real home, parents, and schools where children also never choose to be offer always a hand gesturing comfort and safety?

Gaiman (2013) knows the answer and offers Lettie, an eternal eleven-year-old embodying the kindness of strangers:

I said, "I'm sorry I let go of your hand, Lettie."

"Oh, hush," she said. "It's always too late for sorries, but I appreciate the sentiment. And next time, you'll keep hold of my hand no matter what she throws at us."

I nodded. The ice chip in my heart seemed to warm then, and melt, and I began to feel whole and safe once more. (p. 103)

Thank you, Neil Gaiman, for bringing Lettie to my world because I now love her as I do eleven-year-old Rachel and Uncle Buck. As I love childhood as the one true thing we must cling to as humans: "children guessed (but only a few/and down they forgot as up they grew" (Cummings, 1991). Here's to never forgetting that we all are children—and, thus, they are all our children.

25

"What These Children Are Like": Rejecting Deficit Views of Poverty and Language

"I am an invisible man," begins Ralph Ellison's (1995, p. 3) enduring modern classic *Invisible Man*, which transforms a science fiction standard into a metaphor for the African American condition in the U.S. Less recognized, however, is Ellison's extensive non-fiction work, including a lecture from 1963 at a seminar for teachers—"What These Children Are Like."

More than 50 years ago, Ellison was asked to speak about "'these children,' the difficult thirty percent," the disproportionate challenges facing African American children in U.S. schools. Ellison's (2003) discussion of language among African Americans, especially in the South, offers a powerful rejection of enduring cultural and racial stereotypes:

> Some of us look at the Negro community in the South and say that these kids have no capacity to manipulate language. Well, these are not the Negroes I know. Because I know that the wordplay of Negro kids in the South would make the experimental poets, the modern poets, green with envy. I don't mean that these kids possess broad dictionary knowl-

edge, but within the bounds of their familiar environment and within the bounds of their rich oral culture, they possess a great virtuosity with the music and poetry of words. The question is how can you get this skill into the mainstream of the language, because it is without doubt there. And much of it finds its way into the broader language. Now I know this just as William Faulkner knew it. This does not require a lot of testing; all you have to do is to walk into a Negro church....

But how can we keep the daring and resourcefulness which we often find among the dropouts? I ask this as one whose work depends upon the freshness of language. How can we keep the discord flowing into the mainstream of the language without destroying it? One of the characteristics of a healthy society is its ability to rationalize and contain social chaos. It is the steady filtering of diverse types and cultural influences that keeps us a healthy and growing nation. The American language is a great instrument for poets and novelists precisely because it could absorb the contributions of those Negroes back there saying "dese" and "dose" and forcing the language to sound and bend under the pressure of their need to express their sense of the real. The damage done to formal grammar is frightful, but it isn't absolutely bad, for here is one of the streams of verbal richness....

I'm fascinated by this whole question of language because when you get people who come from a Southern background, where language is manipulated with great skill and verve, and who upon coming north become inarticulate, then you *know* that the proper function of language is being frustrated.

The great body of Negro slang–that unorthodox language–exists precisely because Negroes need words which will communicate, which will designate the objects, processes, manners and subtleties of their urban experience with the least amount of distortion from the outside. So the problem is, once again, what do we choose and what do we reject of that which the greater society makes available? These kids with whom we're concerned, these dropouts, are living critics of their environment, of our society and our educational system, and they are quite savage critics of some of their teachers. (pp. 548-549, 550, 554-555)

What Ellison is rejecting is a deficit view of language as well as a deficit view of people living in poverty, both blurred with racial prejudices. This deficit view is not some remnant of history, however; in fact, a deficit view of language and impoverished people is one of the most resilient and often repeated claims among a wide range of political and educational ideologies. For example, Robert Pondiscio (2014) notes in a blog post:

We know that low-SES kids tend to come to school with smaller vocabularies and less "schema" than affluent kids, and both of these are correlated with (and probably caused by) poverty. Low-SES kids have heard far fewer words and enjoyed few to no opportunities for enrichment. (n.p.)

When I posted a challenge to this deficit view at Pondiscio's (2014) blog post, Labor Lawyer [screen name] added this comment:

How about the seminal research outlined in Hart & Risley's "Meaningful Differences"? Their research showed that there were significant differences in how low-SES parents and high-SES parents verbally interacted with their children + that the low-SES parents' interactions were generically inferior, not just reflective of different vocabularies. The low-SES parents spoke less often to their children, used fewer words, used fewer different words, initiated fewer interactions, responded less frequently to the child's attempt to initiate an interaction, used fewer encouraging words, and used more prohibitive words. (n.p.)

Two important points must be addressed about deficit views of language among impoverished people:

1. Ellison's argument against a deficit view from 1963

is strongly supported by linguists, anthropologists, and sociologists.

2. The flawed Hart and Risley (1995) study remains compelling, not because the research is credible (it isn't), but because their claims match cultural assumptions about race and class, assumptions that are rooted in prejudices and stereotypes.

One powerful example of the popularity of a deficit view of language and poverty is the success of Ruby Payne's framework of poverty books and teacher training workshops—despite a strong body of research refuting her claims and despite her entire framework lacking any credible research (Thomas, 2010, July). To understand the problems associated with deficit views of language and poverty, the Hart and Risley (1995) research must be examined critically (Dudley-Marling and Lucas, 2009).

Hart and Risley: Six African American Families on Welfare in Kansas City

Dudley-Marling and Lucas (2009) reject the deficit view of poverty and language, calling instead for an asset view. They note that deficit views place an accusatory gaze on impoverished parents, and thus, blaming those parents reinforces stereotypes of people in poverty and allows more credible sources of disproportionate failure by students in poverty and minority students to be ignored. Since the political, social, and educational embracing of deficit views is commonly justified by citing Hart and Risley (1995), Dudley-Marling and Lucas carefully detail what the study entails and how the claims made by Hart and Risley lack credibility because of an inadequate sample size (p. 363). Thus, Dudley-Marling and Lucas stress:

> What is particularly striking about Hart and Risley's data analysis is their willingness to make strong, evaluative claims about the quality of the language parents directed to their children....

> Many educational researchers and policy makers have

generalized the findings about the language and culture of the 6 welfare families in Hart and Risley's study to all poor families. Yet, Hart and Risley offer no compelling reason to believe that the poor families they studied have much in common with poor families in other communities, or even in Kansas City for that matter. The primary selection criterion for participation in this study was socioeconomic status; therefore, all the 6 welfare families had in common was income, a willingness to participate in the study, race (all the welfare families were Black), and geography (all lived in the Kansas City area). (pp. 363, 364)

In other words, Hart and Risley (1995) make *causational* claims based on a very limited sample, and those claims are widely embraced because they speak to the dominant culture's assumptions about race and class. Dudley-Marling and Lucas (2009) explain:

> Conflating correlation with causation in this way illustrates the "magical thinking" that emerges when researchers separate theory from method (Bloome et al., 2005). Hart and Risley make causal claims based on the co-occurrence of linguistic and academic variables, but what's missing is an interpretive (theoretical) framework for articulating the relationship between their data and their claims....

> The discourse of "scientifically based research," which equates the scientific method with technique, has led to a body of research that is resistant to meaningful (theoretical) critique. Hart and Risley's conclusions about the language practices of families living in poverty, for example, are emblematic of a discourse of language deprivation that "seems impervious to counter evidence, stubbornly aligning itself with powerful negative stereotypes of poor and working-class families...."

> [T]hey are establishing a norm thoroughly biased in favor of middle- and upper-middle-class children. This common-sense rendering of the data pathologizes the language and culture of poor families, reflecting harmful, long-standing

stereotypes that hold the poor primarily responsible for their economic and academic struggles (Nunberg, 2002). (p. 367)

The accusatory blame, then, focusing on impoverished parents is a powerful and detrimental consequence of deficit views of poverty and language, as Dudley-Marling and Lucas (2009) add:

> Blaming the poor for their poverty in this way leaves no reason to consider alternative, systemic explanations for poverty or school failure....Recent research in neuroscience, for example, indicates that the stresses of living in poverty can impair children's brain development (Noble, McCandliss, & Farah, 2007). But most Americans do not easily embrace systemic explanations for academic failure. In our highly individualistic, meritocratic society, it is generally assumed that academic underachievement is evidence of personal failure (Mills, 1959). (p. 367)

That deficit views of language and poverty remain compelling is yet another example of a research base being discounted because cultural beliefs offer pacifying blinders:

> The deficit-based research of Hart and Risley, with all of its methodological and theoretical shortcomings, has been more persuasive than linguistic research that considers the language of poor families on its own terms (e.g., Labov, 1970; Heath, 1983; Michaels, 1981; Gee; 1996; see also Michaels, 2005), perhaps because Hart and Risley's findings comport with long-standing prejudices about the language of people living in poverty (Nunberg, 2002). (Dudley-Marling & Lucas, pp. 367-368)

Continuing, then, to cherry-pick one significantly flawed study in order to confirm cultural stereotypes reveals far more about society and education in the U.S. than it does about children living and learning in poverty (see Taylor & Dorsey-Gaines, 1988).

Despite many well-meaning educators embracing this deficit view as well as Hart and Risley's (1995) flawed study, seeking to help students from impoverished backgrounds acquire the cultural capital associated with the dominant grammar, usage, and vocabulary is actually inhibited by that deficit view:

> Finally, Hart and Risley draw attention to a real problem that teachers encounter every day in their classrooms: children enter school with more or less of the linguistic, social, and cultural capital required for school success. However, we take exception to the characterization of this situation in terms of linguistic or cultural *deficiencies*....In this formulation, the ultimate responsibility for this failure lies with parents who pass on to their children inadequate language and flawed culture. But, in our view, the language differences Hart and Risley reported are just that—*differences*. All children come to school with extraordinary linguistic, cultural, and intellectual resources, just not the *same* resources. (Dudley-Marling & Lucas, 2009, p. 369)

A larger point we must confront as well is that all efforts to describe and address any social class as monolithic is flawed: Neither all affluent nor all impoverished children are easily described by what they have and don't have. In fact, social classifications and claims about a culture of poverty are equally problematic as deficit views of poverty and language.

Just as Ellison (2003) confronted, U.S. society and schools remain places where minority and impoverished children too often fail. Much is left to be done to correct those inequities, both in society and in our schools, but blaming impoverished and minority parents as well as seeing impoverished and minority children (no longer invisible) as *deficient* stereotypes behind a false justification of research has never been and is not now the path we should take.

"I don't know what intelligence is," concludes Ellison (2003) in his lecture:

> But this I do know, both from life and from literature: whenever you reduce human life to two plus two equals four, the human element within the human animal says, "I

don't give a damn." *You* can work on that basis, but the kids cannot. If you can show me how I can cling to that which is real to me, while teaching me a way into the larger society, then I will not only drop my defenses and my hostility, but I will sing your praises and help you to make the desert bear fruit. (p. 555)

Continuing to embrace a deficit view of poverty and language is to embrace a desert that will never bear fruit.

26

On Zombies

While genres and subgenres ride peaks and valleys of popularity and cult fascination, horror and science fiction, for example, appear to hold enduring places in the public's heart and mind, often in conjunction—for example, *Alien* or *The Fly*. Zombies as a subgenre, however, have never gained serious and popular acclaim in quite the way that they have in the first couple of decades of the twenty-first century. Novels, films, and TV series have raised the stature of the zombie as both entertainment and commentary.

Lessons from the Zombie Apocalypse

At the intersection of horror and science fiction (SF) lies a haunting lesson in the allegory rising from narratives such as *The Invasion of the Body Snatchers* (1956): By the time the apocalypse happens, it won't look like we expect, and political and public recognition of the event will come way too late. As a life-long SF fan and educator for three decades, then, I have found that Max Brooks (2007), in his *World War Z*, has inadvertently written a series of lessons for the education reform apocalypse that is already happening, and almost no one is willing to admit it.

I think we must not ignore that the zombie genre is a mythology about the brain: The infection attacks the brain and the only way to kill a zombie is to destroy the brain. For an educator, these are not trivial matters. Brooks crafts an oral history that looks back on the human race barely surviving a zombie apocalypse. As the snippets of interviews reveal, the political and military elites around the world failed to act with clarity and often hid the rising zombie plague from the public in calculated and horrifying ways: Decisions were made, for example, about who should survive and who was expendable.

In one section we learn that to target infected zombies, airplanes killed hundreds of people so that the infected could rise from the carnage and be easily eliminated. Another response to the zombie outbreak involves the government and Big Pharma. Initially, the zombie infection is identified as rabies so a rabies vaccine is mass-produced primarily to allay fear, although the government and pharmaceutical companies knew the vaccine to be ineffective. Money was to be made and the ends justified the means. But one of the most powerful lessons to me is in the Great Panic section, an interview with Maria Zhuganova. This oral history focuses on the actions of the military in conjunction with civilian oversight, a man call "Rat Face."

In Zhuganova's explanation, we discover that the soldiers are forced to enact *decimation*, as she explains:

> "To 'decimate'…I used to think it meant just to wipe out, cause horrible damage, destroy…it actually means to kill by a percentage of ten, one out of every ten must die…and that's exactly what they did to us…."

> "We would be the ones to decide who would be punished. Broken up into groups of ten, we would have to vote on which one of us was going to be executed. And then we… the soldiers, we would be the ones to personally murder our friends…."

> "Brilliance….Conventional executions might have reinforced discipline, might have restored order from the top down, but by making us all accomplices, they held us

together not just by fear, but by guilt as well. We could have said no, could have refused and been shot ourselves, but we didn't. We went right along with it....We relinquished our freedom that day, and we were more than happy to see it go. From that moment on we lived in true freedom, the freedom to point to someone else and say 'They told me to do it! It's their fault, not mine.' The freedom, God help us, to say 'I was only following orders.'" (Brooks, 2007, pp. 81-83)

And here we sit in the second decade of the twenty-first century, with a film version of *World War Z* and pretending that a horror/ SF tale has no value beyond our entertainment.

Our government conspires with Big Testing to implement disaster capitalism policies with our children, but because the public is afraid of our international competitiveness, it does not question the effectiveness of testing, despite the evidence to the contrary. And like the soldiers, teachers are compelled to be accomplices in the implementation of Common Core State Standards and in preparing our students for the tests to follow. The decimation of public education has infected us all.

The only real antidote, unlike the zombie apocalypse, is that educators, students, and parents must all choose *not* to follow orders, *not* to become the accomplices that allow the decimation.

Post-apocalyptic Mindset in a Civilized World

The mass of men lead lives of quiet desperation.
Henry David Thoreau, Walden

Since October 1999, when I experienced several weeks of unrelenting panic attacks, I have been negotiating my lifelong struggle with anxiety—many of those years spent completely unaware of the problem and then coming to recognize and even understand a condition that to most people seems completely irrational (even silly). Not to slip into being simplistic, one of the foundational ways in which I have come to better understand my anxiety is that my body responds to the civilized world in ways that prehistory demanded. In other words, when human existence depended on a constant state of vigilance, the quality of anxiety was passed on from human to human since those humans most vigilant—most aware of the world around them—lived long enough to procreate.

Now, although no mountain lion lies in wait to pounce upon me and make me its lunch, I live in a constant state *as if that were true*—hyper-aware of both the world and *every possibility* about that world. And that is the seemingly irrational part for those who do not experience incessant anxiety. Of course, I know better, but anxiety of the type I experience is beyond rationality. Thus, for me (and possibly my fellow sufferers of anxiety), *The Walking Dead* (both the graphic series and the TV series) serves as a powerful allegory for our condition because surviving humans in that imagined post-apocalyptic world actually must exist always aware of the omnipresent possibility of zombie attack. But there is something here far beyond my personal wrestling with anxiety: The cultural and educational post-apocalyptic mindset in a civilized world.

To survive and thrive as a human has always been, is currently, and likely will be in the context of finite resources for survival and thriving. For much of human history (and in our imagined post-apocalyptic worlds), those finite resources were necessarily the focus of human competition. In the 21st century, humanity has not yet eradicated *existence-as-survival* among large numbers of people—disproportionately children, with no political power—born into and living in extreme poverty. However, in so-called developed countries, we do have pockets of organized societies that have built resources that, although still finite, are adequate to eradicate *existence-as-survival* if those people had the political will to address the distribution of those resources.

The U.S. is one such country that does not suffer under a scarcity of resources. It does suffer, however, under an inequitable distribution of resources, one that allows and even perpetuates scarcity for some and abundance for others—primarily determined by anyone's accident of birth. I want to pose two claims now:

1. The U.S. as a civilized nation could establish an equitable society in which the basic minimum human condition would insure that all have access to those resources that support both the need to survive and the urge to thrive.

2. That ideal cannot be attained as long as the U.S. remains entrenched in ideologies committed to rugged individualism, competition, and institutional pursuits of "grit" and "zero tolerance."

The U.S.'s commitments to (2) are not only counter to achieving (1), but also serve primarily to support the minority elite class that benefits from those ideologies, despite having rarely exhibited those qualities.

In other words, the ruling elite have been born into abundance and haven't experienced the anxiety of scarcity, but they demand that those born into and living in scarcity rise through a manufactured culture of competition—even though we have an abundance of resources to make such Social Darwinism unnecessary. As just one example, researchers and advocates of "grit" actually recommend placing impoverished and minority students in fabricated situations of scarcity to teach them the "grit" those researchers and advocates claim is the source of achievement among the affluent—a claim that, in fact, is at best misleading, and at worst, simply false. And to add insult to injury, those outliers who have risen through scarcity to thrive have been co-opted into the post-apocalyptic mindset, maintaining that since some have fought to survive, others must fight to survive.

The alternative of a society in which such base struggles do not have to occur is either ignored or trivialized as a soft option beneath our ruggedly individualistic culture. We boast, in fact, when we make other people suffer: "I taught him a lesson."

As someone trapped in an irrational existence governed by anxiety—an existence dramatized in the fabricated world beyond the zombie apocalypse—I treasure the possibility of rejecting the post-apocalyptic mindset in a civilized world. We know that scarcity creates anxiety, and that any person will suffer under the weight of scarcity, most notably if that scarcity is in fact avoidable. We also know that everyone benefits from a condition of abundance (Mullainathan & Shafir, 2013).

And thus, I remain offended by the incessant refrain offered by those with the loudest voices in our society, voices that demand the least among us must work twice as hard as everyone else to *earn* the basic dignity of human existence that the privileged simply have handed to them.

It is, ultimately, a shallow call against the *world we could create*, a world unlike our prehistoric past and unlike our fabricated post-apocalyptic future. It is world where we no longer foster competition, but make competition unnecessary—as it already could be if we recognized we are no longer slaves to scarcity, but to the inequitable distribution of resources that erases our humanity in very real ways that have nothing to do with zombies.

Many people throughout the world and in the U.S.—many *children*—lead lives of quiet desperation, desperation about food, shelter, health, and happiness. One new fact of the human condition, however, is that those people do not *have* to lead lives of desperation. For those living in abundance, the choice to end scarcity is ours. That we appear unwilling (not unable) to do so causes me great, and for once, justifiable anxiety.

Zombies, "Scarcity," and Understanding Poverty

The original comic book series *The Walking Dead* opens with "This is not good" in the panel depicting police officers pinned behind their patrol car by gunfire. The page ends with officer Rick Grimes being shot, followed by a full-page panel on the next page of Rick waking with a gasp in the hospital. Zombies are soon to follow. Preceding this first story is an introduction from creator Robert Kirkman, who explains: "I'm not trying to scare anybody" (Kirkman & Moore, 2006, n.p.). But he is interested in how characters react to the most extreme scarcity—the zombie apocalypse.

While the AMC television series is an adaptation of the comic book (and not bound to Kirkman's graphic narrative), this central premise tends to remain true in both the comic book and the TV series, notably in the "Isolation" episode (October 27, 2013):

> AMC's *The Walking Dead* picked up right where it left off, exploring the mental and emotional toll Karen's and David's deaths has had on the group and specifically Tyreese, who experienced the loss of someone close to him for the first time in this new world....
>
> The biggest reveal of the hour, however, came in the final moments after Rick (Andrew Lincoln) uses his sheriff skills and pieces together that it was Carol (Melissa McBride) who was the one who killed Karen and David in a bid to contain the deadly illness threatening the group's safe haven. (Goldberg, 2013)

When asked by Rick and with a calm matter-of-fact detachment, Carol confesses to killing, dragging outside, and then setting on fire Karen and David. While there is certainly tension and shock created by this confession, the more powerful point may be that Carol has acted in a way that she feels is justified by the shared human condition—the pervasive threat of zombies surrounding the prison along with the reality that anybody who dies, including those living in close quarters with Carol and the others, will reanimate as a zombie.

Two of the most compelling aspects of the AMC series are that zombies are omnipresent and that every human is a walking potential for becoming a zombie. Once the main characters have positioned themselves in a prison behind two layers of fences, viewers watch as the characters go about their reduced lives (sometimes casually hoeing the garden) with zombies always moaning and clawing at the fence. There is *only one world* for these characters—a world saturated with zombies. And a world defined by zombies is a world that has redefined the nature of human free will and choice.

On Rationality and Free Will (Choice)

Western culture honors rational behavior above emotional responses, and particularly in the U.S., choice is a nearly sacred value. That prejudice for rationality tends to normalize rational behavior, creating the appearance that rationality is objective. Yet, in fact, rationality is always bound by context. Consider the hiker, Aron Ralston, who would not have been rational for amputating a limb in his day-to-day life, but once Ralston was confronted with being trapped by a boulder while hiking, amputating a limb became not only rational, but also life-saving. The context changes and so does rationality.

In *The Walking Dead* TV series narrative, Carol's murderous acts raise the same sort of debate about her behavior: Considering the threat of the newly spreading flu in the prison, is Carol's behavior rational? Certainly in a world without zombies, Carol has no justification for murdering people and burning the corpses, but in the realities of *The Walking Dead*, context dictates behaviors—and colors our judgment of those behaviors. While rationality is contextual and subjective, choice as a sacred value in the U.S. is popularly idealized and misrepresented. Choice is not a foundational aspect of being human. In fact, being human is about basic behaviors concerning which humans have no choice: breathing, eating, seeking shelter, attending to one's health. And broadly, *survival* (think Ralston).

Zombie narratives are speculative stories of humans reduced to a single basic human necessity, consumption. Zombies are perpetual and relentless consumers—to the extreme that renders them simultaneously campy and terrifying. The Western fetish for choice is an exaggeration of a *great human hope* or quest: The human faith in free will, the human faith that our free will lifts us above the rest of the earth's beasts.

"So it goes" is the now-iconic phrase that provides Kurt Vonnegut's *Slaughterhouse-Five* the coherence of a refrain against the staccato of Vonnegut's time-traveling narrative. At its essence "So it goes" is an acknowledgement of the human condition, one in which humans cling to a belief in free will that doesn't exist. When a Tralfamadorian explains to Billy Pilgrim that Pilgrim is on the planet Tralfamadore, the conversation turns to free will:

"Where am I?" said Billy Pilgrim.

"Trapped in another blob of amber, Mr. Pilgrim...."

"How—how did I get here?"

"It would take another Earthling to explain it to you. Earthlings are the great explainers, explaining why this event is structured as it is, telling how other events may be achieved or avoided. I am a Tralfamadorian, seeing all time as you might see a stretch of the Rocky Mountains. All time is all time. It does not change. It does not lend itself to warnings or explanations. It simply is. Take it moment by moment, and you will find that we are all, as I've said before, bugs in amber."

"You sound to me as though you don't believe in free will," said Billy Pilgrim...

..."If I hadn't spent so much time studying Earthlings," said the Tralfamadorian, "I wouldn't have any idea what was meant by 'free will.' I've visited thirty-one inhabited planets in the universe, and I have studied reports on one hundred more. Only on Earth is there any talk of free will." (Vonnegut, 1991, pp. 85-86)

Do the characters in *The Walking Dead* have the choice to live as if zombies do not exist? Do people living in poverty have the choice to live as if they are not in poverty? Free will and choice, like rationality, are bound by context. But neither free will nor choice is basic to being human since our basic human nature consists of those things about which we have no real choice. *Choice, in fact, is not an essential aspect of a free people. Choice is the result of a free people collectively insuring that all people have the essentials of life protected so that the human longing to choose becomes possible and even ethical.*

Simply stated, choice and being free are luxuries that exist toward the top of the triangle representing Maslow's hierarchy of needs: choosing between a Camry and an Accord is of little importance to a person starving. If nothing else, *The Walking Dead* highlights how trivial our choices about materialistic lives become once the human condition is reduced to survival within an ever-present threat.

Before Free Will: Zombies and Understanding Poverty

Poverty is as omnipresent for the poor as the threat of zombies is for the characters in *The Walking Dead*: "Poverty is surely the most widespread and important example of scarcity....*One cannot take a vacation from poverty* [emphasis added]. Simply deciding not to be poor—even for a bit—is never an option" (Mullainathan & Shafir, 2013, pp. 147, 148). Just as the threat of zombies and reanimation into zombies weigh on the characters' minds and drive their actions 24 hours a day and every day of their lives, poverty too dictates who poor people are and what they do.

Living in constant vigilance against the threat of zombies, ironically, reduces all living humans to their basic compulsions, rendering even living humans more zombie-like than they would want to admit: zombies are only consumers, and humans living under the threat of zombies are primarily survivors. Living under the weight of poverty is a very real condition that zombie narratives represent in metaphor. Human behavior, then, is likely a window into larger social contexts and less a reflection of individual strengths and weaknesses.

Because of cultural stereotypes that marginalize and even demonize people in poverty, Mullainathan and Shafir (2013) caution against drawing conclusions from observable behaviors of people living in the behavior-changing stress of poverty.

In *The Walking Dead*, Carol-as-killer is a consequence of the existence of zombies in the same way people in poverty have their mental capacities drained by the state of poverty in which they are trapped. As well, poverty may be as unavoidable as zombies for people who find themselves born into impoverished homes, considering that in the U.S., affluence and poverty are highly "sticky"—most people remain in the social class into which they are born, especially at the extreme ends of the class spectrum (Bruenig, 2013, June 13).

The Walking Dead's central relevance as it speaks to the power of poverty is that becoming a zombie in this narrative is simply the result of dying; everyone is a potential zombie (unlike the traditional need to be bitten by a zombie). Zombies in *The Walking Dead* and poverty, then, are unavoidable and pervasive. Depending on evidence instead of metaphor, with unintended zombie flair, Mullainathan and Shafir (2013) argue, "Scarcity captures the mind" (p. 7). For example, Carol's entire existence now *tunnels* (Mullainathan and Shafir's term for an intense form of focus) on surviving zombies. Before she kills Karen and David, she offers the children in the prison covert lessons on killing zombies swiftly by using knives and weapons to execute effective blows to the brain. In a world devoid of zombies, Carol's behavior would be warped. In her previous life, in fact, Carol has been a different person.

Zombie narratives as well as Mullainathan and Shafir's (2013) work on scarcity help highlight an understanding of poverty that rejects stereotypes as well as what people and children living and learning in poverty need: Their state of scarcity must be alleviated. Until we alleviate poverty, however, we must be vigilant not to increase the consequences of scarcity (such as artificially ramping up stress for teachers and students), and we can no longer ask children and their teachers to work as if poverty doesn't exist.

Social programs addressing poverty and education reform targeting the achievement gap must begin with embracing a closing claim from Mullainathan and Shafir (2013): "We can go some way toward 'scarcity proofing' our environment" (p. 225). But that goal cannot be achieved within a deforming idealism that asks impoverished people to live as if poverty doesn't exist, that asks children living in poverty to pretend they are not impoverished during the school day. It deserves repeating: "One cannot take a vacation from poverty."

27

Pop Culture and the Mutant Narrative
X-Men Endure

The late 1930s and early 1940s birthed the superhero comic book fascination (Thomas, 2010) that despite several bumps along the way has endured into the twenty-first century where superhero films are huge box-office successes and pop culture gold mines. In both the comic book and film universes, superhero reboots are common: Batman, Superman, and Spider-Man, to name only a few, have all experienced revised origins in the pages of their comics as well as multiple cycles of films dedicated to them. The X-Men films from 2000 to 2006 may have had as much to do with the adaptation success of comic books to film such as Batman, Superman, and Spider-Man.

X-Men: First Class in 2011 was one such re-boot and was enough of a success that *X-Men: Days of Future Past* was released in 2014. Before the release of the 2014 film, Alexander Abad-Santos (2013) discusses how the mutant aspect of X-Men narratives can be found nearly universally in pop culture:

> In about seven months, I along with a lot of X-Men fans will be getting to the theater an hour early, lining up, and then watching to see if *Days of Future Past* is what I've imagined it would be. What's kinda great for an X-Men [fan], though,

is that we don't have to wait until then to get an X-Men story. Pop culture is filled with them. (n.p.)

During the rise of zombie movies and TV shows, I was interviewed by a local journalist about zombie culture; the journalist was investigating why zombies are so popular. I tried to explain that pop culture has all sorts of cycles. Some periods when vampires are hot, some periods when something else is hot. But I also conceded that certain elements of pop culture trends are enduring; for example, something about zombies certainly remains captivating with the public (see Chapter 26).

I believe the same case can be made for mutants: mutant narratives are compelling and ripe for making important social commentary. And to that I examine the X-Men and the Hunger Games trilogy as they speak to wider issues, such as education.

Civil Rights and Civil Wrongs

When research, history, and allegory all converge to tell us the same story, we must pause to ask why we have ignored the message for so long and why are we likely to continue missing the essential thing before us. *The New York Times* and *Education Week* reveal two important lessons in both the message they present and the distinct difference in their framing of that message. "Black Students Face More Discipline, Data Suggests [sic]" headlines the NYT's article with the lead: "Black students, especially boys, face much harsher discipline in public schools than other students, according to new data from the Department of Education" (Lewin, 2012). And *Education Week* announces "Civil Rights Data Show Retention Disparities," opening with:

> New nationwide data collected by the U.S. Department of Education's civil rights office reveal stark racial and ethnic disparities in student retentions, with black and Hispanic students far more likely than white students to repeat a grade, especially in elementary and middle school. (Adams, Robelen, & Shah, 2012, n.p.)

One has to wonder if this is truly news in the sense that this research is revealing something we don't already know because we should already admit this fact: America's public schools and prisons are stark images of the reality of racial, gender, and socioeconomic inequity in our society—inequity that is both perpetuated by and necessary for the ruling elite to maintain their artificial status as that elite. The research coming from the U.S. Department of Education—as well as the media coverage of it—are not evidence we are confronting that reality or that we will address it any time soon. The research and the media coverage are proof we'll spend energy on both the research and the coverage of it in order to mask the racism lingering corrosively in our free state, while continuing to blame the students who fail for their failure and the prisoners for their transgressions.

X-Men and *The Hunger Games*: Allegory as Unmasking

Science fiction allows an artist to pose worlds that appears to be "other worlds" in order for the readers to come to see our own existence more clearly. In the re-boot film version of the Marvel Comics superhero team, *X-Men: First Class*, the powerful allegory of this comic book universe portrays the isolation felt by the mutants—one by one they begin to discover each other and share a common sentiment: "I thought I was the only one."

These mutants feel not only isolation, but also shame—shame for their looks, those things that are not their choices, not within their direct power to control. While this 2011 installment of X-Men on film reveals the coming together of the mutants, the narrative ends with the inevitable division of the mutants into factions: Professor X's assimilationists and Magneto's radicals. It takes only a little imagination to see this allegory in the historical factionalism that rose along with the Civil Rights movement between Martin Luther King Jr. and Malcolm X. In whose interest is this in-fighting?

Although written as young adult literature, *The Hunger Games* trilogy (Collins, 2008, 2009, 2010) has spread into the mainstream popular consciousness. The savage reality show that pits children against children to the death gives the first book in the series its title, but as with the research on racial inequity in our schools, I fear we fail to look at either the purpose of these Hunger Games in that other world of the novel or how it speaks to us now.

In *Catching Fire*, Katniss Everdeen, the narrator, confronts directly that her country, Panem, has created stability by factionalizing the people into Districts, ruled by the Capitol. Panem exists because of the competition among the Districts, daily for resources and once a year personified by two lottery losers, children from each district. In this second book, Katniss learns something horrifying but true when the winners of the most recent Games, Katniss and Peeta, visit District 11, the home of Rue, Katniss's friend who is killed in the Games. During the celebration, the people of District 11 repeat Katniss's act of rebellion:

> What happens next is not an accident. It is too well executed to be spontaneous, because it happens in complete unison. Every person in the crowd presses the three middle fingers of their left hand against their lips and extends them to me. It's our sign from District 12, the last good-bye I gave Rue in the arena. (Collins, 2009, p. 61)

Then as Katniss and Peeta are rushed from the stage, they witness Peacekeepers executing people in the District 11 crowd. As President Snow has warned Katniss about the possibility of uprisings:

> "But they'll follow if the course of things doesn't change. And uprisings have been known to lead to revolution.... Do you have any idea what that would mean? How many people would die? What conditions those left would have to face? Whatever problems anyone may have with the Capitol, believe me when I say that if it released its grip on the districts for even a short time, the entire system would collapse." (Collins, 2009, p. 21)

What maintains the stability of Panem? Competition, division, and *fear*. What threatens the stability of Panem and the inequity it maintains? Solidarity, compassion, cooperation, and rebellion.

Separate, Unequal—and Distracted

U.S. public education has always been and remains, again like our prisons, a map of who Americans are and what we are willing to tolerate. Children of color and children speaking home languages other than English are disproportionately likely to be punished and expelled (especially the boys), disproportionately likely to be retained to suffer the same grade again, disproportionately likely to be in the lowest level classes with the highest student-teacher ratios in order to prepare them for state testing (while affluent and white children sit in advanced classes with low student-teacher ratios), and disproportionately likely to be taught by un- and under-certified teachers with the least experience. And many of these patterns are distinct even in pre-kindergarten (Gilliam, 2005).

We don't really need any more research, or history lessons, or SF allegory, or comic books brought to the silver screen. We need to see the world that our children live in and recognize themselves (just ask an African American young man), and then look in the mirror ourselves. Why do those in power remain committed to testing children in order to label, sort, and punish them? Who does the labeling, sorting, and punishing benefit? And what are the reasons behind these facts, the disproportionate inequity in our schools and in our prisons?

We only need each minute of every day to confront what the recent data from the USDOE reveal, but it is always worth noting that genuine compassion for all humans is often ignored despite its value. How and why? Because this sentiment is dangerous for the Capitol. If we persist in being shocked by the research or enamored by the exciting story of Katniss, we will remain divided and conquered.

Katniss in *Catching Fire* responds to the president with: "'It [Panem] must be very fragile, if a handful of berries can bring it down.'" To which the president replies, "'It is fragile, but not in the way that you suppose'" (Collins, 2009, p. 22). The fragility is masked by the 99% as separate, unequal, and distracted—fighting among ourselves in fear of what we might lose otherwise.

It is time to suppose otherwise.

28

It's Still a Man's (Hostile) World

"He knows, or thinks he knows"

During the spring of 2006 when members of the Duke lacrosse team were first accused of rape (later to be dismissed by North Carolina Attorney General Roy Cooper), I was teaching a freshman English course that focused on Kurt Vonnegut. Although my university is composed of a female majority, this class was mostly male students; and since the university is a small, selective liberal arts university, the students in most ways identified with the lacrosse players. Nonetheless, I was taken aback that the students almost unanimously (including the females) believed the lacrosse players were innocent. Class and race identification was central to these feelings, I believed, but when the case was exposed as a false accusation, I was placed in a much more complex position.

As the accusation against Florida State University quarterback Jameis Winston unfolded, then, I was once again faced with the tension that accompanies high-profile public discourse about rape and sexual abuse. Beyond the issue of Winston's innocence or guilt, however, we have been confronted with something we seem almost unwilling to acknowledge, something Emily Bazelon (2013) frames as, "How Did Jameis Winston Evade a Rape Charge?":

At a press conference that turned weirdly jokey—at one point, a female reporter in the room blurted "Come on" in exasperation—why did Meggs make a point of the fact that the victim "acknowledged having sex with her boyfriend"? I suppose he felt he had to say something about the presence of someone else's DNA, in addition to Winston's, on her clothing. But the effect was to fuel the slut shaming she's already enduring—treatment that has led her to withdraw from her FSU classes.

Here is what's bothering me most: I've been looking for a case in which a woman accuses a big-time college athlete of rape, and he is charged and then convicted. (n.p.)

Bazelon (2013) has found few examples, and adds:

The underlying question about Winston, his accuser, and Meggs' decision is this: Did she lie, or did she make an accusation of rape that is credible but too difficult, in the view of this prosecutor, to prove in court? One thing is clear: It is uncommon for victims to make false accusations of sexual assault. Yes, it happens, causing terrible damage for men who are falsely accused. But the evidence suggests that the vast majority of the time, women who go to the police about rape are telling the truth.

Reading through the police narrative of this alleged victim's account, it is hard for me to imagine that she had consensual sex with Winston and then decided to lie and say it was rape. (n.p.)

Again, beyond the specifics of the Winston case, but in the context of high-profile sexual assault accusations such as those identifying Ben Roethlisberger and Kobe Bryant (both of which were not pursued), how must all women feel when sexual assault of any kind is aired publicly with smiles, smirks, and laughter; and the derision exhibited in the press conferences by Florida State Attorney Willie Meggs and Winston lawyer Tim Jansen? Are we to believe that women targeting athletes, as Jansen claims, is somehow more prevalent and a greater scar on our society than women being sexually assaulted?

As Laurie Penny (2013, November 30) declares in a discussion of Miley Cyrus, the agency of women and girls remains decontextualized from their humanity: "We care about young women as symbols, not as people":

> Another week, another frenzy of concern-fapping over teenage girls. A few days ago, I was invited onto Channel 4 News to discuss a new report detailing how young people, much like not-young people, misunderstand consent and blame girls for rape. The presenter, Matt Frei, tried to orchestrate a fight between myself and the other guest, Labour MP Luciana Berger, because it's not TV feminism unless two women shout at each other....
>
> The tone of the reports on girls' lack of confidence, on the persistence of myths of ignorance about rape and sexual violence, is as patronising as ever. The implication is that girls fret about their appearance, are confused about sex and consent and worried about the future because they are variously frivolous or stupid. (n.p.)

Penny highlights both the specific mansplaining (Rothman, 2012) around Cyrus and the wider mansplaining, paternalism, and objectifying that remain pervasive in the public discourse about girls and women. The slut shaming of women—whether it be aimed at Cyrus (as simultaneous sexualizing and de-sexualizing of females) or the wink-wink-nod-nod discrediting of Winston's accuser by Meggs and Jansen—exposes that it's still a man's (hostile) world for women, including when women are accused of slut shaming women.

A Man's (Hostile) World for Women

A rare safe haven for challenging paternalism and slut shaming is art (Penny, 2013, October 11) where writers (mostly women) and filmmakers have portrayed the aftermath of sexual assault as another sexual assault.

Poet Adrienne Rich's (1994) "Rape" is a stark and powerful recreation of a sexually assaulted woman doubly assaulted during her police interview, beginning:

> There is a cop who is both prowler and father:
> he comes from your block, grew up with your brothers,
> had certain ideals.

And then toward the end:

> You hardly know him but now he thinks he knows you:
> he has taken down your worst moment
> on a machine and filed it in a file.
> He knows, or thinks he knows, how much you
>   imagined;
> he knows, or thinks he knows, what you secretly
>   wanted.

With a dexterity that leaves the reader deeply uncomfortable, Margaret Atwood explores "date rape"—both as an unfolding of the reality of a woman in the context of the possibility of sexual assault by a male blind date and as a complicating of normative views of women having "Rape Fantasies." Atwood builds similar examinations in her *The Handmaid's Tale*.

While it raised considerable attention when released, *The Accused* and the real-life events it was based on—the gang rape of Cheryl Araujo—the film also anticipated discussions of slut shaming by highlighting what was then and still remains the predisposition to blame the victim, especially when the victim is a woman and when the violence is sexual.

But the attention achieved by the film and the sanctuary of poetry and fictional narrative bring us back to Penny's (2013, November 30) charge: "We care about young women as symbols, not as people." For example, Lisbeth Salander is powerful and complex in the Millennium Trilogy, the fictional personification of blaming the victim:

> "Our client on principle does not speak to the police or to other persons of authority, and least of all to psychiatrists. The reason is simple. From the time she was a child she tried time and again to talk to police and social workers to explain that her mother was being abused by Alexander Zalachenko. *The result in every instance was that she was punished* [emphasis added] because government civil servants had decided that Zalachenko was more important than she was." (Larsson, 2012, p. 733)

Salander's entire life is the situation in Rich's "Rape" writ large.

But we must not ignore that even in fiction—Lisbeth as symbol—the first book in the trilogy is given the English title *The Girl with the Dragon Tattoo* (why "girl" not "woman"?), instead of the literal translation from Swedish, "men who hate women," and as in the film *The Accused*, why do we appear more concerned about women being assaulted in books and films than in real life? And is it possible that at least in the U.S. film version, we appear more drawn to Salander as vigilante than morally enraged by the repeated violence and sexual assaults she endures?

It is without question that the human dignity of a man wrongly accused of rape is no less valuable than the human dignity of a woman raped; it is without question that I have no inside knowledge and cannot know the innocence or guilt of Winston or his accuser. But *unknowables* do not excuse us from confronting *knowns*: The smirks and grins, the innuendo, and the direct slut shaming aimed at Winston's accuser were all the sort of double assault we have been warned about, the sort of double assault that affects all women, the sort of double assault that must not be tolerated:

> "The victim and her family appreciate the State Attorney's efforts in attempting to conduct a proper investigation after an inordinate delay by the Tallahassee Police Department,"

Carroll [the accuser's lawyer] said in a statement. "The victim in this case had the courage to immediately report her rape to the police and she relied upon them to seek justice. The victim has grave concerns that her experience, as it unfolded in the public eye and through social media, will discourage other victims of rape from coming forward and reporting." (Boren, 2013, n.p.)

And as Christine Brennan (2013) explains:

There was laughter. There were jokes. There were smiles. The news conference in which Florida state attorney Willie Meggs announced that Jameis Winston was not going to be charged with sexual battery was an extremely light-hearted affair.

Everyone seemed so incredibly happy to be talking about an alleged sexual assault. (n.p.)

The known has confronted us: relief that a football career and national championship would not be derailed combined with a levity not suited for public talk around the possibility of sexual violence—it's still a man's (hostile) world, and as Rich (2002) reminds us in "What Kind of Times Are These?":

...this is not somewhere else but here,
our country moving closer to its own truth and dread,
its own ways of making people disappear.

True Detective: Another Man's (Hostile) World

I started to say *True Detective* (HBO original series) is gold ore and then to pursue a metaphor of finding something of value in an impure original form. But one of the two main characters is named Rust Cohle (Matthew McConaughey) so I will say instead, *True Detective* is iron ore and we can find something of value— something tarnished, yes—in an impure original form. I want to start with the tarnished, the rust, that few people have confronted.

Emily Nussbaum (2014) sees *True Detective* through the lens of all that it fails to achieve:

> Like many critics, I was initially charmed by the show's anthology structure (eight episodes and out; next season a fresh story) and its witty chronology, which chops and dices a serial-killer investigation, using two time lines...
>
> On the other hand, you might take a close look at the show's opening credits, which suggest a simpler tale: one about heroic male outlines and close-ups of female asses. The more episodes that go by, the more I'm starting to suspect that those asses tell the real story. (n.p.)

The women in the episodes, Nussbaum (2014) explains, are "paper-thin"; they serve as women often do in art made by men—as props, as symbols, as embodiments rendered meaningful only in the context of the men who gain most of the attention when the camera isn't focused on the bared curves of women titillating and pleasing those same men—and the audience, mostly men, we may assume. "Wives and sluts and daughters—none with any interior life," she recognizes.

I think Nussbaum's explication is important, not to set *True Detective* aside, but to mine the rust from the ore. I think there is much of value here—even conceding the entrenched failures of men making art as if women truly and inevitably are "paper-thin," a simple prop to occupy [their] time"—to turn a phrase from R.E.M.'s sarcastic and bitter "The One I Love."

Many people have noted that about 5% of pop culture is brilliant and the remaining 95% is trash. From production value to acting, *True Detective* aspires to that 5%, and I think it is often successful. Even (maybe especially) with the mind disengaged in rational ways, each episode is mesmerizing for the senses. But if we approach the series as a work of collaborative art (director, writer, actors) that necessarily involves the viewer as yet another collaborator, we may find that *True Detective* is a tale possibly subtitled "It's Still a Man's (Hostile) World."

Yes, women are cheated in (and cheated on) this narrative from HBO, but women are cheated in (and cheated on) the real world also. Children too are central in the series, often as the victims they are in real life also. And if we are to decide whether to applaud *True Detective* for its often soaring craft or to denounce the series for its clichéd and tone deaf paternalism, misogyny, and chauvinism, I think we must also start with genre—not just what the series is *about* but what *form* the series is taking to shape that tale.

Taken for its commitment to form, *True Detective* is noir fiction, a genre itself both illuminating the sexism of the human condition and flawed because of the sexism of the human condition entrenched in the genre. "Noir fiction has attracted some of the best writers in the United States (mostly) and many of its aficionados are among the most sophisticated readers in the crime genre," explains Otto Penzler (2010). "Having said that, I am constantly baffled by the fact that a huge number of those readers don't seem to know what noir fiction is," adding:

> Look, noir is about losers. The characters in these existential, nihilistic tales are doomed. They may not die, but they probably should, as the life that awaits them is certain to be so ugly, so lost and lonely, that they'd be better off just curling up and getting it over with. And, let's face it, they deserve it.
>
> Pretty much everyone in a noir story (or film) is driven by greed, lust, jealousy or alienation, a path that inevitably sucks them into a downward spiral from which they cannot escape. They couldn't find the exit from their personal highway to hell if flashing neon lights pointed to a town named Hope. It is their own lack of morality that blindly drives them to ruin. (n.p.)

And there is Rust Cohle and his partner Marty Hart—deeply flawed men blinded by their lusts and trapped between justice and injustice.

Are there better ways to do that story? There was Andy Sipowicz in *NYPD Blue*, and Bruce Wayne/Batman endures—both of which are examinations of that exact dynamic of justice/injustice and flawed men. Either these are archetypal characters and narratives or evidence that the paternalism of film and literature have imposed these characters and narratives onto the world by sheer force. But as I watch the first season of the series (concluded after eight episodes), I have been reminded of John Gardner's *The Sunlight Dialogues*, a literary and complex novel that searches the human soul as well as the landscape of justice and injustice, as this excerpt shows:

> His watchmen are blind: they are all ignorant, they are all dumb dogs, they cannot bark.
>
> -Isaiah 56:10

> In late August, 1966, the city jail in Batavia, New York, held four regular prisoners, that is, four prisoners who were being kept on something more than an overnight basis. Three had been bound over for trial; the fourth was being held, by order of the court, until the County could administer a psychiatric examination. The identity of this fourth prisoner was not yet known. He seemed to be about forty. He'd been arrested on August 23rd for painting the word *love* in large, white, official-looking letters across two lanes of Oak Street, just short of the New York State Thruway. As the police were in the act of arresting him he had managed to burn all the papers in his billfold (dancing up and down, shaking like a leaf), and he refused to say now a halfway sensible word about himself, except that he was "an anarchist, a student." His face was slightly disfigured by what looked like a phosphor burn — the kind men get in wars. Whether he was actually a student (he was an anarchist, all right) there was no way of telling. He seemed too old for that, and there was no college in Batavia; but the town was not large and they knew he was not from there. (Gardner, 2007, n.p.)

The Sunlight Dialogues is hard; it demands a great deal of the reader in terms of time as well as concentration.

I think the same of *True Detective* in the sense that we must not take the work on face value only, we must not allow ourselves to be mesmerized, and we must not see the "paper-thin" women as endorsements, but mirrors of the very real ways life remains a man's (hostile) world.

And I remain committed to mining the rust from the ore in this show because we remain faced with much the same in the real world we fail to excavate and then re-imagine each day.

True Detective is flawed as is the human condition. We can do better in both, but not by giving in to the nihilism of the noir that is both creation and mirror.

It's still a man's (hostile) world, but it doesn't have to be.

29

On James Baldwin

The published work of James Baldwin as well as his impressive public presence during his life appears undervalued in academia and in popular consciousness in the U.S. Unlike Ralph Ellison or Martin Luther King, Jr., Baldwin has been pushed to the edges despite his considerable gifts with language and his perceptive mind, both confrontational, and thus here we find why Baldwin is not embraced by the mainstream.

My journey to and with Baldwin has rested on his nonfiction and his public talks—now accessible through and preserved by YouTube and the Internet. I am struck again and again how Baldwin's challenges to racism and ignorance throughout the 1960s and 1970s, specifically, speak just as directly to the twenty-first century. This is a marker of Baldwin's brilliance, and I fear, of the tragic failures of the American people.

James Baldwin at 90: "'I can't believe what you say,' the song goes, 'because I see what you do'"

January 1, 2000, exposed a truly baffling phenomenon about most humans: A silly fascination with numbers that end in zero that completely renders those humans irrational. In the land of the arbitrary where people fear that arbitrary dates can spawn the Apocalypse, the irrational can't even manage those arbitrary dates—for example, January 1, 2001 (not 2000), was the turning point of the millennium. And so we witnessed a flurry of articles about James Baldwin, mostly ignored over the past few decades, because August 2, 2014, would have been Baldwin's 90th birthday—somehow signifying he is more important now than when he would have turned 89.

As someone who has come to cherish Baldwin the essayist and Baldwin the public intellectual, I welcome this sudden burst of sunlight on one of the most daring and perceptive voices ever among writers in the U.S. I cannot stress enough in print that I find Baldwin as valuable today as ever, and often feel deeply inadequate as a writer and would-be public intellectual against the power of Baldwin.

To join in with this celebration, I want to recommend primarily that Baldwin's voice be read and viewed and heard, that we do not allow all being said and written about him to suffice. And on August 2, 2014, and beyond, we have so much of Baldwin before us, so much that we have failed to embrace, to consider carefully, to allow these words to complete their unmasking. But, of course, there is much more we must consider.

Review: *Jimmy's Blues and Other Poems,* James Baldwin

For many, James Baldwin is associated with novels, fiction. But my greatest affinity for Baldwin lies with his nonfiction and his role as a public intellectual. In the volume I co-edited, *James Baldwin: Challenging Authors*, chapter authors examine Baldwin as a powerful voice across genre and form (Henderson & Thomas, 2014). Concurrent with that volume is the publication of *Jimmy's Blues and Other Poems* (Baldwin, 2014b).

Baldwin is rarely examined as a poet, so this collection is significant for those new to Baldwin as well as those who have studied and treasure his complete canon. The slim book of poetry is inviting as a paperback—the cover an electric blue to complement the rich use of "blues" in the title—color, music, mood. "Playing by Ear, Praying for Rain: The Poetry of James Baldwin," the introduction by Nikky Finney, opens the collection passionately and parallels Baldwin's own challenging persona: "Baldwin was dangerous to everybody who had anything to hide," Finney warns (Baldwin, 2014b, p. ix).

Finney introduces readers to Baldwin as well as his poetry—his sexuality and frankness central to both:

> Uninviting Baldwin was often the excuse for the white-washing of his urgent and necessary brilliance from both the conservative black community and from whites who had never heard such a dark genius display such rich and sensory antagonism for them. Into the microphone of the world Baldwin leaned — never afraid to say it. (Baldwin, 2014b, p. xx1)

Finney emphasizes that Baldwin always remained true to himself: "They could listen in or they could ignore him, but he was never their boy, writing something they wanted to hear" (Baldwin, 2014b, p. xiii). Baldwin always sought Truth, compelled to speak the Truth, Finney explains:

> In his work he remained devoted to exposing more and more the ravages of poverty and invisibility on black and poor people....

> Baldwin was never afraid to say it in his novels, in his essays, and in his poetry—because Baldwin saw us long before we saw ourselves. (Baldwin, pp. xix, xxi)

For me, as someone drawn to Baldwin's nonfiction and videos of his speaking, these poems fits into those contexts in ways that give his poetry a vibrancy beyond the grave. Baldwin's poetry is Baldwin's *voice*.

With "Staggerlee wonders," a 16-page poem in four sections, this opening piece sparks, for me, Baldwin's "Who Is the Nigger?" from *Take This Hammer*. Simultaneously, "Staggerlee wonders" is deeply steeped in the U.S. of Baldwin's lifetime and disturbingly relevant to 2014. The speaker mentions Russia, China, the Panama Canal, and Vietnam along with "Mad Charlie," Patty Hearst, John Wayne, Ronald Reagan, and Mohammad Ali. But the historical, political, and pop culture references do not date the poem since Baldwin uses them as vehicles for his truth-telling.

The poem rarely strays too far from colors, or more accurately skin pigmentation. And Baldwin deftly blends slurs and dialects in the voice of the speaker who appears both *of* the situation as well as *above* the situation: the racial and social inequities of being Black in the U.S.:

> I wonder how they think
> the niggers made, make it,
> how come the niggers are still here.
> But, then, again, I don't think they dare
> to think of that: no:
> I'm fairly certain they don't think of that at all. (Bald-
> win, 2014b, 3.1-6)

As an opening poem, "Staggerlee wonders" represents Baldwin's complexity and richness, as well as his tensions—notably his use of Biblical references bracketed with "though theology has absolutely nothing to do/ with what I am trying to say" and "But we are not talking about belief." This poem reveals Baldwin's craft, his ability to be deeply personal and bound by his moments of history while speaking against and to the great questions of being human when humans fail their humanity.

David L. Ulin (2014) poses "James Baldwin, poet? But of course" in his review of this new collection from Baldwin, concluding:

> This new version of "Jimmy's Blues" features six poems that until now have only been available in a limited edition chapbook published after Baldwin's death. Not all of this material is equally resonant, but when he's on, Baldwin has the rare ability to contain contradictions — and not only to contain them, but also to evoke them on the page. (n.p.)

As National Poetry Month 2014 came to a close and as we moved toward Baldwin's 90th birthday in August, the time appeared to be right for exploring Baldwin the poet.

Blacked Out: "you must consider what happens to a life which finds no mirror"

> *First the air is blue and then*
> *it is bluer and then green and then*
> *black I am blacking out*
> *"Diving into the Wreck," Adrienne Rich*

Recently, I have been trying to navigate my own journey toward calling for the next phase in the education reform debate—the primary tension being between my evolving position as it rubs against my sisters and brothers in arms who remain (justifiably) passionate about confronting the misinformed celebrity of the moment or the misguided journalist of the moment.

And then Jose Vilson posted on Twitter (12:50 PM - 10 Aug 2014): "I'm increasingly unimpressed with folks who want me to get riled up about Campbell Brown but won't so much as peep about #MichaelBrown." This moment of concise clarity from Vilson was followed the next morning by a post on R.E.M.'s Facebook page, "Troopers release video showing forceful stop of musician Shamarr Allen":

> As he continued defending his troopers' actions, the Louisiana State Police chief released a dashcam video Tuesday of the forceful stop of a musician in the Lower 9th Ward.

> Shamarr Allen, a trumpeter known for his band, Shamarr Allen and the Underdawgs, has claimed in TV interviews that he felt in danger and that he was treated unfairly because of his race.

> "It's just wrong," Allen told NOLA.com | The Times-Picayune on Tuesday after watching the video. "I don't drink,

I don't smoke, I don't do none of that. I don't live wrong at all. It's just, this is the life of a black man in the Lower 9th Ward." (Martin, 2014, n.p.)

Occurring with cruel relevance at the nexus of disaster capitalism and education reform, New Orleans, Allen's "life of a black man" rests in the wake of Michael Brown's death as a black young man:

An 18-year-old Missouri man was shot dead by a cop Saturday, triggering outrage among residents who gathered at the scene shouting "kill the police."

Michael Brown was on his way to his grandmother's house in the city of Ferguson when he was gunned down at about 2:15 p.m., police and relatives said.

What prompted the Ferguson officer to open fire wasn't immediately clear.

Multiple witnesses told KMOV that Brown was unarmed and had his hands up in the air when he was cut down.

The officer "shot again and once my friend felt that shot, he turned around and put his hands in the air," said witness Dorian Johnson. "He started to get down and the officer still approached with his weapon drawn and fired several more shots." (Schapiro, 2014, n.p.)

This feeling has come to me before, a sense that outrage remains mostly token outrage, misguided outrage. Outrage over Whoopi Goldberg, Campbell Brown, and Tony Stewart filled social media, blacking out Brown and Allen as well as dozens and dozens of black men who will never be named.

50 Years Later

August of 2014 marked the month James Baldwin would have turned 90. 18 December 2014 marked 50 years since Baldwin spoke at The Non-Violent Action Committee (N-VAC). There Baldwin built a passionate message, challenging his audience with "you must consider what happens to a life which finds no mirror." Baldwin inspired author Walter Dean Myers (2014), who echoed a similar message just before his own death:

> But by then I was beginning the quest for my own identity. To an extent I found who I was in the books I read....
>
> But there was something missing. I needed more than the characters in the Bible to identify with, or even the characters in Arthur Miller's plays or my beloved Balzac. As I discovered who I was, a black teenager in a white-dominated world, I saw that these characters, these lives, were not mine. I didn't want to become the "black" representative, or some shining example of diversity. What I wanted, needed really, was to become an integral and valued part of the mosaic that I saw around me....
>
> Then I read a story by James Baldwin: "Sonny's Blues." I didn't love the story, but I was lifted by it, for it took place in Harlem, and it was a story concerned with black people like those I knew. By humanizing the people who were like me, Baldwin's story also humanized me. The story gave me a permission that I didn't know I needed, the permission to write about my own landscape, my own map. (n.p.)

There is a beauty, a symmetry to the lineage from Baldwin to Myers—and then to the countless young people for whom Myers paid it forward.

But I must pose a counter-point about Baldwin's speeches and essays: Why must Baldwin remain relevant 50 years later? Baldwin's words in 1964—"it is late in the day for this country to pretend I am not a part of it"—fit just as well in Allen's mouth, pulled over in New Orleans because he committed the crime of approaching his car and then reversing himself *while black*. And then Baldwin (1966) in "A Report from Occupied Territory":

> Here is the boy, Daniel Hamm, speaking—speaking of his country, which has sworn to bring peace and freedom to so many millions. "They don't want us here. They don't

want us—period! All they want us to do is work on these penny-ante jobs for them—and that's it. And beat our heads in whenever they feel like it. They don't want us on the street 'cause the World's Fair is coming. And they figure that all black people are hoodlums anyway, or bums, with no character of our own. So they put us off the streets, so their friends from Europe, Paris or Vietnam—wherever they come from—can come and see this supposed-to-be great city."

There is a very bitter prescience in what this boy—this "bad nigger"—is saying, and he was not born knowing it. We taught it to him in seventeen years. He is draft age now, and if he were not in jail, would very probably be on his way to Southeast Asia. Many of his contemporaries are there, and the American Government and the American press are extremely proud of them. They are dying there like flies; they are dying in the streets of all our Harlems far more hideously than flies. (n.p.)

Here Baldwin is echoing Baldwin from 1963 asking, *Who is the nigger?* in "Take This Hammer." In 2014, the list of blacked out names grew—Trayvon Martin, Jordan Davis, Michael Brown—with the unnamed list even longer, mostly ignored, invisible.

When Baldwin's 90th birthday passed, many expressed how Baldwin as a writer and powerful public voice has himself become mostly unseen, unheard, unread, but each day suggests that in the U.S. we prove Baldwin's words to be disturbingly relevant. At the end of his 1964 speech, Baldwin asserts: "[I]t is not we the American negro who is to be saved here; it is you the American republic, and you ain't got much time."

"I came to explore the wreck," explains Rich's (2002) speaker, the "wreck" a metaphor for the U.S.:

the wreck and not the story of the wreck
the thing itself and not the myth
the drowned face always staring
toward the sun…

a book of myths
in which
our names do not appear.

The narrative of the U.S. remains a redacted myth, names and lives blacked out. Yes, as Baldwin noted, "it is late in the day for this country to pretend I am not a part of it."

Let us hope it isn't too late.

30

On Superheroes: Spider-Man, Captain America, Wonder Woman

Risking hyperbole, I believe Spider-Man saved my life, much as the superhero did for Max Dillon/Electro in the film *The Amazing Spider-Man 2*—except mine was metaphorical.

Watching the sequel to the 2012 reboot that had the cinematic guts to replicate possibly the most important moment in the Spider-Man Universe (and even the entire Marvel Universe)—"The Night Gwen Stacy Died," the iconic issues 121-122 of *The Amazing Spider-Man* from June/July 1973 (Lee, Conway, Kane, & Romita, 2012)—I was powerfully forced into two minds paralleling the Peter Parker/Spider-Man duality. My 53-year-old academic mind stood in conflict with my teenaged self, a traumatic period in the 1970s when I found myself strapped into a full body brace in hopes I could overcome scoliosis without major back surgery.

In the summer of 1975, I was diagnosed with scoliosis, a medical shock tossed on top of my frail self-concept wallowing in the typical throes of adolescence. I was scrawny like Peter Parker, and I was destined not to become the strapping young male and athlete I believed my father wanted. And then, scoliosis—a curving spine and an affliction mostly common among females. Perfect.

The body brace I wore was a torture device of straps, metal

rods, and a solid plastic body mold, designed to force my spine straight so that the defective vertebrae could regain their proper shape. Wearing the brace 23 of 24 hours a day was how I spent my ninth grade, an adventure horrifying all on its own without the brace waving out to everyone, "Hey, look at the nerdy cripple kid!"

And then there was Spider-Man.

The Power of Superhero Mythology

My wonderful parents not only sacrificed financially for the brace and seemingly never-ending visits to the orthopedist, but also scrambled to find anything that would help off-set what they must have recognized as a significant blow to who I was becoming, how I saw myself.

The saving choice was comic books. And to this day, I cannot set aside how hard that must have been for my very-1950s, rugged, working-class father, a four-sport athlete in high school who lost all of his teeth to sports and fights before graduation.

At first, I began buying comics mostly to stand at the long bar separating our kitchen/living room and draw, starting with tracing, and then freehand with pencil followed by teaching myself how to ink those pencil drawing as comic book artists did. Drawing led to reading, and reading, to collecting. One of our spare bedrooms became my comic book room. In my ninth-grade wood working class at school, I built a chest to store my comics.

Those familiar with Peter Parker/Spider-Man likely already anticipate what had to happen; I fell in love with Spider-Man comics—the Holy Grail of low self-esteem nerd superhero mythologies.

Science nerd, orphaned, painfully thin and wearing glasses, Peter Parker walked into my life both as a stark reflection of my Self and a promise that transformation was possible, although with a price. But in 1975, I was dropped into the post-Gwen Stacy world of Peter Parker/Spider-Man, although that was about to change.

"The Night Gwen Stacy Died"

As my comic book fascination grew, somehow my father was snagged in the collecting bug, taking me to the local pharmacies and quick shops in my small hometown that carried comics, and even to one comic book convention in Atlanta, GA. But he also noticed comic collections being sold in the ads of the newspaper.

After seeing a newspaper ad by a 20-something still living at home but obviously making a decision to shift into adulthood, we bought about 1000 comics during two separate trips, his entire collection and essentially a complete run of Marvel comics spanning most of the 1970s.

Sorting, cataloguing, and carefully placing each comic in the prerequisite plastic bags of true comic book nerdom—these were my solitude. I also ravenously began to piece together the Peter Parker/Spider-Man Universe, significantly the death of Gwen Stacy.

In *The Power of Myth*, an interview between Bill Moyers and popular comparative religion guru Joseph Campbell, I came to understand many years later the mythological patterns in superhero comics and the science fiction I would also begin to consume. Throughout 30-plus years of teaching, I have grown more and more fascinated with genre and form; and as a reader, I can now trace my early comic book love that fed into Arthur C. Clarke to the logical path through Kurt Vonnegut and Margaret Atwood, leading then to Neil Gaiman and Haruki Murakami.

Mine is the story of the power of *secular mythology*—as Campbell has explained, the Truth beyond the narrative that need not be factually true in contrast to the literalist Christianity of my Southern childhood.

That brings me back to watching *The Amazing Spider-Man 2* as both teenage-Me and current-Me.

The updating of the Gwen Stacy arc (set in contemporary times, for example) hurts my soul, but I found the film ambitious for remaining true to the only conclusion possible in the Peter Parker/

Spider-Man narrative, the death of Gwen Stacy.

Peter Parker/Spider-Man has always been a bit about working-class insecurity, but the current-Me feels deeply uncomfortable about the failures in the original Silver Age storylines that lack sophisticated portrayals of race and gender, the latter captured in the character of Gwen Stacy, blonde, pretty, and more symbol than person.

I want to set aside, however, a critical re-reading of Spider-Man to embrace again why I believe the myth remains enduring and ultimately important, despite its many flaws. Peter Parker/Spider-Man is grounded in the central superhero motif of *duality*: the mere human and the masked superhero.

Spider-Man grew out of the seminal Marvel method—personified by Stan Lee, Steve Ditko, and Jack Kirby—of collaborative creation and genre blurring among superhero, romance, science fiction, fantasy, etc. As the domain of child, teen, and young adult males, comic books from Marvel in the 1960s succeeded by tapping into teenage angst and alienation, relationships, and the transition from formal school to work.

While often misquoted, however, the ethical dilemma of Peter Parker/Spider-Man endures: "WITH GREAT POWER THERE MUST ALSO COME — GREAT RESPONSIBILITY!"—anchoring the final panels of *Amazing Fantasy #15*, the origin of Spider-Man ("With great power comes great responsibility," 2012).

The duality motif in Spider-Man is about much more than hiding Peter behind a mask. Peter the nerd, before the spider bite, is lonely and alienated; and then, Peter Parker (Spider-Man) discovers over and over that he remains lonely and alienated not because of his super powers, but because of his great responsibility. Silver Age Spider-Man, from his origin in 1962 until the death of Gwen Stacy in 1973, confronts the mythology of the individual heart in battle with that individual's social responsibility.

Despite all the villains the Marvel bullpen could muster, Peter Parker's greatest battle has always been with himself. And the one moment that matters above all others is captured in a way that sequential art demands. In five vertical panels of *The Amazing Spider-Man* 121, Gwen Stacy falls from a bridge that leads to Spider-Man's webbing snagging her at the last second, followed by the tragic "snap" near her head (Lee, Conway, Kane, & Romita, 2012, p. 124).

The Peter Parker/Gwen Stacy storyline, despite all the camp and flaws, remains in mythological terms a disturbing and fatalistic story of the sacrifice of the individual heart against our obligations, about the limitations of the human need to connect and then protect.

As a parent/grandparent and teacher, I lay on the couch and re-watched *The Amazing Spider-Man 2* through layers of *me* and then tears because I have lived and live a very real battle with myself that is our essential humanity: how do we follow our hearts *and* offer those we love *and* the world the selflessness it deserves?

Beneath the mask of superhero lies a secular myth of duality that is each one of us, a calling not for superheroes but for every human. *All of which we can find in classic mythology about gods and humans.*

In Peter Parker's universe, Gwen Stacy had to die, and then she had to die again in the re-imagined universe of film. Gwen Stacy's neck breaking is the frailty of human limitation, ironically, at the end of Spider-Man's web—Gwen's own mortality intersecting with Peter's humanity, even as Spider-Man.

In existential terms, our passions are our suffering—the essential duality of being human. As we watch Peter Parker fight himself, it is ours to recognize that to avoid our passions is to avoid living, to avoid the very humanity that should be our joy.

Max Dillon/Electro fumbles badly the gift of being saved by Spider-Man in the film; I continue to try to find ways to serve it while parenting, grand-parenting, teaching, although I do so in the only way a human can—I race forward, I trip, I pause on the ground, and then I stand again, committed to doing better the next time.

Each time, the spider webs are metaphorical.

Eyes of the Beholder

Rain and cold at the beginning of my holiday break in late December 2014 forced me onto the bicycle trainer, something I loath doing. But to off-set that torture, I was pleased to find *Eternal Sunshine of the Spotless Mind* (2004), one of my short list of favorite movies that I watch over and over: *Blade Runner* (1982), *Solaris* (2002), *Lost Highway* (1997). These films draw me in part because of genre—surrealism, fantasy, science fiction—and the allure of considering alternate worlds, alternate consciousness, and alternate minds. But there are thematic threads pulling these films together as well.

The folding of time, or the urge and then the opportunity to relive, revisit opportunities; questions about reality and what constitutes basic humanity, specifically the human mind and will/spirit; the complicated relationship/tension with each person between mind and heart—these are dramatized and personified in those films in ways that continue to help me wrestle with those realities, but also to imagine beyond this temporal existence that is inevitably linear and cumulative.

As a university professor, I am reminded each semester of how perception shapes reality when I read my student feedback forms, almost always including *both* a few students who think I am the best professor ever *and* a few students who think I was pure torture and failure. *In the same course, the same classroom.*

As a parent, I experienced similar swings from my daughter's own perception of me, especially in those volatile teen years. Few things sting or hurt as much as disappointing those you love and care for, or for whom you are seeking to do nothing except the best in their interests.

I still flinch a bit each time—and it happens regularly—when students inform me that I seem "mean," that students are "afraid of me." How, oh how, could I possibly have sent such completely opposite messages?

Above, I touch on superheroes' internal struggles as those intersect with the duality motif common in superhero narratives (Peter Parker/Spider-Man, Bruce Wayne/Batman, etc.). But another pattern found especially in the Spider-Man narrative is the contrast between what Peter Parker/Spider-Man *intends* and how Spider-Man is *perceived*. The graphic novel *Death of the Stacys* collects *The Amazing Spider-Man* 88-92, 121-122, combining the deaths of Captain Stacy and his daughter/Peter's girlfriend Gwen (Lee, Conway, Kane, & Romita, 2012). The stories are about the collateral damage of vigilante justice.

After Captain Stacy's death, the public and Gwen begin to view Spider-Man as the villain, and thus, Peter's internal struggle over great power/great responsibility is magnified by the social construction of him as evil.

At the end of each semester, I am typically concerned about which students I have failed to reach as I intended, which students are apt to see the professor I never intended to be. This cycle is very powerful in teaching, and although somewhat anxiety triggering, it also helps drive me to be a better teacher next time; teaching affords us those opportunities of *another chance* without having to be in a dystopian future or a mind-bending David Lynch nightmare.

The winter of 2014, however, offered me the most significant moment yet in terms of having another chance: my granddaughter, who has recently begun to look at me (and everything) quite intensely. I have, then, started to contemplate what she will come to think of me—who will I be in here eyes?

I still walk extremely fast—I do almost everything extremely fast—and I admit to having raced through much of my 20s, 30s, and 40s, sometimes dragging my daughter along the way. A granddaughter's five-month-old stare has made the world slow down somewhat, or at least those eyes have asked of me: Who do I think I am? Who do I want to be? Yes, these existential questions remain throughout our lives; they are not things to be answered in youth.

In my advancing age, I am more capable, I hope, and at least I am more aware that there isn't necessarily a tension between *who we are* and *who others think we are/want us to be*, but there is the need to negotiate those parallel realities.

I will continue to gift myself re-watching the films I love, re-reading the books that move me, but through those, I hope to live *better*, recognizing that today is the only today I will have, and then again tomorrow—not as an act of regret, but as an act of being fully human.

The Epilogue in *The Amazing Spider-Man* 122 is one page of nine panels. In the wake of Gwen's death, for which he feels responsible, Peter Parker lashes out at Mary Jane, who turns to leave but in the final three wordless panels (except for the onomatopoeia "click" in the final panel) she closes the door and turns back to Peter. Mary Jane is looking at the distraught Peter. In her eyes, he is worth it (Lee, Conway, Kane, & Romita, 2012, p. 147).

I think that is what we are hoping for from the ones we love. I think that is what is ours to offer.

Should We Marvel at a Black Captain America?

Technically, in order to celebrate the first black Captain America, we'd have to resort to the sort of contortions common in the comic book universe—the time machine. *Truth: Red, White & Black* was a seven-issue series in 2003 with, yes, a black Captain America (Connors, 2013), as Joshua Yehl (2014) noted when the more recent announcement of a black Captain America surfaced: "While it is notable that this will be a black Captain America, it turns out that he's not the first. Isaiah Bradley was not only the first black Captain America, but he held the mantle even before Steve Rogers."

But the comic book universe has also been noted for decades for acting as if the same-old-same-old is *New!!!*—with reboots, and more reboots, renumbering long-standing titles, killing superheroes, having those superheroes' sidekicks take over for the dead superheroes, and then resurrecting the superheroes.

It's exhausting.

But in 2012, Marvel rebooted *Captain America* again after recently killing off Steve Rogers, having his sidekick, Bucky Barnes (aka The Winter Soldier) take over, and then bringing Rogers back, building a two-year journey to issue 25 announcing the new Captain America, as Yehl (2014) explains:

> Tonight on The Colbert Report, Marvel Comics' Chief Creative Officer Joe Quesada revealed that the new Captain America is Sam Wilson aka The Falcon.
>
> With Steve Rogers losing his super powers in the pages of his solo series written by Rick Remender, readers have been guessing who the new Captain America would be, and now we have our answer. General audiences will recognize Falcon from this summer's Captain America: The Winter Soldier movie with Anthony Mackie playing the winged superhero.

A few aspects of this move to have a black Captain America are worth noting. First, as the announcement above shows, Marvel's commitment to films is significantly impacting their comics. As well, making Sam Wilson/The Falcon the new Captain America takes a step further the decision by Marvel in 2011 to create a biracial Spider-Man in the alternate universe *Ultimate Spider-Man* (Cavna, 2011).

Sam Wilson/Captain America appears to be solidly in the mainstream Marvel Universe, and Captain America as superhero comic character reaches back to 1941.

What Good a Black Superhero?

My serious comic book collecting years were mainly in the 1970s, and I was always drawn to Captain America because The Falcon was one of my favorite characters. The series featured The Falcon by name and image on each issue's cover for most of the 1970s, in fact.

My teenaged self lurking below a few decades of the 50+ self is, then, quite excited about Sam Wilson/Captain America. However, that adolescent nerd-glee is significantly tempered by the social justice adult I have become, leaving me to ask: Should we marvel at a black Captain America?

Captain America 25 opens with Steve Rogers remembering Sam Wilson—Wilson's warrior nature, his losing both parents (minister and community organizer) and raising a brother and sister, his resilience in the face of prejudice. Notably as well, Sam Wilson was, according to Rogers, "just a man. A man dedicated to showing what one person could accomplish after a lifetime of misfortune" (Remender, Pancheco, & Immonen, 2015).

Too often, comic book narratives remain firmly entrenched in the cliché—of course, if your audience is primarily children/teens, most anything can seem new to them, and is. But where comic book narratives have failed over about eight decades is that they mostly *reflect* social norms, even the biases and stereotypes, uncritically.

Readers in the first pages of issue 25 are led to believe, as the surrounding superheroes do, that Wilson has died heroically—and Rogers is about to pronounce Wilson a martyr. Until Wilson speaks.

The issue then turns to the aging Steve Rogers, no longer invigorated by super-soldier serum, who speaks to The Avengers in order to announce Sam Wilson/Captain America. This reboot ends with Wilson/Captain America in a hybrid uniform—red, white, and blue, Captain's shield, and Falcon wings—shouting, "Avengers assemble!" (Remender, Pancheco, & Immonen, 2015).

The *All-New Captain America* 1, interestingly, comes in a variant edition—all-white cardboard cover with only the title blazoned across the top. And with a somber and powerful opening page in which Sam Wilson recalls his father's sermons and death, and his mother's murder soon after, it builds to a refrain alluding to Martin

Luther King Jr.'s dream, as the black Captain America takes flight (Remender & Immonen, 2015).

And there I am stuck about the black Captain America, built up in *Captain America* 25 as the rugged individual, the exceptional human (superhuman) who lifted himself up by his bootstraps (wings didn't hurt, there) and overcame every obstacle, including racism.

And there I am haunted by Ta-Nehisi Coates (2014):

> There is no evidence that black people are less responsible, less moral, or less upstanding in their dealings with America nor with themselves. But there is overwhelming evidence that America is irresponsible, immoral, and unconscionable in its dealings with black people and with itself. Urging African-Americans to become superhuman is great advice if you are concerned with creating extraordinary individuals. It is terrible advice if you are concerned with creating an equitable society. The black freedom struggle is not about raising a race of hyper-moral super-humans. It is about all people garnering the right to live like the normal humans they are.

If a black Captain America reinforces the "terrible advice" confronted by Coates, if black Captain American continues to perpetuate crass militarism and unbridled vigilante violence, I am left to ask, what good a black superhero?

Wonder Woman and a (Surprising) Brief History of U.S. Feminism

By sheer coincidence, or at the bidding of the book gods, I discovered a connection between U.S. poet E.E. Cummings and Wonder Woman creator William Moulton Marston:

> And then, on Thursday, June 24, 1915, an unseasonably cold day, Marston graduated from Harvard. In exercises held at Sanders Theatre, E.E. Cummings, a member of Marston's class, delivered a speech about modernism called 'The New Art' (Lepore, p. 42).

After reading Susan Cheever's (2014) compact and engaging *E.E. Cummings: A Life*, I turned to Jill Lepore's (2014) *The Secret History of Wonder Woman*, completely unaware of the connection. Paired, however, these well written and researched books are also powerful histories that reveal the possibly distorted influence of Harvard in the U.S. as well as insight into the intersection of early twentieth century intelligentsia, art, and pop culture.

My initial interest in Lepore's (2014) examination of Wonder Woman rested on my comic book background—although I was a Marvel collector in the day and *quite* not DC. However, Lepore's volume is about much more than Wonder Woman or even a solid biography of Marston; this is a somewhat shocking story about U.S. feminism and sexual politics, commercialization, pop culture, and the enduring power of myth.

As a lifelong educator who essentially hid my comic book reading/collecting throughout junior and high school, I was initially sympathetic to Marston, who struggled at Harvard:

> "I had to take a lot of courses that I hated," [William Moulton Marston] explained. English A: Rhetoric and Composition was a required course for freshmen. "I wanted to write and English A, at Harvard, wouldn't let you write," he complained. "It made you spell and punctuate. If you wrote anything you felt like writing, enjoyed writing, your paper was marked flunk in red pencil." (Lepore, 2014, p. 6)

Especially in the wake of reading again about how Cummings developed while at Harvard, I recognized in Marston's life, among his proclivities for living with and fathering children by multiple women, the development of creativity as an act *against* the norms of one's time or community.

The short version of Lepore's (2014) work is that Marston stumbled, often badly, through a career as a scholar/academic and inventor of the lie detector test until he created Wonder Woman in the foundational years of superhero comic books, the 1930s-1940s. However, what Lepore details well is that Marston's creation grew significantly from the U.S. feminism movement in the early twentieth century and through his relationships with Sadie Elizabeth Holloway, Margaret Sanger, and Olive Byrne.

While comic books and superheroes in the early decades of the medium from the 1930s and into the 1950s were often discredited and even savagely attacked as corrupting of children, Lepore builds a case not for Marston, who certainly comes off poorly as often a charlatan and essentially a self-centered hypocrite, but for the potential of pop culture as social activism.

Wonder Woman was created and written by Marston with significant help, it appears, from the many women in his life as a manifesto for women's liberation and equality—sexual liberation, reproductive rights, work-place equality. The further Wonder Woman drifted from Marston, who wrote most of her comic book adventures from the early to the late 1940s, the less that ideal held against the influence of the market, where traditional womanhood sold better than radical feminism—or least, that is what publishers believed (Lepore, 2014).

Superheroes as pop icons have entered the U.S. consciousness through many media—comic books, television (Batman, The Hulk, and Wonder Woman, notably), and film. At any given moment in history, then, the "hot" superhero is often dictated by the medium of prominence. As a result, few people are likely aware that Wonder Woman was among the first big three in superhero comics, along with Superman and Batman.

And while all three have endured 70-plus years in pop culture—with all three having peaks, valleys, and fairly dramatic reboots—Wonder Woman has certainly not maintained either Marston's original intent or the same weight as Superman and Batman. That in itself is a message about how far women have yet to go in the journey to equality so well detailed by Lepore (2014) in her portrayals of Holloway, Sanger, Byrnes, and others.

Regretfully, after reading *The Secret History of Wonder Woman*, I have a parallel question to the one I raise above about a black

Captain America: If Wonder Woman reinforces female stereotypes, objectifies women, what good a woman superhero?

Hugh Ryan (2014) shares this concern by considering both the new team who are writing and drawing Wonder Woman—David and Meredith Finch—and how that essentially spits in the face of Wonder Woman as a feminist ideal:

> That comics are a bastion of sexism is a truism so banal it almost goes without saying. But it is particularly galling to watch *the* feminist superhero be treated in such a way. The Finches have made no small point of the fact that Meredith is one of only a handful of women to ever write Wonder Woman. "I love the idea that it's a woman writing a woman," David said in an interview with *USA Today*, "because we're trying to appeal to more female readers now."
>
> Seeking to be celebrated for simply hiring a woman is tokenizing and offensive. From writer Gail Simone to artist Fiona Staples, there are incredible women already working in the industry. Let's celebrate them. The Finch's ideas of feminism, strength, and what appeals to women today seem retrograde, borderline misogynistic, and—to be frank—boring. Wonder Woman deserves better.

Cheever's biography of Cummings and Lepore's exploration of Wonder Woman reveal that truly flawed men (in these two cases) are often behind genuinely marvelous creation. And thus, the irony increases: Just as Cummings and Marston created as often flawed reactionaries, in spite of their environments, against the norms, we are now faced with *rejecting* a popular media failing not just Wonder Woman, but women once again.

Epilogue

A Child's Story: "Because she's older and the teacher, she's right and I'm not"

A child's birthday should be a ritual of joy, a celebration of living as well as of *being* a child. Rachel sits in class on her eleventh birthday in Sandra Cisneros's (Cisneros, 2004, p. 6) "Eleven," however, feeling many things except joy:

> Only today I wish I didn't have only eleven years rattling inside me like pennies in a tin Band-Aid box. Today I wish I was one hundred and two instead of eleven because if I was one hundred and two I'd have known what to say when Mrs. Price put the red sweater on my desk. I would've known how to tell her it wasn't mine instead of just sitting there with that look on my face and nothing coming out of my mouth. (p. 7)

Even before her day turns against her, Rachel has offered a glimpse of her world, the life she brings with her each day to school:

> And maybe one day when you're all grown up maybe you will need to cry like if you're three, and that's okay. That's what I tell Mama when she's sad and needs to cry. Maybe she's feeling three. (Cisneros, 2004, p. 6)

On this day of Rachel turning eleven, Mrs. Price, her math teacher, discovers a red sweater, and when the teacher asks for its owner, Sylvia Saldivar says the sweater is Rachel's. The teacher adds she has *seen* it on Rachel so she "takes the sweater and puts it right on [Rachel's] desk" (Cisneros, 2004, p. 7). In a voice that almost isn't a voice, Rachel tries to explain that the sweater isn't hers, but to no avail "[b]ecause she's older and the teacher, she's right and I'm not," Rachel recognizes (Cisneros, p. 7). Rachel struggles with her rising powerlessness and anger, crying and prompting the teacher to reprimand her:

> "Now, Rachel, that's enough," because she sees I've shoved the red sweater to the tippy-tip corner of my desk and it's hanging all over the edge like a waterfall, but I don't care.
>
> "Rachel," Mrs. Price says. She says it like she's getting mad. "You put that sweater on right now and no more nonsense."
>
> "But it's not—"
>
> "Now!" Mrs. Price says. (Cisneros, p. 8)

The sweater stinks. It itches. Rachel soon crumbles for everyone to see, a nightmare in the world of childhood:

> That's when everything I've been holding in since this morning, since when Mrs. Price put the sweater on my desk, finally lets go, and all of a sudden I'm crying in front of everybody. I wish I was invisible but I'm not. I'm eleven and it's my birthday today and I'm crying like I'm three in front of everybody. I put my head down on the desk and bury my face in my stupid clown-sweater arms. My face all hot and spit coming out of my mouth because I can't stop the little animal noises from coming out of me, until there aren't any more tears left in my eyes, and it's just my body shaking like when you have the hiccups, and my whole head hurts like when you drink milk too fast. (Cisneros, 2004, p. 9)

And then, Phyllis Lopez claims the sweater—adding insult to

Rachel's embarrassment. But "Mrs. Price pretends like everything's okay" even though, for Rachel, "it's too late," her birthday has been ruined (Cisneros, 2004, p. 9).

While it may be compelling to read "Eleven" as a powerful narrative of a child's ruined birthday, it is important not to ignore how Cisneros offers us all important messages about how schools and teachers impact the children they are intended to serve, how teachers often become *calloused* and hurtful especially as they fail to recognize the frailty and humanity of each child. Here, then, are some lessons from the story:

- Children do not and cannot leave their lives behind when they walk through the doors of a school or a classroom. To pretend that they can is dehumanizing and hurtful.

- How a child *feels* about the world and her/himself is at least as important if not more important than what a child *thinks* about the world. Emotions should not be ignored or marginalized as "childish." A child's affective and cognitive selves are dialogic and inseparable.

- The authoritarian teacher is the failed teacher.

- "We know of course there's really no such thing as the 'voiceless'. There are only the deliberately silenced, or the preferably unheard," cautions Arundhati Roy in her 2004 Sydney Peace Prize lecture.

- All education should begin with the child, and then always hold the dignity of each child sacred.

Rachel knows a certain sadness in her home, and on her eleventh birthday, her teacher, her peers, and her school make her want to disappear, and force her to deny her*self* and her *childhood*:

I'm eleven today. I'm eleven, ten, nine, eight, seven, six, five, four, three, two, and one, but I wish I was one hundred and two. I wish I was anything but eleven, because I want today to be far away already, far away like a runaway balloon, like a tiny *o* in the sky, so tiny-tiny you have to close your eyes to see it. (Cisneros, 2004, p. 9)

Every child that we teach needs our relentless love and patience because childhood is a *frail becoming* that leads to this thing we call adulthood, which we fail each time we allow ourselves to be callous to the laughter or tears of a child—especially when we do so in the name of education.

I teach and I write, I think, because I love students (represented by Rachel), or more accurately, the *student of each of us*—the eternal child, the Other, the marginalized, and the silenced. So I end this book, this collection of pieces, seeking ways to make literature and texts of all kinds those words we turn to when, like Rachel, we know we are right but feel "[b]ecause she's older and the teacher, she's right and I'm not."

Armed with books and films and words of all kinds, like the academics and scholars at the end of Bradbury's *Fahrenheit 451* who have memorized precious, precious books, we can join each other in refrain:

Beware the roadbuilders.

References

2013 data book: State trends in child well-being. (2013). *Kids Count.* The Annie E. Casey Foundation. Retrieved from http://www.aecf.org/m/resourcedoc/AECF-2013KIDSCOUNTDataBook-2013.pdf

Abad-Santos, A. (2013, October 22). The best X-Men stories you're going to see aren't called X-Men stories. *The Wire.* Retrieved from http://www.thewire.com/entertainment/2013/10/best-x-men-stories-youre-going-see-arent-called-x-men-stories/70807/

Adams, C.J., Robelen, E.W., & Shah, N. (2012, March 6). Civil rights data show retention disparities. *Education Week.* Retrieved from http://www.edweek.org/ew/articles/2012/03/07/23data_ep.h31.html

Adelson, A. (2014, June 30). NCAA again investigating UNC. ESPN. Retrieved from http://espn.go.com/college-sports/story/_/id/11157920/ncaa-reopens-investigation-academic-scandal-north-carolina

Alexander, M. (2012). *The new Jim Crow: Mass incarceration in the age of colorblindness* (Rev. ed.). New York, NY: New Press.

Anderson, M.T. (2012). *Feed.* Somerville, MA: Candlewick.

Applebee, A.N., & Langer, J.A. (2013). *Writing instruction that works: Proven methods for middle and high school classrooms.* New York, NY: Teachers College Press.

Asimov, I. (1980, January 21). A cult of ignorance. *Newsweek,* p. 19.

Attenborough, R., director, & Briley, J., writer. (1982) *Gandhi.* UK: International Film Investors.

Atwood, M. (2013, January 18). My hero: George Orwell by Margaret Atwood. *The Guardian.* Retrieved from http://www.guardian.co.uk/books/2013/jan/18/my-hero-george-orwell-atwood

Atwood, M. (2012, January 20). Haunted by The Handmaid's Tale. *The Guardian.* Retrieved from http://www.guardian.co.uk/books/2012/jan/20/handmaids-tale-margaret-atwood

Atwood, M. (2011). *In other worlds: SF and the human imagination.* New York: Nan A.

Talese.

Atwood, M. (2005). *Writing with intent: Essays, reviews, personal prose--1983-2005.* New York: Carroll and Graf.

Atwood, M. (1998). *The handmaid's tale.* New York: Anchor Books.

Baker, B. (2012, January 7). Fire first, ask questions later? Comments on recent teacher effectiveness studies [Web log]. *School Finance 101.* Retrieved from http://school-finance101.wordpress.com/2012/01/07/fire-first-ask-questions-later-comments-on-recent-teacher-effectiveness-studies/

Baldwin, J. (2014a). *James Baldwin: The last interview and other conversations.* Brooklyn, NY: Melville House.

Baldwin, J. (2014b). *Jimmy's blues and other poems.* Boston, MA: Beacon Press.

Baldwin, J. (1966, July 11). A report from occupied territory. *The Nation.* Retrieved from http://www.thenation.com/article/159618/report-occupied-territory

Bazelon, E. (2013, December 6). How did Jameis Winston evade a rape charge? *Slate.* Retrieved from http://www.slate.com/articles/sports/jurisprudence/2013/12/jameis_winston_sexual_assault_how_did_the_florida_state_quarterback_evade.html

Bennett, B. (2014, March 27). Northwestern players get union vote. EPSN. Retrieved from http://espn.go.com/college-football/story/_/id/10677763/northwestern-wildcats-football-players-win-bid-unionize

Benson, H. (2005, March 29). In a world of violence, inequality and moral chaos, Adrienne Rich's voice will be neither silent nor content. *SFGate.* Retrieved from http://www.sfgate.com/entertainment/article/In-a-world-of-violence-inequality-and-moral-2689262.php

Bessie, A. (2013, November 14). School‾: Resist the feed, feed the resistance. *Truthout.* Retrieved from http://truth-out.org/speakout/item/20045-school-resist-the-feed-feed-the-resistance

Bessie, A. (2010, December 30). To fix education: Fire human teachers, hire holograms. *BuzzFlash.com.* Retrieved from http://www.truth-out.org/buzzflash/commentary/to-fix-education-fire-human-teachers-hire-holograms-satire/10270-to-fix-education-fire-human-teachers-hire-holograms-satire

Bessie, A. (2010, October 15). The myth of the bad teacher. *Truthout.* Retrieved from http://archive.truthout.org/the-myth-bad-teacher64223

Bigelow, B., & Menkart, D. (2013, January 26). Honoring Howard Zinn's life by teaching people's history. Zinn Education Project. Retrieved from http://zinnedproject.org/2013/01/honoring-howard-zinns-life-by-teaching-peoples-history/

Bingham, C., Dejene, A., Krilic, A., & Sadowski, E. (2012). Can the taught book speak? In C.W. Ruitenberg, ed., *Philosophy of Education 2012* (pp. 199-206). Urbana, IL: Philosophy of Education Society. Retrieved from http://ojs.ed.uiuc.edu/index.php/pes/article/viewFile/3625/1246

Boren, C. (2013, December 5). Jameis Winston will not be charged. *The Washington Post*. Retrieved from http://www.washingtonpost.com/blogs/early-lead/wp/2013/12/05/jameis-winston-will-not-be-charged/

Bracey, G. W. (2003). April foolishness: The 20th anniversary of *A Nation at Risk*. *Phi Delta Kappan, 84*(8), 616-621.

Bradbury, R. (2013). *Fahrenheit 451*. 60th anniversary ed. New York: Simon and Schuster.

Brennan, C. (2013, December 5). Brennan: Laughter about Winston sex assault case disturbing. *USA Today*. Retrieved from http://www.usatoday.com/story/sports/ncaaf/2013/12/05/christine-brennan-jameis-winston-case/3881903/

Brooks, M. (2007). *World war Z: An oral history of the zombie war*. New York: Broadway Paperbacks.

Brown, M. (2013, October 14). Neil Gaiman: Let children read the books they love. *The Guardian*. Retrieved from http://www.theguardian.com/books/2013/oct/14/neil-gaiman-children-books-reading-lecture

Bruenig, M. (2013, June 13). What's more important: a college degree or being born rich? *Matt Bruenig Politics*. Retrieved from http://mattbruenig.com/2013/06/13/whats-more-important-a-college-degree-or-being-born-rich/

Buck, S. (2006, September 5). Other people's children [Web log]. *The Buck Stops Here*. Retrieved from http://stuartbuck.blogspot.com/2006/09/other-peoples-children.html

Bump, P. (2014, March 10). People — including cops — see black kids as less innocent and less young than white kids. *The Wire*. Retrieved from http://www.thewire.com/politics/2014/03/people-including-cops-view-black-kids-less-innocent-and-less-young-white-kids/359026/

Carnevale. A.P., & Strohl, J. (2013, July). Separate & unequal: How higher education reinforces the intergenerational reproduction of white racial privilege. Georgetown University. Georgetown Public Policy Institute. Retrieved from https://georgetown.app.box.com/s/vjfxgz8tlxgwd10c5xn2

Carr, S. (2013). *Hope against hope: Three schools, one city, and the struggle to educate America's children*. New York, NY: Bloomsbury Press.

Cavna, M. (2011, August 4). Miles Morales & me: Why the new biracial Spider-Man matters [Web log]. Comic Riffs. *The Washington Post*. Retrieved from http://www.washingtonpost.com/blogs/comic-riffs/post/miles-morales-and-me-why-the-new-biracial-spider-man-matters/2011/08/04/gIQABzlGuI_blog.html

Cheever, S. (2014). *E.E. Cummings: A life*. New York, NY: Pantheon Books.

Cisneros, S. (2004). *Vintage Cisneros*. New York: Vintage Books.

Classen, C., & Howes, D. (2014). Margaret Atwood: Two-headed woman. *Canadian Icon*. Retrieved from http://canadianicon.org/table-of-contents/margaret-atwood-two-headed-woman/

Coates, T. (2014, March 21). Black pathology and the closing of the progressive mind. *The Atlantic*. Retrieved from http://www.theatlantic.com/politics/archive/2014/03/black-pathology-and-the-closing-of-the-progressive-mind/284523/

Cody, A. (2013, May 16). Dystopia: A possible future of teacher evaluation. Living in Dialogue. *Education Week/ Teacher*. Retrieved from http://blogs.edweek.org/teachers/living-in-dialogue/2013/05/dystopia_a_possible_future_of_.html

Collins, J. (2014, June 20). Why NBA center Jason Collins is coming out now. *Sports Illustrated*. Retrieved from http://sportsillustrated.cnn.com/magazine/news/20130429/jason-collins-gay-nba-player/

Collins, S. (2010). *Mocking jay*. New York: Scholastic Press.

Collins, S. (2009). *Catching fire*. New York: Scholastic Press.

Collins, S. (2008). *The hunger games*. New York: Scholastic Inc.

Connelly, S. (2013, June 16). "The ocean at the end of the lane": Book review. *Daily News*. Retrieved from http://www.nydailynews.com/entertainment/music-arts/ocean-lane-book-review-article-1.1369838

Connors, S.P. (2013). "It's a bird . . . It's a plane . . . It's . . . a comic book in theclassroom?": Truth: Red, white, and black as test case for teaching superhero comics. In P. L. Thomas (Ed.), *Science fiction and speculative fiction: Challenging genres* (pp. 165-184). Boston, MA: Sense Publishers.

Cottom, T.M. (2014, May 29). No, college isn't the answer. Reparations are. *The Washington Post*. Retrieved from http://www.washingtonpost.com/posteverything/wp/2014/05/29/no-college-isnt-the-answer-reparations-are/

Cronin, D., & Lewin, B. (2000). *Click, clack, moo: Cows that type*. New York, NY: Athenuem Books for Young Readers.

Cuaron, A., director/writer. (2013). *Gravity*. USA: Warner Brothers.

Cummings, E.E. (1991). anyone lived in a pretty how town. *Poets.org*. Retrieved from http://www.poets.org/poetsorg/poem/anyone-lived-pretty-how-town

DeBellis, R. J., & Zdanawicz, M. (2000, November). *Bacteria battle back: Addressing antibiotic resistance*. Boston: Massachusetts College of Pharmacy and Health Science. Retrieved from www.tufts.edu/med/apua/research/completed_projects_5_1888322820.pdf

Debs, E.V. (1918, September 18). Statement to the court: Upon being convicted of violating the Sedition Act. E.V. Debs Internet Archive. Retrieved from http://www.dailykos.com/story/2012/03/12/1073629/-Eugene-V-Debs-Statement-September-18-1918

Deleuze, G. (1992, Winter). Postscript on the societies of control. *October, 59*, 3-7.

Delpit, L. (2006). *Other people's children: Cultural conflict in the classroom*. New York: New Press.

Delpit, L.D. (1988). *The silenced dialogue: Power and pedagogy in educating other people's children. Harvard Educational Review, 58,* 280–298.

Di Carlo, M. (2012a, January 8). The persistence of both teacher effects and misinterpretations of research about them. *Shanker Blog.* Retrieved from http://shanker-blog.org/?p=74

Dodenhoff, D. (2007, October). Fixing the Milwaukee public schools: The limits of parent-driven reform. *Wisconsin Policy Research Institute Report, 20*(8). Retrieved from http://www.wpri.org/WPRI-Files/Special-Reports/Reports-Documents/vol20no8.pdf

Domhoff, G. W. (2008/2013). Wealth, income, and power. *Who Rules America?* Retrieved from http://www2.ucsc.edu/whorulesamerica/power/wealth.html

Dreier, P. (2013, January 21). Martin Luther King was a radical, not a saint. *Common Dreams.* Retrieved from http://www.commondreams.org/view/2013/01/21-2

Dudley-Marling, C. (2007, Winter). Return of the deficit. *Journal of Educational Controversy, 2*(1), Retrieved from http://www.wce.wwu.edu/Resources/CEP/eJournal/v002n001/a004.shtml

Dudley-Marling, C., & Lucas, K. (2009, May). Pathologizing the language and culture of poor children. *Language Arts, 86*(5), 362-370.

Duncan, A. (2010, December 7). Secretary Arne Duncan's remarks at OECD's release of the Program for International Student Assessment (PISA) 2009 results. Washington DC: U. S. Department of Education. Retrieved from http://www.ed.gov/news/speeches/secretary-arne-duncans-remarks-oecds-release-program-international-student-assessment-

Eggers, D. (2013). *The circle.* New York: Knopf.

Ellison, R. (2003). *The collected essay of Ralph Ellison.* Ed. J.F. Callahan. New York: The Modern Library.

Ellison, R. (1995). *Invisible man.* New York: Vintage International.

Eugenides, J. (2003). *Middlesex: A novel.* New York, NY: Picador.

Fassler, J. (2014, June 24). *The Leftovers, Our Town,* and the brutal power of ordinary details. *The Atlantic.* Retrieved from http://www.theatlantic.com/entertainment/archive/2014/06/the-brutal-power-of-the-ordinary-details/373327/

Ferguson, D.E. (2013/2014, Winter). Martin Luther King Jr. and the Common Core: A critical reading of close reading. *Rethinking Schools, 28*(2). Retrieved from http://www.rethinkingschools.org/archive/28_02/28_02_ferguson.shtml

Fishkin, J. (2014, April 28). Bottlenecks: The real opportunity challenge. Brookings. Retrieved from http://www.brookings.edu/blogs/social-mobility-memos/posts/2014/04/28-bottlenecks-real-opportunity-challenge

Fitzgerald, F.S. (2004). *The great Gatsby.* New York: Scribner.

Florio, M. (2009, December 13). Chargers' Cromartie singled out in ESPN report on Florida State. Pro Football Talk. *NBC Sports.* Retrieved from http://profootball-talk.nbcsports.com/2009/12/13/chargers-cromartie-singled-out-in-espn-report-on-florida-state/

Foucault, M. (1984). *The Foucault reader.* Ed. P. Rabinow. New York, NY: Pantheon Books.

Fox, M. (2012, March 28). Adrienne Rich, influential feminist poet, dies at 82. *The New York Times.* Retrieved from http://www.nytimes.com/2012/03/29/books/adrienne-rich-feminist-poet-and-author-dies-at-82.html

Freire, P. (1998). *Pedagogy of freedom: Ethics, democracy, and civic courage* (P. Clarke, Trans.). Lanham, MD: Rowman and Littlefield.

Freire, P. (1993). *Pedagogy of the oppressed.* New York, NY: Continuum.

Gaiman, N. (2013, October 14). Neil Gaiman lecture in full: Reading and obligation. *The Reading Agency.* Retrieved from http://readingagency.org.uk/news/blog/neil-gaiman-lecture-in-full.html

Gaiman, N. (2013). *The ocean at the end of the lane.* New York: William Morrow.

Gardner, J. (2007, June 4). Excerpt: "The sunlight dialogues." *NPR.* Retrieved from http://www.npr.org/templates/story/story.php?storyId=10530224

Gardner, W. (2012, January 27). Who determines what is taught? [Web lob]. Walt Gardner's Reality Check. *Education Week.* Retrieved from http://blogs.edweek.org/edweek/walt_gardners_reality_check/2012/01/who_determines_what_is_taught.html

Gay, R. (2014). *An untamed state.* New York: Black Cat.

Gay, R. (2010, October 1). There is no "e" in zombie which means there can be no you or me. *Guernica.* Retrieved from http://www.guernicamag.com/fiction/gay_10_1_10/

"A gesture can blow up a town." (2011, August 2). [Web log]. *South/South.* Retrieved from http://southissouth.wordpress.com/2011/08/02/a-gesture-can-blow-up-a-town/

Gilliam, W. S. (2005, May). Pre-kindergarteners left behind: Expulsion rates in state prekindergarten systems. FCD Policy Brief Series No. 3. Yale University Child Study Center. Retrieved from http://www.hartfordinfo.org/issues/wsd/education/NationalPreKExpulsionPaper.pdf

Goff, P.A., et al. (2014). The essence of innocence: Consequences of dehumanizing black children. *Journal of Personality and Social Psychology, 106*(4) 526-545). Retrieved from http://www.apa.org/pubs/journals/releases/psp-a0035663.pdf

Goldberg, L. (2013, October 27). "Walking dead" dissection: Robert Kirkman talks Carol's shocking confession. *The Hollywood Reporter.* Retrieved from http://www.hollywoodreporter.com/live-feed/walking-dead-season-4-spoilers-651084

Gonzolez, M. (2014, March 17). The walking dead recap: Look at the flowers. *Entertainment Weekly*. Retrieved from http://tvrecaps.ew.com/recap/the-walking-dead-recap-season-4-episode-14/

Gonzolez, M. (2013, October 21). The walking dead recap: Under my skin. *Entertainment Weekly*. Retrieved from http://tvrecaps.ew.com/recap/the-walking-dead-season-4-episode-2/

Graves, B. (2010, March 23). Prisons don't use reading scores to predict future inmate populations. *The Oregonian*. Retrieved from http://www.oregonlive.com/education/index.ssf/2010/03/prisons_dont_use_reading_score.html

Green. J. (2013, March 8). Two against the world. *The New York Times*. Retrieved from http://www.nytimes.com/2013/03/10/books/review/eleanor-park-by-rainbow-rowell.html

Greene, M. (1995). *Releasing the imagination: Essays on education, the arts, and social change*. San Francisco, CA: Jossey-Bass.

Hart, B., & Risley, T. R. (1995). *Meaningful differences in the everyday experiences of young American children*. Baltimore, MD: Brookes.

Heilig, J. V., & Jez, S. J. (2010). Teach for America: A review of the evidence. Boulder and Tempe: Education and the Public Interest Center & Education Policy Research Unit. Retrieved from http://epicpolicy.org/publication/teach-foramerica

Henderson, S., & Thomas, P.L. (Eds.). (2014). *Challenging authors: James Baldwin*. Netherlands: Sense Publishers.

Hess, R. (2013, January 25). "Counting on character" as NHA [Web log]. Rick Hess Straight Up. *Education Week*. Retrieved from http://blogs.edweek.org/edweek/rick_hess_straight_up/2013/01/counting_on_character_at_nha.html

Hicks, G. (1952, August 17). The engineers take over. *The New York Times*. Retrieved from http://www.nytimes.com/books/97/09/28/lifetimes/vonnegut-player.html

Holton, G. (2003, April 25). An insider's view of "A Nation at Risk" and why it still matters. *The Chronicle Review, 49*(33), B13. Retrieved from http://chronicle.com/article/An-Insider-s-View-of-A/20696

Hopkins, N. (2013, March 5). Is school reform about replacing blackness? The Answer Sheet. *The Washington Post*. Retrieved from http://www.washingtonpost.com/blogs/answer-sheet/wp/2013/03/05/is-school-reform-about-replacing-blackness/

Jacobs, J. (2013, January). Counting on character: National Heritage Academies and civic Education. Policy Brief 5. AEI Program on American Citizenship. Retrieved from http://www.citizenship-aei.org/wp-content/uploads/American-Citizenship_Counting-on-Character-05_Jacobs.pdf

Johnson, E.M. (2013, May 3). Survival of the…nicest? Check out the other theory of evolution. *Yes!* Retrieved from http://www.yesmagazine.org/issues/how-cooperatives-are-driving-the-new-economy/survival-of-the-nicest-the-other-theory-of-evolution

Judd, A., & Torres, K. (2010, August 3). Commission reports evidence of cheating on tests. *The Atlanta Journal-Constitution*. Retrieved from http://www.ajc.com/news/news/local/investigative-panel-calls-cultural-changes-superin/nW69H/

Kafka, F. (2007, February 7). In the penal colony. Trans. I. Johnston. Retrieved from http://records.viu.ca/~johnstoi/kafka/inthepenalcolony.htm

Kappala-Ramsamy, G. (2013, May 11). Barbara Kingsolver: "Motherhood is so sentimentalised in our culture." *The Guardian*. Retrieved from http://www.theguardian.com/books/2013/may/11/barbara-kingsolver-interview-flight-behaviour

Kimberly, M. (2014, June 1). Police target black children. *Truthout*. Retrieved from http://truth-out.org/opinion/item/24063-police-target-black-children

King, S. (2013). *Doctor sleep*. New York: Scribner.

Kingsolver, B. (2012). *Flight behavior*. New York: Harper Perennial.

Kingsolver, B. (1998). *Another America/otra America*. Berkeley, CA: Seal Press.

Kingsolver, B. (1992, February 9). Everybody's somebody's baby. *The New York Times*. Retrieved from http://www.nytimes.com/books/98/10/18/specials/kingsolver-hers.html

Kirkman, R., & Moore, T. (2006). *The walking dead, vol. 1: Days gone by*. Berkeley, CA: Image Comics, Inc.

Klugman, B., & Sternthal, L., directors. (2012). *The words*. USA: Also Known as Pictures.

Krashen, S. (2011, January 2). The freedom in education act. *SusanOhanian.org*. Retrieved from http://susanohanian.org/outrage_fetch.php?id=840

LaBrant, L. (1949, May). Analysis of clichés and abstractions. *English Journal, 38*(5), 275-278.

Landsberg, M. (2009, May 31). Spitting in the eye of mainstream education. *The Los Angeles Times*. Retrieved from http://www.latimes.com/local/la-me-charter31-2009may31-story.html

Larsson, S. (2012). *The girl who kicked the hornet's nest*. New York: Vintage Crime.

Layton, L. (2014, May 28). In New Orleans, major school district closes traditional public schools for good. *The Washington Post*. Retrieved from http://www.washingtonpost.com/local/education/in-new-orleans-traditional-public-schools-close-for-good/2014/05/28/ae4f5724-e5de-11e3-8f90-73e071f3d637_story.html

Lee, N. (2014, July 7). Ride like a girl [Web log]. *Medium*. Retrieved from https://medium.com/@nkkl/ride-like-a-girl-1d5524e25d3a

Lee, S. (writer), Conway, G. (writer), Kane, G. (penciler), & Romita, Sr., J. (penciler). (2012). *Death of the Stacys*. New York, NY: Marvel Worldwide, Inc.

Le Guin, U.K. (1975). *The wind's twelve quarters*. New York, NY: Harper Perennial.

Lepore, J. (2014). *The secret history of Wonder Woman*. New York, NY: Alfred A. Knopf.

Lewin, T. (2012, March 6). Black students face more discipline, data suggests. *The New York Times*. Retrieved from http://www.nytimes.com/2012/03/06/education/black-students-face-more-harsh-discipline-data-shows.html

Lienhard, J.H. (1997). No.1199: Gallop poll. *Engines of Our Ingenuity*. Retrieved from http://www.uh.edu/engines/epi1199.htm

Lowry, A. (2012, January 6). Big study links good teachers to lasting gains. *The New York Times*. Retrieved from http://www.nytimes.com/2012/01/06/education/big-study-links-good-teachers-to-lasting-gain.html

Martin, N. (2014, August 5). Troopers release video showing forceful stop of musician Shamarr Allen. *The Times-Picayune*. Retrieved from http://www.nola.com/crime/index.ssf/2014/08/state_police_releases_dashcam.html

Mathis, W. (2012). Common Core State Standards. Research-based options for education policymaking. Boulder, CO: National Education Policy Center. Retrieved from http://nepc.colorado.edu/files/pb-options-2-commcore-final.pdf

McAdams, J. (2007, October 29). WPRI school choice study: Clarification or recantation? [Web log]. *Marquette Warrior*. Retrieved from http://www.mu-warrior.blogspot.com/2007/10/wpri-school-choice-study-clarification.html

McDonough, K. (2014, March 11). Study: Police see black children as less innocent and less young than white children. *Salon*. Retrieved from http://www.salon.com/2014/03/11/study_police_see_black_children_as_less_innocent_and_less_young_than_white_children/

McKenzie, M. (2014, June 2). The white teachers I wish I never had [Web log]. *Black Girl Dangerous*. Retrieved from http://www.blackgirldangerous.org/2014/06/white-teachers-wish-never/

Meier, D. (2013a, March 4). Harass them til it hurts! [Web log]. *Deborah Meier on Education*. Retrieved from http://deborahmeier.com/2013/03/04/harass-them-til-it-hurts/

Meier, D. (2013b, March 1). Where we disagree: Let's discuss [Web log]. Bridging Differences. *Education Week*. Retrieved from http://blogs.edweek.org/edweek/Bridging-Differences/2013/03/where_we_disagree_lets_discuss.html

Michell, R., Dir., & Curtis, R., Writer. (1999). *Notting hill*. United Kingdom: Polygram Filmed Entertainment.

Michie, G. (2011, January 9). How to be taken seriously as a reformer (don't be an educator) [Web log]. The Answer Sheet. *The Washington Post*. Retrieved from http://voices.washingtonpost.com/answer-sheet/guest-bloggers/how-to-be-taken-seriously-as-a.html

Mullainathan, S., & Shafir, E. (2013). *Scarcity: Why having too little means so much*. New York: Holt.

Myers, W.D. (2014, March 15). Where are the people of color in children's books? *The*

New York Times. Retrieved from http://www.nytimes.com/2014/03/16/opinion/sunday/where-are-the-people-of-color-in-childrens-books.html

Niccol, A., director/writer. (2011). *In time.* USA: Regency Enterprises.

Noah, T. (2010, September 3). The United States of inequality. *Slate.* Retrieved from http://www.slate.com/articles/news_and_politics/the_great_divergence/features/2010/the_united_states_of_inequality/introducing_the_great_divergence.html

Nolan, K. (2011). *Police in the hallways: Discipline in an urban high school.* Minneapolis, MN: University of Minnesota Press.

Nussbaum, E. (2014, March 3). Cool story, bro. *The New Yorker.* Retrieved from http://www.newyorker.com/arts/critics/television/2014/03/03/140303crte_television_nussbaum

Obama, B. (2012). The 2012 State of the Union: An America built to last. Retrieved from http://www.whitehouse.gov/state-of-the-union-2012

O'Hara, B. (2012, November 8). How did Nate Silver predict the US election? *The Guardian.* Retrieved from http://www.theguardian.com/science/grrlscientist/2012/nov/08/nate-sliver-predict-us-election

Ong, S., et al. (2007, September). Antibiotic use for emergency department patients with upper respiratory infections: Prescribing practices, patient expectations, and patient satisfaction. *Annals of Emergency Medicine, 50*(3), 213-220.

Parramore, L. S. (2012, July 12). Fifty shades of capitalism: Pain and bondage in the American workplace. *AlterNet.* Retrieved from http://www.alternet.org/story/156291/fifty_shades_of_capitalism_pain_and_bondage_in_the_american_workplace

Penny, L. (2013, November 30). Laurie Penny on girl trouble: We care about young women as symbols, not as people. *New Statesman.* Retrieved from http://www.newstatesman.com/media/2013/11/girl-trouble-we-care-about-young-women-symbols-not-people

Penny, L. (2013, October 11). The Miley Cyrus complex – an ontology of slut shaming. *New Statesman.* Retrieved from http://www.newstatesman.com/music-and-performance/2013/10/miley-cyrus-complex-ontology-slut shaming

Penzler, O. (2010, August 10). Noir fiction is about losers, not private eyes. *The Huffington Post.* Retrieved from http://www.huffingtonpost.com/otto-penzler/noir-fiction-is-about-los_b_676200.html

Perrotta, T. (2011). *The leftovers.* New York: St. Martin's Press.

Perry, A. (2014, June 2). The education-reform movement is too white to do any good. *The Washington Post.* Retrieved from http://www.washingtonpost.com/posteverything/wp/2014/06/02/the-education-reform-movement-is-too-white-to-do-any-good/

Perry, A. (2014, January 6). Black athletes must pick up the ball on graduation rates.

The Hechinger Report. Retrieved from http://hechingerreport.org/content/black-athletes-must-pick-up-the-ball-on-graduation-rates_14363/

Peske, H. G., & Haycock, K. (2006, June). *Teaching inequality: How poor and minority students are shortchanged on teacher quality*. Washington DC: The Education Trust, Inc. Retrieved from http://www.edtrust.org/sites/edtrust.org/files/publications/files/TQReportJune2006.pdf

Petrilli, M.J. (2011, May 4). Alfie Kohn: Read your Lisa Delpit [Web log]. Flypaper. Thomas B. Fordham Institute. Retrieved from http://www.educationgadfly.net/flypaper/2011/05/alfie-kohn-read-your-lisa-delpit/

Piketty, T. (2014). *Capital in the twenty-first century*. Cambridge, MA: Belknap Press.

Pondiscio, R. (2014, February 6). Be excellent at simple [Web log]. Bridging Differences. *Education Week*. Retrieved from http://blogs.edweek.org/edweek/Bridging-Differences/2014/02/be_excellent_at_simple.html

Popova, M. (2014, June 6). Kafka on books and what reading does for the human soul. *brain pickings*. Retrieved from http://www.brainpickings.org/index.php/2014/06/06/kafka-on-books-and-reading/

Randerson, J. (2008, May 12). Childish superstition: Einstein's letter makes vie of religion relatively clear. *The Guardian*. Retrieved from http://www.theguardian.com/science/2008/may/12/peopleinscience.religion

Ravitch, D. (2013, March 29). Vouchers don't work: Evidence from Milwaukee [Web log]. *Diane Ravitch's Blog*. Retrieved from http://dianeravitch.net/2013/03/29/vouchers-dont-work-evidence-from-milwaukee/

Ravitch, D. (2012, January 31). Does President Obama know what Race to the Top is? [Web log]. Bridging Differences. *Education Week*. Retrieved from http://blogs.edweek.org/edweek/Bridging-Differences/2012/01/does_president_obama_know_what.html

Reardon, S. F. (2013, April 27). No rich child left behind. *The New York Times*. Retrieved from http://opinionator.blogs.nytimes.com/2013/04/27/no-rich-child-left-behind/

Redeaux, M. (2011). The culture of poverty reloaded. *Monthly Review, 63*(3). Retrieved from http://monthlyreview.org/2011/07/01/the-culture-of-poverty-reloaded

Remender, R. (writer), & Immonen, S. (penciler). (2015, January). *All-New Captain America 1*. New York, NY: Marvel Worldwide, Inc.

Remender, R. (writer), Pancheco, C. (penciler), & Immonen, S. (penciler). (2015, January). *Captain America 25*. New York, NY: Marvel Worldwide, Inc.

Rich, A. (2002). *The fact of a doorframe: Selected poems 1950-2001*. New York, NY: W. W. Norton and Company.

Rich, A. (2002). The school among the ruins. *Seattle Journal for Social Justice, 1*(3), 535-539. Retrieved from http://digitalcommons.law.seattleu.edu/sjsj/vol1/iss3/50

Rich, A. (2001). *Arts of the possible: Essays and conversations*. New York, NY: W. W. Norton and Company.

Rich, A. (1994). *Diving into the wreck: Poems 1971-1972*. New York: W.W. Norton and Company.

Roberts, A. (2103, December 3). Best science fiction books of 2013. *The Guardian*. Retrieved from http://www.theguardian.com/books/2013/dec/03/best-science-fiction-2013

Robinson, C. (2014, January 22). The loneliness of the long-distance reader. *The New York Times*. Retrieved from http://www.nytimes.com/2014/01/05/opinion/sunday/the-loneliness-of-the-long-distance-reader.html

Rosenblatt, L. (1995). *Literature as exploration*. 5th ed. New York: The Modern Language Association of America.

Ross, D. (2014, March 16). "The walking dead": Did the show go too far? *Entertainment Weekly*. Retrieved from http://popwatch.ew.com/2014/03/16/walking-dead-the-grove/

Rothman, L. (2012, November 1). A cultural history of mansplaining. *The Atlantic*. Retrieved from http://www.theatlantic.com/sexes/archive/2012/11/a-cultural-history-of-mansplaining/264380/

Rowell, R. (2013). *Eleanor & Park*. New York: St. Martin's Press.

Roy, A. (2004, November 8). The 2004 Sydney Peace Prize lecture. *Real Voice*. Retrieved from http://realvoice.blogspot.com/2004/11/arundhati-roy-2004-sydney-peace-prize.html

Ryan, H. (2014, December 16). Wonder Woman takes a big step back. *The Daily Beast*. Retrieved from http://www.thedailybeast.com/articles/2014/12/16/wonder-woman-takes-a-big-step-back.html

Sanders, K. (2013, July 16). Kathleen Ford says private prisons use third-grade data to plan for prison beds. *PolitiFact Florida*. Retrieved from http://www.politifact.com/florida/statements/2013/jul/16/kathleen-ford/kathleen-ford-says-private-prisons-use-third-grade/

Saunders, G., & Smith, L. (2000). *The very persistent gappers of Frip*. San Francisco, CA: McSweeney's Books.

Schapiro, R. (2014, August 10). Unarmed 18-year-old man shot dead by police in Missouri: witnesses. *Daily News*. Retrieved from http://www.nydailynews.com/news/national/18-year-old-shot-dead-missouri-witnesses-article-1.1898333

Schneider, M. (2013, April 2). In Ravitch's defense: Milwaukee voucher study found wanting [Web log]. *deutsch29*. Retrieved from http://deutsch29.wordpress.com/2013/04/02/in-ravitchs-defense-milwaukee-voucher-study-found-wanting/

Sinclair, U. (2001). *The jungle*. Mineola, NY: Dover Thrift Editions.

Singer, A. (2013, November 22). Reading without understanding – Common Core versus Abraham Lincoln. The Blog. *Huffington Post*. Retrieved from http://www. huffingtonpost.com/alan-singer/reading-without-understan_b_4323239.html

Smyth, C. (2014, March 19). Rethinking Gandhi on film (1982). *Making History Matter*. Retrieved from http://www.makinghistorymatter.ca/articles/rethinking-gandhi-on-film-1982

Strauss, V. (2013, April 12). Why not subpoena everyone in D.C. cheating scandal—Rhee included? (update) [Web log]. The Answer Sheet. *The Washington Post*. Retrieved from http://www.washingtonpost.com/blogs/answer-sheet/ wp/2013/04/12/why-not-subpoena-everyone-in-d-c-cheating-scandal-rhee-included/

Strauss, V. (2010, December 6). Do international test comparisons make sense? [Web log]. The Answer Sheet. *The Washington Post*. Retrieved from http://voices.washingtonpost.com/answer-sheet/standardized-tests/so-what-if-the-us-is-not-no-1. html

Sumner, G.D. (2011). *Unstuck in time: A journey through Kurt Vonnegut's life and novels*. New York: Seven Stories Press.

Taylor, D., & Dorsey-Gaines, C. (1988). *Growing up literate: Learning from Inner-city families*. Portsmouth, NH: Heinemann.

Thomas, P. L. (2014, May 16). Racial segregation return to US schools, 60 years after the Supreme Court banned it. *The Conversation UK*. Retrieved from https:// theconversation.com/racial-segregation-returns-to-us-schools-60-years-after-the-supreme-court-banned-it-25850

Thomas, P.L. (2014, April 13). Devaluing teachers in the age of value-added [Web log]. *The Becoming Radical*. Retrieved from http://radicalscholarship.wordpress. com/2014/04/13/devaluing-teachers-in-the-age-of-value-added/

Thomas, P.L. (2013, December 3). Why are we (still) failing writing instruction? [Web log]. *The Becoming Radical*. Retrieved from http://radicalscholarship.wordpress. com/2013/12/03/why-are-we-still-failing-writing-instruction/

Thomas, P. L. (2013, May 17). Education reform in the New Jim Crow era. *Truthout*. Retrieved from http://truth-out.org/opinion/item/16406-education-reform-in-the-new-jim-crow-era

Thomas, P.L. (2013, March 6). Why sending your child to a charter school hurts other children. *AlterNet*. Retrieved from http://www.alternet.org/education/why-sending-your-child-charter-school-hurts-other-children

Thomas, P.L. (2013, January 3). Review [updated]: "How to evaluate and retain effective teachers" (League of Women Voters of SC) [Web log]. *The Becoming Radical*. http://radicalscholarship.wordpress.com/2013/01/03/review-how-to-evaluate-and-retain-effective-teachers-league-of-women-voters-of-south-carolina/

Thomas, P.L. (2012, January). "A richer, not a narrower, aesthetic"—The rise of New Criticism in *English Journal*. *English Journal, 101*(3), 52-57.

Thomas, P.L. (2012). *Ignoring poverty in the U. S.: The corporate takeover of public edu-*

cation. Charlotte NC: Information Age Publishing, Inc.

Thomas, P. L. (2012, May 15). Studies suggest economic inequity is built into, and worsened by, school systems. *Truthout*. Retrieved from http://truth-out.org/news/item/8993-studies-suggest-economic-inequity-is-built-into-and-worsened-by-school-systems

Thomas, P.L. (2011, January 26). Belief culture: "We don't need no education." *Truthout*. Retrieved from http://truth-out.org/archive/component/k2/item/94104:belief-culture-we-dont-need-no-education

Thomas, P.L. (2010, November 14). The teaching profession as a service industry. *The Daily Censored*. Retrieved from http://www.dailycensored.com/the-teaching-profession-as-a-service-industry/

Thomas, P.L. (2010, July). The Payne of addressing race and poverty in public education: Utopian accountability and deficit assumptions of middle class America. *Souls, 12*(3), 262-283.

Thomas, P.L. (2010). *Challenging genres: Comic books and graphic novels*. Netherlands: Sense Publishers.

Thomas, P. L. (2007). *Reading, learning, teaching Margaret Atwood*. New York: Peter Lang USA.

Thomas, P. L. (2006). *Reading, learning, teaching Kurt Vonnegut*. New York: Peter Lang USA.

Thomas, P. L. (2005). *Reading, learning, teaching Barbara Kingsolver*. New York: Peter Lang USA.

Thomas, P. L., Porfilio, B.J., Gorlewski, J., & Carr, P.R. (eds.). (2014). *Social context reform: A pedagogy of equity and opportunity*. New York, NY: Routledge.

Tucker, J. (2013, June 26). No reprieve for Oakland Indian charter schools. *SFGate*. Retrieved from http://www.sfgate.com/education/article/No-reprieve-for-Oakland-Indian-charter-schools-4622492.php

Ulin, D. L. (2014, April 21). James Baldwin, poet? But of course. *Los Angeles Times*. Retrieved from http://www.latimes.com/books/jacketcopy/la-et-jc-james-baldwin-poet-20140420,0,4219677.story

Ventura, J. (2013, October 7). Do prisons use third grade reading scores to predict the number of prison beds they'll need? *Reading Partners*. Retrieved from http://readingpartners.org/blog/do-prisons-use-third-grade-reading-scores-to-predict-the-number-of-prison-beds-theyll-need/

Vonnegut, K. (1991). *Slaughterhouse-five*. New York: Dell.

Vonnegut, K. (1964). *God bless you, Mr. Rosewater*. New York: Delta.

Vonnegut, K. (1963). *Cat's Cradle*. New York: Delta.

Vonnegut, K. (1952). *Player piano*. New York: Delta.

Walker, A. (1982). *The color purple*. New York: Pocket Books.

Whitman, D. (2008a, Fall). An appeal to authority. *Education Next, 8*(4). Retrieved from http://educationnext.org/an-appeal-to-authority/

Whitman, D. (2008b, June). *Sweating the small stuff: Inner-city schools and the new paternalism*. Thomas B. Fordham Institute.

Wilder, T. (2003). *Our town*. New York: Perennial Classic.

Willen, L. (2013, November 10). Tolstoy endures—but here's why the liberal arts might not [Web log]. The Answer Sheet. *The Washington Post*. Retrieved from http://www.washingtonpost.com/blogs/answer-sheet/wp/2013/11/10/tolstoy-endures-but-heres-why-the-liberal-arts-might-not/

Williams, T. (2004). *Cat on a hot tin roof*. New York: New Directions Books.

"With great power comes great responsibility." (2012, July 5). [Web log]. *quote/counterquote*. Retrieved from http://www.quotecounterquote.com/2012/07/with-great-power-comes-great.html

Wolf, P.J. (2013, April 1). Ravitch blow-up on school choice. *Education Next*. Retrieved from http://educationnext.org/ravitch-blow-up-on-school-choice/

Wray, J. (2004, Summer). Interviews: Haruki Murakami, The art of citation No. 182. *The Paris Review* (170). Retrieved from http://www.theparisreview.org/interviews/2/the-art-of-fiction-no-182-haruki-murakami

Yehl, J. (2014, July 16). Marvel Comics reveals The Falcon is the new Captain America. *IGN*. Retrieved from http://www.ign.com/articles/2014/07/17/marvel-comics-reveals-the-falcon-is-the-new-captain-america

Zinn, H. (2006, April 10). America's blinders. *The Progressive*. Retrieved from http://www.progressive.org/mag_zinn0406

Zinn, H. (2009, March 11). Sacco and Vanzetti. *ZNet*. Retrieved from http://zcomm.org/znetarticle/sacco-and-vanzetti-by-howard-zinn/

Zinn. H. (1995). *A people's history of the United States: 1492-present*. Rev. and updated ed. New York: Harper Perennial.

Zinn, H. (1994). *You can't be neutral on a moving train: A personal history of our times*. Boston, MA: Beacon Press.

Zirin, D. (2014, March 23). It's the racism, stupid: Meet the Press's epic NCAA fail. *The Nation*. Retrieved from http://www.thenation.com/blog/178969/its-racism-stupid-meet-presss-epic-ncaa-fail

About the Author

P.L. Thomas

P. L. Thomas, a recipient of the NCTE's George Orwell Award in 2013, engages the public in the most profound and controversial topics of our day, exposing the terrifying truths of the times in which we live. His commentaries have been published in *AlterNet*, *The Conversation UK/US*, *Room for Debate (The New York Times)*, *The Answer Sheet (The Washington Post)*, *The Guardian* (UK), *Truthout*, *Education Week*, *The Daily Censored*, *OpEdNews*, *The State* (Columbia, S.C.), *The Charlotte Observer*, *The Post and Courier* (Charleston, S.C.), and *The Greenville News* (Greenville, S.C.).

He has published books on Barbara Kingsolver, Kurt Vonnegut, Margaret Atwood, Ralph Ellison, and James Baldwin; his recent books include *Ignoring Poverty in the U.S.*, *Parental Choice?*, *Becoming and Being a Teacher* , *De-Testing and De-Grading Schools*, and *Social Context Reform*. His scholarly work has been published in major journals—*English Journal, English Education, Souls, Notes on American Literature, Journal of Educational Controversy, Journal of Teaching Writing*, and others.

He taught high school English in rural South Carolina before moving to teacher education. He has worked on major committees with the National Council of Teachers of English (NCTE), is a column editor for *English Journal* published by NCTE, and currently serves as NCTE Council Historian (2013-2015).

He is the series editor for the Critical Literacy Teaching Series: Challenging Authors and Genres (Sense Publishers), in which he authored the first volume—*Challenging Genres: Comics and Graphic Novels* (2010)—and co-edited a volume on James Baldwin (2014).

His work can be followed at *the becoming radical* blog and @ plthomasEdD on twitter.

Other Books by

P.L. Thomas

Social context reform: A pedagogy of equity and opportunity (edited book, with B.J. Porfilio, J. Gorlewski & P.R. Carr). (2014)

James Baldwin: Challenging author (edited book, with A.S. Henderson) (2014)

Science fiction and speculative fiction: Challenging genres (edited book). (2013)

De-testing and de-grading schools: Authentic alternatives to accountability and standardization (edited book, with J. Bower). (2013)

Becoming and Being a Teacher: Confronting Traditional Norms to Create New Democratic Realities (edited book). (2013)

Ignoring poverty in the U. S.: The corporate takeover of public education. (2012)

Challenging genres: Comic books and graphic novels. (2010)

Parental choice? A critical reconsideration of choice and the debate about choice. (2010)

21st century literacy: If we are scripted, are we literate? (co-authored with R. Schmidt). (2009)

Reading, learning, teaching Ralph Ellison. (2008)

Reading, learning, teaching Margaret Atwood. (2007)

Reading, learning, teaching Kurt Vonnegut. (2006)

Reading, writing, and thinking: The Postformal basics (co-authored with J.L. Kincheloe). (2006)

Reading, learning, teaching Barbara Kingsolver. (2005)

Teaching writing primer. (2005)

Numbers games—Measuring and mandating American education. (2001)

Vivid language: Writer as reader, reader as writer. (2004)

Lou LaBrant: A woman's life, a teacher's life. (2001)

Made in the USA
Lexington, KY
27 June 2016